Creating Inclusion and Well-being for Marginalized Students

Creating Inclusion and **Well-being** for **Marginalized Students**

Whole-School Approaches to Supporting Children's Grief, Loss, and Trauma

EDITED BY LINDA GOLDMAN

Jessica Kingsley *Publishers*
London and Philadelphia

Quote on p. 42 from "A Grief Observed" by CS Lewis
© copyright CS Lewis Pte Ltd. 1961.

First published in 2017
by Jessica Kingsley Publishers
73 Collier Street
London N1 9BE, UK
and
400 Market Street, Suite 400
Philadelphia, PA 19106, USA

www.jkp.com

Library of Congress Cataloging in Publication Data
Names: Goldman, Linda, 1946- editor.
Title: Creating inclusion and well-being for marginalized students: whole-school
approaches to supporting children's grief, loss, and trauma/ edited by Linda Goldman.
Description: London ; Philadelphia : Jessica Kingsley Publishers, 2017.
Identifiers: LCCN 2017033971 (print) | LCCN 2017008831 (ebook)
| ISBN 9781784502935 () | ISBN 9781785927119 (alk. paper)
Subjects: LCSH: Students with social disabilities--Counseling of. |
Students--Mental health. | Students--Mental health services.
| Grief in children. | Psychic trauma in children.
Classification: LCC LB4065 (print) | LCC LB4065 .C74 2017 (ebook) | DDC
371.826/94--dc23

British Library Cataloguing in Publication Data
A CIP catalogue record for this book is available from the British Library

ISBN 978 1 78592 711 9
eISBN 978 1 78450 293 5

Printed and bound in Great Britain

This book is dedicated to the children that feel invisible—

and the adults who have eyes to see them.

Contents

Preface

Once again, Linda Goldman has reached out across cultures to break down barriers and rally caregivers and educators to the aid of our most vulnerable citizens, children who are traumatically bereaved and in desperate need of trauma-informed care. Those who serve and support these precious children now have an extraordinary resource to rely upon, *Creating Inclusion and Well-being for Marginalized Students.* It is an essential reference for teachers and caregivers and all those who yearn to profoundly impact—and quite possibly save—a child's life.

Bonnie Carroll

President and Founder of TAPS, Tragedy Assistance Program for Survivors

Recipient of the Presidential Medal of Freedom (2015)

Introduction

As educators, parents, clinicians, and caring adults we often ponder what kind of a world we are creating for our future generations. We are charged with the creation of a global human family whereby every child is important and the conditions under which she or he learns and grows are equally important. One goal is to vigilantly battle, inwardly and outwardly, the war on exclusion, polarization, and multi-separate thinking that creates endless obstacles for the many already marginalized youth in our classrooms. Social exclusion has painful consequences. Students cast off by society tend to suffer unjustly, and may become vulnerable, fragile victims of a culture that views them as insignificant, faceless, and voiceless.

Creating Inclusion and Well-being for Marginalized Students is a resource that addresses the children truly *left behind* in a system whereby legal accountability may be equated with services, expedience can outweigh human need, and tremendously difficult and challenging life issues are often disregarded to meet a phantom norm often seeking to satisfy the needs of a system, not the needs of each and every student.

As an editor, I was driven to not necessarily answer questions, but to create an open-ended and inclusive *conversation* that embraces diverse viewpoints. Each contributor shares their perspective of the subject matter, presenting emerging paradigms as a forum for discussion that can lift dialogues toward a higher level of awareness and understanding. One gift of an edited resource is reader exposure to different voices to ultimately establish a welcoming educational environment whereby our underserved students can best learn and grow.

The mandatory questions we need to ask include: How can we help our young people with issues such as poverty, human sex trafficking, and a broad range of stereotyping and scapegoating? How can we help girls and boys with special conditions that may inhibit learning such as immigration, deportation, incarceration, deployment, nutritional challenges, school violence, LGBT concerns, and traumatic death in the military?

Working with grieving and traumatized children has been my life's work and passion. Personal experiences with students and loss began after college, in 1968, as I entered the field of teaching, where I would remain for 20 years as a first grade, second grade, kindergarten, and reading teacher, as well as guidance counselor, before becoming a grief therapist with children. The following story was my initial teaching experience and the valuable lessons learned (adapted from Stillion and Attig, 2015).

My first class was a group of 22 second grade repeaters. Being a novice as an educator, I was given a class labeled "throw away kids," students no one wanted to teach, and placed in an aluminum trailer far removed from the rest of the school building. At the onset of the school year these girls and boys looked sad, withdrawn, and disinterested. During this time in the field of education, many children repeated a grade when they could not achieve the desired academic standards, without insight into the factors that may have inhibited their learning and school performance.

Luckily, I was given free rein in my approach to teaching. I decided on a three-fold plan. The first step was to start at the beginning of the first grade curriculum and re-teach what the children may not have been able to absorb in order to create a uniform foundation for learning. The next step was to enhance self-esteem by creating positive learning experiences, and the third step was allowing children time each day to process their life issues. These simple steps became the seed point for my future work. Thus, I introduced the paradigm that children's grief and loss issues deeply impact their school performance and potential and influence their ability to learn and grow.

We worked together with these guidelines in mind, each day building concepts based on what the children knew, and each day creating a safe space for sharing life issues. Many of these kids had experienced death at a young age, divorce, multiple moves, and family issues such as alcoholism and abuse. I began to realize that as these young people shared emotional issues, their learning capacity increased.

Our principal visited the classroom that spring, and marveled at the academic progress and the enthusiasm for learning he witnessed. "How did you do this?" he remarked. The answer became my life's work to develop and share. It also became the goal and foundation of this book.

The first two chapters of *Creating Inclusion and Well-being for Marginalized Students* present childhood losses, common signs of grieving children, and a comprehensive plan for educators to create awareness of the multiple loss, grief, and trauma issues students face in our schools, often without the accountability, dialogue, or interventions necessary to help them with challenging circumstances and still grow, learn, and thrive. The third chapter offers a teacher's perspective by Kyle Schwartz, who contributes one lesson that gave voice to her students to share life circumstances highlighted in many of these chapters. She merely asked kids in her class to respond to the phrase: "I wish my teacher knew...." Their answers were incredible, covering a range of topics from poverty, illness, deportation, and incarceration to bullying, loneliness, and peer rejection. In Chapter 4 Susan Craig gives an overview of a trauma-informed school that prepares the reader for chapters on specific challenging issues.

Part II addresses individual life circumstances too many marginalized youth encounter. These challenges are recognized and highlighted, and practical ways educators can work with students experiencing issues such as poverty, death, nutrition, stereotyping, sexual exploitation, imprisonment, immigration, military deployment, and LGBT issues are emphasized.

In Part III, this resource offers solutions to working with students in the classroom. It focuses on a strengths-based approach to learning, impact of social media in supporting children and families, the expressive arts as a forum for teaching, a principal's practical application of a trauma-informed school, resilience techniques to support students, and a community-based volunteer project focused on enhancing the well-being of children. These solutions inspire students to become all they can be, in an educational environment of caring and protection.

This is a necessary tool for educators in today's world. No longer can teachers merely teach to the curriculum, or a specific age group, without having a deeper understanding of the loss, grief, and trauma issues young people face that impact their learning, safety, and well-being. A worthy goal is to carry these children from being the *marginalized* and bring them to the *mainstream*, with equal opportunities for learning and growing within and without of our school systems.

Creating Inclusion and Well-being for Marginalized Students is a snapshot into the diverse world our kids live in, and a mandate to accommodate all children by providing them the resources necessary to cope with difficulties that for some seem insurmountable. Our first step is recognition. Our second step is actualizing a successful outcome. Our third step is a commitment to action that promises our schools will be a safe haven for support and learning. Opening the minds and hearts of all of our children is the core of education. In order to accomplish this feat, we must comprehend the challenges young people face, the issues that impact their lives and learning, and the steps crucial in creating change. We must see what existing conditions there are, what can be done, and what is being done to catch our students before they fall.

Let us *hope* to gain a clear vision of the intrinsic value of each and every student.

Let us *recognize* that undermining or exclusion of any group defeats the purpose of providing a broad and inclusive learning environment for all young people.

Let us *create* a conscious effort to evoke justice for all children that are living, struggling, and suffering in our classrooms on a daily basis.

References

Stillion, J. and Attig, T. (2015). *Death, Dying, and Bereavement: Contemporary Perspectives, Institutions, and Practices.* Goldman, L. Chapter, Supporting Grieving Children. Springer Publishing Company.

Part I

THE PROBLEM

Impact of Grief, Loss, and Trauma on Students

"One child, one teacher, one book and one pen can change the world."

Malala Yousafzai (2015, p.310)[1]

---

1   Yousafzai, M. (2015) *I Am Malala.* New York: Back Bay Books.

Chapter 1

Loss and Grief in Our Schools

THE IMPACT ON LEARNING AND GROWTH

Linda Goldman

Students don't care about how much you know until they know how much you care.

Anonymous

Educators, parents, and all caring adults need to build the muscle of moral courage to wage the war against marginalization, disenfranchisement, stereotyping, and neglect that can ultimately lead to our underserving of school students. In September 2015 the United Nations General Assembly presented new global goals affecting our children "that will combat hunger, eradicate poverty, and improve the quality of life" (Lowenberg, 2015). These 17 goals impact young people in every nation marginalized and treated with inequality in their homes, schools, and communities.

Can the solution to the problem of educating our underserved young people be as simple as loving them? Shall we dare to use the word *love*, as it is often not found in higher institutions teaching educators to educate children? It is often not found in classroom curriculums or psychological techniques. Yet it is the underlying cure for the malady of this population of disenfranchised children that yearns to be acknowledged, embraced, and cared for, within the breadth and scope of life circumstances and challenging feelings that all too often contribute to difficulties in learning and an inability to be fully present.

Perhaps some in our current educational system have a predisposition to teach to the test rather than the child, to highlight the textbook rather than the heart of a trauma, to focus on a phantom norm rather than see the brilliance of the individual child. If so, it is understandable. With a groundswell of students, a heavy pressure to meet standards, and countless, unconscionable circumstances related to grief and trauma, how can an educator find the time or the energy to meet the needs of each and every girl and boy?

A voice and a choice may be the key that unlocks the door to empowerment for our children. Throughout this book each contributor has presented their specific area of expertise and each has included a heartfelt solution as well as conventional paradigms. Both are important and worthy. A system emerges whereby students who would otherwise hide in the shadows, feel isolated, or become withdrawn or act out are instead recognized individually and given resourceful activities that meet the specific difficulty they are facing with safety and compassion. Each author has witnessed the growth of those they work with by honing in on what children say they need, hearing their voice, and presenting them with options in the kindest of ways.

Understanding children's loss and grief

It is important to understand the complex relationship between loss issues and a child's ability to function in and out of the classroom. Children's grief can be seen as an ongoing life process that is approachable through words, activities, non-verbal communication, and accountability. This grief can be processed in a safe environment that acknowledges and respects challenging emotions and thoughts.

Often teachers, parents, and even health professionals feel inadequate to speak to kids about death, and may consciously or unconsciously restrain feelings in children. Adults often mistakenly feel they should avoid topics that might make a child cry. In order to reduce anxiety and fear and create a "safe oasis," adults must become familiar with concepts involving childhood losses, myths about grieving children, tasks of grief, and common signs of grieving children.

The following are typical childhood losses students face: loss of relationship, loss of environment, loss of skills and abilities, loss of routines and habits, loss of self/self-esteem, loss of external objects, loss of privacy, loss of a future, and loss of the safety and protection of the adult world. Often any one of these life events may lead to secondary loss in another category. Olivia's father died when she was five. Her mom was forced to move to another home, and work full time. Olivia not only experienced the death of a relationship and the loss of friends, but the loss of environment, routines, and habits, and the subsequent loss of skills and abilities in school.

Many of today's students are being raised on the same myths of grief and loss that adults were raised on in past generations. These myths include the following:

Grief and mourning are the same experience.

Adults can instantly give explanations to children about death and spirituality.

The experience of grief and mourning has orderly stages.

The grief of adults does not have an impact on the bereaved child.

Adults should avoid topics that cause a child to cry.

An active, playing child is not a grieving child.

Infants and toddlers are too young to grieve.

Parents and professionals are always prepared and qualified to explain loss and grief.

Children need to "get over" their grief and move on.

Children are better off not attending funerals. (Goldman, 2014a, p.25)

So often adults rely on the prevailing myth that children are too young to grieve. When a child is capable of loving, he is capable of grieving. Yet many of today's children are born into a world of grief issues that await them inside their homes and outside in their neighborhoods. Girls and boys are becoming increasingly traumatized by these prevailing social and societal loss issues in their homes, in their schools, and in their communities.

The four basic psychological tasks of grief are: understanding, grieving, commemorating, and going on (Fox, 1988; Goldman, 2014a; Worden, 2001).

Presenting children's perceptions of death at different developmental stages can broaden the conceptualization of the first task, understanding. The Swiss educator Piaget (Wadsworth, 2003) explained children's cognitive understanding of death through the following developmental stages:

- *Sensorimotor Stage: Approximately 0–2.* A child's concept of death is characterized by "out of sight, out of mind."

- *Preoperational Stage: Approximately 2–7.* A child's concept of death includes magical thinking, egocentricity, reversibility, and causality.

- *Concrete Operations: Approximately 7–12.* A child's concept of death is curious and realistic.

- *Formal Operations: Approximately 13 and up.* An adolescent's concept of death is self-absorbed and they see death as remote and rely on their peers for support. (Goldman, 2014a)

Often the young child thinks their words and thoughts can cause a person to die, and magical thinking is common for our grieving children. After her mom died at the Pentagon terrorist attack, five-year-old Brigit whispered in my ear, "It's my fault Mommy died. She had a cold and I didn't make her stay home from work that day." Mathew was seven when his dad died. Even though he had gone to the funeral, the gravesite, and felt Dad was in heaven, he wrote him a letter, mailed it, and waited for a response, magically thinking death was reversible.

It is crucial to provide children with age-appropriate language to allow them a forum for a comfortable dialogue. Death for youngsters can be defined in the following way:

> Death is when the body stops working. Usually someone dies when they are very, very old or very, very sick, or their bodies are so injured that the doctors and nurses can't make their bodies work again. (Goldman, 2005, p.75)

Common clichés can inhibit the grief process. Children often take language literally and need direct and simple, age-appropriate explanations. The examples below are adapted from Goldman (2014a):

> "Dad went on a long trip." Child might respond, "Why didn't he take me?"

"Isabella lost her mother." Child might respond, "How could she lose her mother, she was so big?"

"Uncle Joe is watching over you." Child might respond, "That could be very embarrassing."

"We put your dog Cooper to sleep and he died." Child might respond, "Will I die if I go to sleep?"

"God loved Grandma so much he took her to heaven." Child might respond, "Why didn't God take me? Can I go too? Doesn't God love me?"

The new normal

A high percentage of our children globally face the loss of the protection of the adult world, as grief-related issues of homicide, violence, and abuse infiltrate their outer and inner worlds. Causes of death involving shame and secretiveness, such as suicide and AIDS, often create fear, isolation, and loneliness that can be far more damaging than the original loss (see Chapter 2). Natural disasters ranging from earthquakes to tornados wreak havoc involving death and destruction of property. In our modern world, family challenges involving poverty, hunger, homelessness, abuse, immigration, deployment, and imprisonment lead to young people losing family through separation. Many statistics underscore the reality of the emergence of a new normal. This fast-growing group of diverse students often runs the risk of becoming underserved in our educational systems if the understanding of the life issues they face are not incorporated into their learning environment.

According to the Children's Defense Fund, the following applies to the United States:

> Every fifth child (16.1 million) is poor, and every tenth child (7.1 million) is extremely poor. Children are the poorest age group and the younger they are the poorer they are... But millions of them are unready for school, poorly educated and unprepared to face the future. Nearly 60 percent of all our children and more than 80 percent of our Black and nearly 75 percent of our Latino children cannot read or compute at grade level in fourth and eighth grade and so many drop out of school before graduating. (2014, p.2)

The Children's Defense Fund (2014) also present the following statistics.

Racial and ethnic diversity

- For the first time the majority of children in America under age two were children of color in 2012. Nearly one in three children of color—11.2 million children—were poor.

- The largest group of poor children was Hispanic children (5.8 million), followed by white children (5.2 million) and black children (4.1 million). (p.4)

Child poverty

- One in five children—16.1 million—were poor in 2012.

- The youngest most vulnerable children were the poorest age group. Over one in four children under age five—nearly 5 million—were poor. (p.4)

Child homelessness and hunger

- Nearly 1.2 million public school students were homeless in 2011–2012, 73 percent more than before the recession.

- More than one in nine children lacked access to adequate food in 2012.

- Black and Hispanic households with children were more than twice as likely as white households to lack access to adequate food in 2012. (pp.4–5)

Child nutrition

- One in three children in the United States are overweight or obese.

- In 2010, one in nine children—16 million in total—lived in households struggling to afford the food they needed to ensure their children would not go to sleep or to school hungry.

- Over 20.7 million children received free or reduced-price lunch through the National School Lunch Program in 2011. (p.28)

Child welfare

- A child is abused or neglected every 47 seconds. Of all child maltreatment victims:
    » 78.6 percent are victims of neglect
    » 17.5 percent are victims of physical abuse
    » 9.3 percent are victims of sexual abuse
    » 7.5 percent are victims of psychological maltreatment
    » 2.3 percent are victims of medical neglect
    » 10.5 percent are victims of other or unknown types of maltreatment. (p.43)

Gun violence

- In 2010, 2,694 children and teens were killed by guns and 15,576 were injured by guns.
- U.S. children and teens were 17 times more likely to be killed by a gun than children in 25 other high-income countries combined. (p.6)

Educational outcomes

- Over half a million public school students dropped out of grades 9–12 during the 2009–2010 school year. (p.5)
- Lower income fourth and eighth grade public school students were over one-and-a-half times more likely to be below grade level in reading or math than higher income students. (p.68)
- Nationally, 66 percent of public school eighth graders were below grade level in reading, and the same percent were below grade level in math. (p.67)
- Thirty-two percent of students who spent more than half of their childhoods in poverty do not graduate. (p.36)

Abuse and neglect

- Poor children and children of color have worse health outcomes and worse access to health and mental health care than higher income children and white children. Nearly 40 percent of children who needed mental health treatment or counseling did not receive it. (p.56)

- Over 60,000 children and youth in the juvenile justice system were held in residential placement on an average night in 2011. Black children were disproportionately likely to be in residential placement. (p.80)

- Close to one million children were raised by grandparents with no parent present in the home. (p.78)

Common signs of grieving children

Today's educators first need to become familiar with the common signs of grief in order to normalize them for parents and students. We then can develop ways to work with the grieving child within the school system.

Goldman (2009) lists the following normal behaviors for bereaved children:

- Child retells *events* of the deceased's death and funeral.
- Child *dreams* of the deceased.
- Child *idolizes or imitates behaviors* of the deceased.
- Child *feels the deceased is with him or her* in some way.
- Child *speaks of his or her loved* one in the present.
- Child *wants to "appear normal."*
- Child *enjoys wearing or holding* something of the loved one's.
- Child *rejects old friends and seeks new friends* with a similar loss.
- Child *asks to call home* during the school day.
- Child *can't concentrate* on homework or class work.
- Child *bursts into tears* in the middle of class.
- Child *seeks medical information* on death of deceased.

- Child *worries excessively* about his or her own health.

- Child sometimes *appears to be unfeeling* about loss.

- Child becomes the *"class clown"* to get attention.

- Child is *overly concerned* with caretaking. (pp. 104–105)

SOPHIE

Sophie was a fourth grade client whose dad had died of cancer on her birthday. During our grief therapy session, she explained her rage at her teacher, Mrs. Martin. Sophie had told her the first week of school that her father had died of cancer during the summer. Mrs. Martin never responded to her and never addressed the subject again. Sophie was furious and swore never to tell anyone else in school about this death.

I asked Sophie what she wished her teacher had said. She replied, "I wish she would have given me a hug, said she was sorry, and promised she would be there if I ever wanted to talk about my dad or the way he died."

Often our grieving students don't like to feel different, especially with peers. When they have experienced the death of a parent, they sometimes choose not to talk about it. Not talking about the death allows some kids to feel some control over normalizing their life.

THOMAS

Thomas was playing on the school basketball team, and the final tournament was a major event. Most of the moms and dads of the team members came to support their children for the game. Thomas scored the final basket that won the victory for his team. Charlie, Thomas's coach, ran over to Thomas to congratulate him, and all the other boys and their parents joined in the celebration.

"Where's your dad?" Coach Charlie asked. "He's working today, and couldn't come," Thomas replied. Coach Charlie was unaware that Thomas's dad had died of cancer three months earlier. Thomas needed to save face and avoid his dad's death in order to "appear normal." Educators can develop ways to normalize and discuss these delicate subjects with children by recognizing common behaviors and feelings in bereaved students and normalizing them to children and parents.

Grief and loss inventory for educators

If the school system had implemented a mandatory policy of requiring a "grief and loss inventory," Coach Charlie could have reviewed this tool for all of his students in order to identify Thomas as a grieving child. The school guidance counselor can serve as a liaison to identify grieving children to all faculty members who currently work with the child.

The following grief and loss inventory (Goldman, 2014a, pp.175–177) can become an invaluable instrument for communication and an ongoing source of information on students identified with a specific challenging life circumstance.

GRIEF AND LOSS INVENTORY:
IDENTIFY THE WHOLE CHILD

Name _____ Age _____ Grade _____

Address _____

_____

_____ Date of birth _____

Home phone/cell number _____

Email _____ Today's date _____

Referral Information

Reason for referral _____

_____

Source for referral _____

Identify Recent Significant Loss

Relationship of deceased to the child _____

Facts about the loss (who, what, where, when?) _____

_____

_____

_____

Was it a military death? _____

Who told the child? _____

How was the child told? _____

_____

Deceased's date of birth _____ Date of death _____

✓

Previous Loss and Grief History (Include significant dates involved in prior losses)

Divorce or separation _____ Date _____

Moving _____ Date _____

Friend moved away _____ Date _____

Past deaths. Who? _____ Date _____

Pet deaths. Who? _____ Date _____

Parent(s) changing job _____ Date _____

Parent(s) losing jobs _____ Date _____

Fire _____ Date _____

Robbery _____ Date _____

Natural disaster _____ Date _____

Incarceration _____ Date _____

Deployment _____ Date _____

Deportation _____ Date _____

Other _____ Date _____

Inherited Family Loss (Examples: grandparent killed in a war, sibling death before birth)

_____

_____

Family Unit

Single parent _____ Divorce _____

Unmarried _____ Adoption _____

Natural parents _____ Blended family _____

Same sex parents _____

Living with grandparents _____

Family History of Chronic Cultural Loss

Drugs _____ Injury _____

Crime _____ Unemployment _____

Medical History

Significant parent illness _____

Significant child's illness _____

Previous School History

Grades _____

Progress _____

Participation _____

Assessment History

Standardized tests _____

_____ Date _____

Speech and language evaluation _____

_____ Date _____

Educational assessment _____

_____ Date _____

Psychological evaluation _____

_____ Date _____

Identify Child's Attitude toward Significant Others/Self

Siblings _____

Parents _____

✓

Friends _____

Pets _____

Self _____

Likes and dislikes:

Interests likes _____

Interests dislikes _____

Abilities likes _____

Abilities dislikes _____

Present Behavior at School (Check those that apply)

Disruptive in school _____ Failing grades _____

Inability to concentrate _____ Increased absenteeism _____

Fighting with peers _____ Withdrawn _____

Using bad language _____ Very tired _____

Physical complaints (headache, stomach ache, etc.) _____

Nervousness _____

Other _____

Identify Present Behaviors at Home
(Check those that apply)

Less interaction _____ Sleeplessness _____

Poor eating _____ Bed wetting _____

Clinging to parents _____ Nightmares _____

Increased perfectionism _____ Crying _____

Talks constantly about loss _____

Fighting with siblings or parents _____

Fears (of dark, noise, robbers, etc.) _____

Other _____

Identify Present Behaviors with
Peers (Tick those that apply)

More arguing ☐

Less interest in play dates ☐

Less communication with peers ☐

Others ☐

Recommendations

Team conference _____

In-school individual counseling _____

Referral to a counseling agency _____

In-school group counseling _____

Referral to a support group _____

Referral to a medical doctor _____

Testing _____

Follow-Up

Monthly _____ Source _____ Date _____

Creating grief awareness in schools

One of the misunderstood myths of grief and loss is that young people "need to move on and get over their loss." As educators, parents, and mental health professionals, we need to recognize and develop awareness of the ongoing journey of processing grief. Each child's grief is unique, and the grief experience is unique to each individual.

Grief work can be incorporated into teaching, communicating, and connecting with girls and boys. The following interventions are examples of techniques that can be used to facilitate grieving and traumatized students.

VANESSA: LOSS OF ENVIRONMENT

Poetry is an expressive art that can be used by educators as a creative vehicle for expression about challenging life situations. Students living in poverty and homelessness often feel shame and stigma. Dr. Ruby Payne presents an in-depth approach to working with children and poverty in Chapter 5, sharing the extraordinary challenges poverty presents in the classroom. Poetry assignments can become an avenue to explore difficult situations and feelings. The following poem, written by a young child, shares her daily losses while living in poverty.

Six People, Five Eat

There are six people in our family.
But only five sit down to dinner.
That's because my mom doesn't eat.
She wants to make sure we have enough food.

Vanessa, age 6 (Children's Defense Fund, 2014, p.7)

ASHLEY: MOTHER'S DAY

Ashley was a third grader whose mom had died of a sudden heart attack when she was in first grade. Ashley's art class was making Mother's Day gifts, and she was flooded with memories as class members began talking about their moms. She burst into tears and ran out of the room. Mr. Barry, her teacher, rushed after her. Ashley explained that her mom had died two years ago, and it was still painful to remember her. Mr. Barry admonished Ashley: "It's been two years since your mom has died. You need to get over it and move on!" Ashley said she hated her teacher for saying that. The last thing she wanted to do was forget her mom. What she needed, instead, were concrete ways to remember her. Perhaps Mr. Barry could have responded to Ashley in a more compassionate way that would have enabled her to safely express challenging feelings in school. He could have created an agreement with Ashley to choose a designated safe adult in school to speak with when she missed her mom.

Another effective intervention was to invite Ashley to make a symbolic Mother's Day card for her mom, write a letter to Mom (Figure 1.1), create a poem, or plant a flower in her memory. Letter and poetry writing are grief therapy techniques that allow children to create concrete ways to commemorate the death of a loved one.

Figure 1.1 Letter (Goldman, 2014a, p.60)

MICHELLE: CHILDREN'S QUESTIONS

Students' questions are often a useful tool for educators. They are a window into their soul, and a mirror of hidden thoughts and feelings. They can act as a key to unlock emotions. Michelle's mom was killed suddenly in a terrible car crash. Mrs. Simpson, Michelle's teacher, knew this was very painful for her and was acutely aware of her grief.

At recess one day, Michelle wondered aloud to her teacher: "What do you think heaven is?" The teacher honored that question by responding to Michelle: "What do you think heaven is?" Michelle created the following explanation and drawing (Figure 1.2). Her teacher wisely knew her question about heaven was a reflection of what was on Michelle's mind. Drawing and writing about heaven allowed Michelle to create positive imagery to sit alongside the difficult visions of her mom's accident, as well as a vehicle to lovingly honor her mom.

What is heaven?

This is what heaven is to me. It's a beautiful place. Everyone is waiting for a new person, so they can be friends. They are also waiting for their family. They are still having fun. They get to meet all the people they always wanted to meet (like Elvis). There are lots of castles where only the great live, like my mom. There's all the food you want and all the stuff to do. There's also dancing places, disco. My mom loved to dance. I think she's dancing in heaven. Animals are always welcome. (My mom loved animals.)

Ask her how Trixie is. That's her dog that died.

Tell her I love her.

Michelle, age 11

Figure 1.2 Heaven (Goldman, 2014a, p.71)

TARA: LETTER WRITING

Tara was a second grader who experienced multiple deaths. Mr. Walker, her teacher, was aware that she worried a lot, and knew that was a common sign of grieving children. Mr. Walker knew many kids worried about things in his classroom, and asked them to make a list of their top five worries. Benjamin worried about his dad smoking, Marco worried about his brother in prison, and Tamika's top worry was that her dad just lost his job. Tara's worry was about her father. With so many deaths in her family, she worried about her dad's safety because he didn't wear his seatbelt.

Mr. Walker invited the children to write to the person they were worrying about, and then give the letter to them if they wanted to. Tara wrote her dad a letter about wearing his seatbelt. She thought it was a great idea.

Below is what Tara came up with, plus her dad's response (Figures 1.3–1.5). She decorated her letter with glitter and stickers. Tara told Mr. Walker the letter made her feel a lot safer and less worried.

Figure 1.3 Wear your seatbelt   Figure 1.4 The letter

Figure 1.5 Dad's response (Goldman, 2014a, pp.61–62)

CLASSROOM REMEMBERS

Mrs. Simpson's class was very sad. Their pet bunny rabbit Cooper died suddenly over the weekend. When the children came to school on Monday, Cooper was gone. They didn't get to say goodbye. Mrs. Simpson explained that Cooper died. His body stopped working. She invited her class to process their feelings and ask questions. She read **Lucy Lets Go** (Goldman, 2014b), a storybook about a pet being sick and then dying, with the children.

Many of the girls and boys wanted to do something for Cooper. One little girl drew a life-size picture of herself and how she felt (Figure 1.6). She made a sock puppet of Cooper and began to dialogue with it, telling Cooper: "I love you, I miss you, I'm sorry I didn't get to say goodbye."

Figure 1.6 How I feel (Goldman, 2014a, p.83)

Sammy made a heart for Cooper, Angela drew a sad face, Richard decided to make a holiday ornament for Cooper, and Thomas made a picture frame with jewels and glitter and put a special picture inside (Figure 1.7). The kindergarteners felt better after talking about Cooper's death and participating in activities that validated their feelings and helped them to heal.

Figure 1.7 Activities (Goldman, 2014a, p.74)

Recommendations for educators

Children gain a greater understanding of themselves when they can express previously hidden emotions. Awareness of unrecognized feelings also allows adults to become more in touch with a child's grief process. Grief feelings and thoughts are ever-changing and continuous, often inundating children without warning. Students can feel unprepared for their enormity in a school setting. The following are helpful recommendations for educators.

Educators can recognize the signs of bereaved children.

- Bereaved students need to acknowledge a loss of a relationship due to death, deportation, imprisonment, etc. by using the person's name or sharing a memory.

- Bereaved students need to tell their stories over and over again. They can use tools such as drawing, writing, role-playing, and reenactment to project feelings and thoughts about the loss safely and present life outside of themselves.

- Bereaved students can use memory work to create a physical way to remember their feelings and share them. Memory books are a collection of drawn or written feelings and thoughts that allow the child to re-experience memories in a safe way.

  Memory books serve as useful tools to share about the person who died, and open discussion about funny, happy, or sad memories. The page shown in Figure 1.8 illustrates how a student felt before and after the loss of a parent.

Figure 1.8 Memory book (Goldman, 2014a, p.75)

- Bereaved students need to be allowed to go to a safe place outside the classroom when these unexpected, overwhelming feelings arise, without needing to explain why in front of fellow classmates.

- Bereaved students are often preoccupied with their own health and the health of loved ones. Providing a reality check—such as allowing the child to phone the surviving parent during the school day or to visit the school nurse—can reassure kids that they and their families are OK. (Adapted from Goldman, 2012, p.29)

Educators can use a grief and loss inventory (Goldman, 2014a) as a tool for creating and storing history on the grieving child throughout his or her academic life. This history includes all losses and deaths of loved ones, and dates of important birthdays, that may have a great impact on the child through the years.

Educators can also use the concept of "teachable moments" to create a spontaneous lesson calling upon a life experience that is happening in "The Now." The death of Mrs. Arnold's class's goldfish, Goldie, was a huge loss to the kindergarteners. Goldie's death during school provided a "teachable moment" whereby the children could express their feelings about death and commemorate their loss with a burial ritual and memorial service. John Holland's (2016) book *Responding to Loss and Bereavement in Schools* is a useful training resource created to assess, evaluate, and improve the school response to grief and loss. It includes material for teachers to copy and use with grieving students.

Classroom teachers can provide a safe haven for the grieving child by:

- allowing the child to leave the room if needed

- allowing the child to call home if necessary

- creating a visit to the school nurse and guidance counselor periodically

- changing some work assignments

- assigning a class helper

- creating some private time in the day

- giving more academic progress reports. (Goldman, 2012, p.29)

Schools can help children commemorate a death in the school by:

- creating a ceremony, releasing a balloon with a special note, or lighting a candle

- making a memorial wall with stories and pictures of shared events

- having an assembly about the student

- planting a memory garden

- initiating a scholarship fund

- establishing an ongoing fundraiser such as a car wash or bake sale, with the proceeds going toward the family's designated charity

- placing a memorial page or picture in the school yearbook or school newspaper

- sending flowers to the grieving family.

Educators can build a loss and grief resource library to support teachable moments. With the myriad of grief and loss issues our students face, the following may be helpful additions to the library: *Malala Yousafzai* (Abouraya and Wheatley, 2014), *Last Stop on Market Street* (De La Pena, 2016), *Bart Speaks Out on Suicide* (Goldman, 1998), *Children Also Grieve* (Goldman, 2005), *Lucy Lets Go* (Goldman, 2014b), *A Season for Mangoes* (Hanson, 2005), *Goodbye Mousie* (Harris, 2004), *Gentle Willow* (Mills, 2004), and *And Still They Bloom* (Rovere, 2012).

Conclusion

The framework for a new paradigm must answer these questions: How can educators create customized support for groups that do not fit into institutionalized norms and standardized requirements? How do we support a model for helping kids who fall outside of an institutionalized educational system built upon benchmarks of what *every* student should know? Too many of today's varied population of students are outliers of that system.

The answers to those questions are simple ones—empathy and understanding. If we, as educators and caring adults, provide a compassionate heart to practical techniques and learning tools, a new model can emerge that implements not an abandonment of the old system, but broadens that system to become more inclusive for all students and their necessary accommodations. Often educators feel this is a daunting task with so many responsibilities they already are accountable for. Yet, the question is not really: "Can we expand a system to adapt to and focus on the individual needs of our kids, supporting *all* girls and boys in our schools equally?" The question really is: "How can we not?"

Our task is two-fold. Academic learning and enhancing life skills will be more successful and more easily manifested for educators and students if a system is implemented that creates an empathetic and understanding model for underserved students, and gives a framework for that model to support that understanding with educational tools and compassionate support. Then, and only then, can we produce a transformed educational system that meets the needs of each and every student by opening their minds and hearts, and also facilitates for educators a more accessible framework for learning and living for so many of our diverse population of students.

References

Abouraya, K. and Wheatley, L.C. (2014) *Malala Yousafzai: Warrior with Words.* NY: StarWalk Kids Media Publisher.

Children's Defense Fund (2014) *The State of America's Children.* Washington, DC. Available at www.childrensdefense.org/library/each-day-in-america.html, accessed on 03/23/17.

De La Pena, M. (2016) *Last Stop on Market Street.* NY: G.P. Putnam Books.

Fox, S. (1988) *Good Grief: Helping Groups of Children When a Friend Dies.* Boston, MA: New England Association for the Education of Young People.

Goldman, L. (1998) *Bart Speaks Out.* CA: WPS Publisher.

Goldman, L. (2005) *Children Also Grieve: Talking about Death and Healing.* London: Jessica Kingsley Publishers.

Goldman, L. (2009) *Great Answers to Difficult Questions about Death: What Children Need to Know.* London: Jessica Kingsley Publishers.

Goldman, L. (2012) 'Helping the grieving child in the schools.' *Healing Magazine,* 26–29.

Goldman, L. (2014a) *Life and Loss: A Guide to Help Grieving Children, 3rd Edition.* New York: Taylor and Francis.

Goldman, L. (2014b) *Lucy Lets Go: Helping Children Love a Pet through Death and Dying.* Omaha, NE: Centering Corporation.

Hanson, R. (2005) *A Season for Mangoes.* WY: Clarion Books.

Harris, R. (2004) *Goodbye Mousie.* NY: Atlanta, Aladdin.

Holland, J. (2016) *Responding to Loss and Bereavement in Schools.* London: Jessica Kingsley Publishers.

Lowenberg, O. (2015) 'UN's 17 global goals: What's on the list?' *The Christian Science Monitor*, September 26. Available at www.csmonitor.com/World/Global-News/2015/0926/UN-s-17-global-goals-What-s-on-the-list, accessed on 05/02/17.

Mills, J. (2004). Gentle Willow: *A Story for Children about Dying*. Washington DC, Magination Press.

Rovere, A. (2012). *And Still They Bloom*. Atlanta, Georgia: American Cancer Society.

Wadsworth, B. (2003) *Piaget's Theory of Cognitive and Affective Development: Foundations of Constructivism, 5th Edition*. New York: Pearson.

Worden, W. (2001) *Children and Grief: When a Parent Dies*. New York: Guilford.

Chapter 2

What Complicates Grief, Loss, and Trauma for Students

Linda Goldman

"I never knew grief could feel so much like fear."

C.S. Lewis (2015, p.3)

Parents, educators, and health professionals must recognize the need for special considerations for their underserved student population. Foremost is the complex relationship between loss, grief, and trauma issues and a child's ability to function in and out of the classroom. The needs of grieving, traumatized children can be provided for with a kinder, more loving approach within our homes, schools, and communities, in order to achieve a safe haven for learning and self-esteem.

Many mental health professionals have identified unresolved grief and loss as a condition termed complicated grief: sometimes manifested in prolonged, intensified, or unresolved grief that can overwhelm children and possibly produce depression and isolation. Dr. Teresa Rando (2013) clarifies that complicated grief can be manifested in many ways. The Mayo Clinic Staff (2015) explains that for some people "feelings of loss are debilitating and don't improve even after time passes."

Complexities in grief

Life events such as suicide, homicide, bullying, school shootings, divorce, poverty, homelessness, LGBT issues, incarceration, immigration, and abuse can create complex grief issues that will be discussed in the following chapters. Many of our youth today are underserved in these areas, and fall below the radar screen of what parents and educators know about students and what they can do to help them. "Inability to discuss these topics openly can create an atmosphere of fear, isolation, and loneliness that can be far more damaging than the actual death of a loved one" (Goldman, 2002, p.13).

Categories that contribute to complicated grief

- *Sudden or traumatic loss* (violent death, deportation, incarceration, etc.) can create an unstable environment, producing a frozen state of overwhelming feelings, as a child may think, "If my dad can be sent back to Mexico, can I be sent there too?"

- *Social stigma of loss* (imprisonment, homelessness, etc.) can possibly cause isolation, repressed feelings, and prolonged grief. Isabella's family kept secret her brother's imprisonment. She felt unable to tell friends that her brother was away without saying *why* he was gone.

- *Multiple, recurring losses* may produce fears of abandonment and self-doubt. Sara's dad had been deployed three times, beginning at age four. At eight, he was killed in combat. Sara and her family moved immediately. She lost her home, her friends, and her school. She began experiencing excessive nightmares and fears.

- *Past relationships can impact a child, especially if abused or neglected.* Secret feelings of relief or anger may emerge and feel shameful. Sophia could feel relieved that her uncle who sexually abused her died, yet too ashamed or afraid to share.

- *The grief process of the caretaking adult serves as a model for children* and may impact them. Matt told his teacher he gets bullied on the playground a lot and started to cry. His teacher responded, "Don't act like a girl. Be strong." He felt he must "act like a man" and not cry. The message Matt's teacher gave was: "Don't openly express feelings, and don't think I will protect you." (Adapted from Goldman, 2015, p.3)

These complex issues exist in our schools and need to be addressed in order for children to grow and learn. Fear, shock, or secrecy may emerge, acting like a wall of ice between the child and his or her grief process and their ability to learn. Girls and boys may no longer have direct access to working on and processing these common tasks of grieving as "fear may override the grief response" (Goldman, 2009, p.91). The traumatic emotional issues can become frozen in the psyche as an impenetrable wall that prevents kids from accessing underlying grief. Caring adults can help children safely melt down that wall.

Pain-based behavior: A new look at "acting out"

A crucial paradigm is the concept of pain-based behavior as an adaptive mechanism to an overwhelming life event. Too often educators and caregivers resort to ineffective or even harmful punitive measures for attention-seeking behaviors propelled by pain. As Anglin (2014) points out, "Young people who have experienced trauma are literally living in a world of pain which shows in their challenging behavior" (p.4). He defines the term *pain-based behavior* as "behavior, either of an 'acting out' or withdrawn nature…triggered by the re-experiencing of psycho-emotional pain." "Pain based behavior is a common human experience" (p.54) that can be triggered by students' unresolved problems, often producing volatility and chaos in the classroom.

"Unfortunately professionals and caregivers often react in ways that perpetuate conflict and pain" (Anglin, 2014, p.53). Tyler, in the case study below, is a perfect example. Tyler appeared defiant, and displayed troubling behaviors with outbursts, emotional explosions, and an overreaction to authority that often escalated into teacher/student conflict. He was labeled "a trouble maker" by many on his school faculty. When I asked his teacher to share something good about Tyler, she responded, "I can't think of anything." The result was continuous time outs, punishments, and even exclusion and school expulsion. If we can change the mindset of staff to one that incorporates love, understanding, and respect for these students, problems can be transformed into opportunities for learning and growth.

Sporleder, in Chapter 15, explains the pitfalls of a system that only uses punishment to shape behavior, and describes the benefits of establishing heartfelt connections with students that help modify destructive or unproductive ways of acting.

TYLER: A CASE STUDY OF ISSUES COMPLICATING GRIEF

Seven-year-old Tyler's dad, Joe, was murdered in a street fight while he was at school. Tyler's father had abandoned him at age two. Joe's visits were infrequent and explosive, with Joe often going into an alcoholic rage of physical and emotional abuse that terrified Tyler and his mother. These outbursts of violence remained silently buried in Tyler after his dad's sudden death.

Tyler was referred to counseling because of a history of repeated emotional outbursts in school, inability to stay in the classroom, and poor school performance and conduct. He had moved five times and lived with many relatives during his mom's frequent illnesses. Tyler's behaviors fluctuated from rage to helpfulness for his teachers and friends.

Melting down frozen feelings

Tyler was unable or unwilling to talk about his father's death or his life before that. Projective techniques were helpful in unlocking hidden feelings. Tyler shares his sadness through his picture of life with his family before his dad died (Figure 2.1). He drew a large figure screaming "Go to bed!" and a very small figure with a big tear saying, "Help me." His sadness and feelings of being overwhelmed by his dad were represented in this picture.

Figure 2.1 Memory page (Goldman, 2002, p.123)

Tyler was withdrawn in one grief therapy session. He drew a scribble picture and I asked him if he could see something inside, and give it a name. He called it a tornado. "What would the tornado say?" I asked. He replied, "Help me!" (See Figure 2.2.)

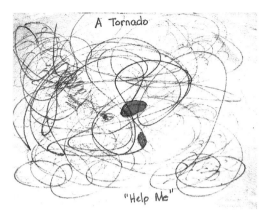

Figure 2.2 "Help me" (Goldman, 2002, p.124)

Tyler liked to create stories, reproduce them with toy figures, and take photographs to share with others. By projecting his feelings onto drawings and written work, Tyler was beginning to safely place them outside of himself.

The Tyler contracts

Specific single goal behavioral contracts were made with Tyler. The following was one of our first contracts:

> *I agree to raise my hand in math class when I want to say something for one week. If I get frustrated I can tell . . .*
>
> - *My teacher*
> - *Linda*
> - *The Guidance counselor*
> - *My journal*
>
> *I will get my favorite treat at the snack bar from Linda at the end of the week.*
>
> *Linda*
>
> *Tyler*

Children may need to repeat back in their own words the terms of the contract to be sure they understand what they are agreeing to. Tyler's math teacher reported that there was a significant improvement in his ability to raise his hand in class. When he did, she created a meaningful reward for this behavior.

Dissolving anger

Tyler shared with me his frustration and anger at school. "I hate my coach. I'd like to sock him!!!" he shouted over and over. "I wish I was a superhero." Then he stopped talking, drew a big superhero, and wrote: "If I was a superhero I would use my power to make people be good—be nice—and hypnotize the bad people and make the sun stop." He said he felt better.

Tyler's angry outbursts towards children and adults, profanity, and impulsivity when storming out of uncomfortable situations are examples of projected anger. Children can learn to vent anger safely without hurting themselves or others. They can create clay figures, dialogue their anger with them, or even choose to destroy the figures. Tyler made clay figures of his dad and himself, explaining that his father was yelling at him to go to bed. "GO AWAY!" he screamed as he battered the father figure until it was unrecognizable. "I wish you were dead!"

Tyler was furious at the school principal for suspending him because he had walked out of class. He knew it was safe to rip up magazines in my office, and soon felt a sense of release from some anger and calmed enough to talk about what happened. "I had to leave the classroom! My math was too hard. I couldn't do it and everyone knew." We picked up the paper, rounded up the scraps into balls, and tried to make a basket as we threw them away.

A punching bag can be a safe means to express anger. Tyler explained that his teacher forced him to sit on the bench at recess because he was fighting with Malcolm. He was enraged; so sure it was Malcolm's fault. He began hitting the punching bag in therapy as he screamed, "I hate your guts." Then he drew Malcolm's face and taped it to the punching bag. Tyler safely identified his anger and vented it without hurting anyone. He realized he could express anger by punching a pillow at home, shouting in the shower, talking into a tape recorder, writing in a journal, or blowing up a paper bag and popping it.

With complex issues, emotions such as fear, shock, or secrecy can dominate, freezing underlying loss and grief. Tyler drew a picture in one therapy session (Figure 2.3).

He explained, "This is me and this is my soul. It's kind of like a disease. Sometimes I feel like killing myself so I won't feel the pain." Although Tyler's pain appears excruciating, he (as many young children do) has masked it with a smile on his face. The drawing illustrates an archetype of a young person disconnected from his soul because of unexpressed and unresolved emotions.

Tyler then shared a memory of his dad. He began explaining how his dad and his mom would get into terrible fights. He shared, "I would sit in school and feel like the walls were closing in on me." I asked him, "If you could draw those walls and give them a name, what would they look like?"

Tyler drew the walls and named them Mom and Dad (Figure 2.4). This opened up a discussion of labeling his feelings, addressing his pain, and releasing pent-up emotions through using the arts.

Figure 2.3 My soul (Goldman, 2002, p.40)

Figure 2.4 The walls (Goldman, 2002, p.41)

Outcome of Tyler's case

A team conference was held at Tyler's school to evaluate school performance, behavior, and possible specialized placement to meet Tyler's specific needs. The team consisted of the principal, guidance counselor, teacher, school nurse, psychologist, Tyler's mom, and me. Each person offered his or her assessment. This team's eventual decision was a special placement for Tyler. Other recommendations included professional evaluations to determine if medication or other resources were needed. Exercise and sports were advised. Resources were suggested such as *After a Murder* (Dougy Center, 2002), *The Boy Who Didn't Want to Be Sad* (Goldblatt, 2004), *Worry Busters* (Weaver, 2011), and *Cool Down and Work Through Anger* (Meiners, 2010).

I remained a consultant to the new school personnel and a support for his mom, as the new school services provided Tyler with daily counseling, small classes, and many academic and therapeutic resources. Six months later Tyler was chosen as the "Student of the Month." His outbursts of rage had decreased, and he was more communicative with teachers and classmates.

Trauma-informed care

Young people like Tyler experiencing trauma can exhibit many pain-based behaviors that manifest as hyper-arousal, hyperactivity, inability to concentrate, and fear and anxiety. Greenwald (2005) explains, "Parents, counselors, teachers, coaches…and others are all in a position to help a child heal" (p.37). Establishing a safe environment in schools with an understanding that many of the behaviors and difficulties in learning are pain-based rather than merely "oppositional" or an indicator of attention deficit disorder can quicken the healing process for our students. Bath (2008) maintains that "one does not need to be a therapist to help address these three crucial elements of healing: the development of safety, the promotion of healing relationships, and the teaching of self-management and coping skills…the three critical pillars for intervention outlined here are fundamental and universal" (p.18).

These three pillars of trauma-informed care for students are safety, connections, and managing emotions. Bath (2008) explains, "Unfortunately, the defining experience of any child who has experienced complex trauma is that of feeling unsafe. The first imperative is creating a safe place for them" (p.19). Including children in decision making, giving them choices, maintaining consistency, and being honest, and reliable are factors that can help educators to create and sustain that "oasis of safety" for kids.

Connections, the second pillar, are essential in developing trust that leads to safety. Educators who are available, honest, and able to become mentors and cheerleaders for students provide an integral step for their healing, their growth, and their learning. Bath (2008) suggests the following:

> From a neurodevelopmental perspective, it appears that the brains of traumatized children have learned to associate adults with negative

emotions by suspicion, avoidance, and/or outright hostility. The task for care providers and other mentors is to help restructure these associations so that the children can develop positive emotional responses (e.g., happiness, joy, feelings of security) with some adults and can learn to accurately distinguish between those who threaten harm and those that do not. If the establishment of safety is the first consideration with traumatized children and yet it is the responses of adults that often bring further pain to the children, Anglin's (2002) central challenge might be re-formulated as follows: How to prevent the corrections adults use from sabotaging connections they need! Too often educators unknowingly create a punitive environment that adds to their perception that school is not safe for them. (p.20)

The third pillar highlighted is emotion and impulse management. Reactivity is a common reaction of students exposed to trauma and complex grief issues that can lead to challenging behaviors. Bath maintains, "A primary focus of work with traumatized children needs to be on teaching and supporting them to learn new ways of effectively managing their emotions and impulses" (2008, p.20). As discussed in Chapter 1, many of the seemingly acting-out incidents of our students who have experienced grief and trauma stems from pain that needs to be recognized and acknowledged. Trauma-informed approaches to teaching self-regulation to students can include parental figures who can model calming techniques, actually labeling feelings for girls and boys, and active listening leading to self-reflection (Bath, 2008; Lieberman *et al.*, 2007; van der Kolk, 2003).

Recommendations for educators

Educators, parents, and health professionals need to responsibly help children cope with trauma, loss, and grief within their homes, schools, communities, and nations. Providing information, understanding, and skills on these essential issues may well aid them in becoming more compassionate, caring human beings and thereby increase their chances of living in a future world of inner and outer peace. (Goldman, 2012, p.14)

The following are suggestions for school systems.

Common signs of complicated loss and grief may become red flags indicating needed help, and are characterized by their increase in frequency, intensity, and duration. In Tyler's case, the following signs were present:

- outbursts of aggressiveness and rage

- extreme feelings of unworthiness and despair

- nightmares and bedwetting

- conflicted relationship with father

- poor grades, impulsivity, and inability to concentrate.

Other possible signs include poor eating habits, difficulties with relationships, isolation, and acting as if nothing happened. Tyler's history of previous multiple losses and the sudden, traumatic nature of his dad's death are significant, related factors.

Memory work is a useful tool for grieving kids suffering with complex grief issues. It provides a creative outlet to help remember a person, release past memories, and discharge pain. Memory books can be interactive story and workbooks that allow children to express feelings and thoughts (Goldman, 2005, 2014b). Examples of questions or ideas children can use to reflect on or discuss thoughts and feelings include the following:

- If you could see your loved one one more time, what would you say?

- If you could change one thing or do one thing over, what would it be?

- Draw what your family was like before your loved one died, and after.

- Write a letter to your loved one. Tell him or her how you feel.

- List or draw your top five worries. (Goldman, 2014a, p.74)

Memory boxes provide a place to store treasured items of a loved one. They can be made from a painted shoebox decorated to house precious belongings. A special memory table can be displayed in bedrooms, classrooms, or grief support groups with meaningful pictures and objects a child has chosen. Photographs, videos, and tape recordings are concrete ways to stimulate visual and auditory memories of a loved one. A photo album of pictures chosen by kids, "My Life," records important times and events and motivates discussion.

Projective techniques such as storytelling, drawing, clay, anger props, and toys offer ways to safely project difficult feelings and help release frozen feelings. In Chapter 13, Green and colleagues expand on the use of the expressive arts in our schools. New York preschool students after the Twin Towers attack began reenacting the disaster. Using props of fire trucks, toy figures, etc., they re-created the terrorist event and became helpers for others. One little boy pretended to be a fireman, to "save as many people as possible."

Tanya, aged four, watched the towers explode, and her Uncle Jim was inside and was killed. She constantly replayed the scene of the airplane hitting the towers, by using kindergarten blocks and knocking them down with a toy airplane. Through projective play, she projected "good guy/bad guy" scenarios over and over again. "Play allows children to use symbolic expression, so that they often feel safer to reveal difficult feelings… Children who are considered to have avoidance symptoms may be more able to articulate their traumatic experiences in a play therapy setting" (Ogawa, 2004, p.25).

Second grader Shannon shared the following drawing after 9/11 (Figure 2.5). Her school was located two blocks from the World Trade Center. Students explained that they could smell the smoke, hear the cries, and see the crash. The intensity of her drawing illustrates how proximity to the event can create more vulnerability.

Figure 2.5 9/11 (Goldman, 2006, p.139)

One of her classmates drew a similar picture, and wrote at the bottom: "Run for your life!!!" Both students had outbursts in class, inattention, and an over-reactivity to stimulus.

Professional help may be needed when signs of complex issues become a red flag. Evaluations, therapy, school team conference, and possible referrals or placement can facilitate a child's grief process.[1]

Educator awareness of characteristics of students with chronic psycho-emotional pain is important. The following combinations of feelings and thoughts were found in young people who had experienced abuse, neglect, or other overwhelming life events that carried deep-seated and prolonged pain (Anglin, 2014, p.54):

- grief at abandonment and loss, often the death of someone close to them

- persistent anxiety about themselves and their situation

- fear, or even terror, of a disintegrating present and a hopeless future

- depression and dispiritedness as a lack of meaning or purpose in their lives

- psycho-emotional paralysis in a state of numbness and withdrawal.

Educator training on pain-based behavior opens doors to communication and healing.

The manner in which adults respond to pain is a key indicator of the quality of care experienced by the youth... Lingering effects of abuse, rejection, or neglect (of staff members) can be re-awakened in the intense interaction with these youth in pain. This highlights the critical importance of self-awareness training and personal development. This entails ongoing supervision of practice, especially in relation to worker "anxiety" which is pain-based fear... Effective intervention requires a deeper understanding of the origins and

---

1   The following national resources may be helpful: American Academy of Experts in Traumatic Stress (www.schoolcrisisresponse.com), National Association of School Psychologists (www.nasponline.org), and National Child Traumatic Stress Network (www.nctsnet.org).

management of this pain-based behavior so that responsive human relationships can help these young people heal. (Anglin, 2014, p.55)

Maintain a library of children's trauma resources. This library may include: *A Safe Place for Caleb* (Chara, 2005), *A Terrible Thing Happened* (Holmes, 2000), *Talking About Domestic Abuse: A Photo Activity Workbook* (Humpreys *et al.*, 2006), *When Mommy Got Hurt* (Lee and Sylvester, 2011), *The PTSD Workbook for Teens* (Palmer, 2012), *But I Didn't Say Goodbye* (Rubel, 2009), and *Hear My Roar* (Watts and Hodson, 2009).

Conclusion

Tyler's case study illustrates several complexities involved with children's loss, grief, and trauma in our schools. His history includes challenging issues such as the sudden, traumatic murder of his dad, the social stigma of homicide, multiple losses from his dad's abandonment and death, numerous residences, his mom's frequent illnesses, and a conflicted relationship with the deceased. His rage at his father was the beginning of the meltdown process. By identifying and separating his feelings through projective techniques and memory work, he was able to move forward with grieving.

Tyler's new academic environment provided daily services for multi-faceted, complex grief issues. Counseling and therapy within and outside of the educational system act as a bridge to help discover, recognize, and treat the severe underlying problems that needed to be acknowledged and addressed in a case like Tyler's, and to eventually seek out and establish the best possible environment to promote healing.

What we can mention, we can manage. This idea is a useful paradigm for educators to understand when formulating a safe environment for the grieving child. "If professionals in the school system can acknowledge and express thoughts and feelings involving grief and loss, they can serve as role models for the ever-increasing population of students experiencing traumatic loss" (Goldman, 2017, p.171).

References

Anglin, J.P. (2002) *Pain, Normality, and the Struggle for Congruence: Reinterpreting Residential Care for Children and Youth.* New York: Haworth Press.

Anglin, J.P. (2014) 'Pain-based behavior with children and adolescents in conflict.' *Reclaiming Children and Youth 22,* 4, 53–55.

Bath, H. (2008) 'The three pillars of trauma-informed care.' *Reclaiming Children and Youth 17,* 3, 17–21.

Chara, K., Chara Jr., and J. Paul (2005). *A Safe Place for Caleb.* London: Jessica Kingsley Publishers.

Dougy Center (2002) *After a Murder.* Portland, OR: Dougy Center.

Goldblatt, R. (2004) *The Boy Who Didn't Want to Be Sad.* Washington, DC: Magination Press.

Goldman, L. (2002) *Breaking the Silence: A Guide to Help Children with Complicated Grief, 2nd Edition.* New York: Taylor and Francis.

Goldman, L. (2005) *Children Also Grieve: Talking about Death and Healing.* London: Jessica Kingsley Publishers.

Goldman, L. (2006) *Raising Our Children to Be Resilient: A Guide to Helping Children Cope with Trauma in Today's World.* New York: Routledge.

Goldman, L. (2009) *Great Answers to Difficult Questions About Death: What Children Need to Know.* London: Jessica Kingsley Publishers.

Goldman, L. (2012) 'Trauma and children: What can we do?' *Healing Magazine,* 12–14.

Goldman, L. (2014a) *Life and Loss: A Guide to Help Grieving Children, 3rd Edition.* New York: Taylor and Francis.

Goldman, L. (2014b) *Lucy Lets Go: Helping Children Love a Pet Through Death and Dying.* Omaha, NE: Centering Corporation.

Goldman, L. (2015) 'What complicates grief for children: A case study.' *Healing Magazine,* 1–4.

Goldman, L. (2017) 'Helping Bereaved Children in Schools.' In R. Stevenson and G. Cox (eds) *Children, Adolescents, and Death: Questions and Answers.* New York: Routledge.

Greenwald, R. (2005) *Child Trauma Handbook: A Guide for Helping Trauma-Exposed Children and Adolescents.* New York: The Haworth Maltreatment and Trauma Press.

Holmes, M. (2000) *A Terrible Thing Happened.* Washington, DC: Magination Press.

Humphreys, C. *et al.* (2006). *Talking About Domestic Abuse: A Photo Activity Workbook.* London: Jessica Kingsley.

Lee, I., and Sylvester, K. (2011). *When Mommy Got Hurt.* Oakland, CA: Storymine Press.

Lewis, C.S. (2015) *A Grief Observed.* New York: HarperOne.

Lieberman, M., Eisenberger, N., Crockett, M., Tom, S., Pfeifer, J., and Way, B. (2007) 'Putting feelings into words: Affect labeling disrupts amygdala activity in response to affective stimuli.' *Psychological Sciences 18,* 5, 421–428.

Mayo Clinic Staff (2015) *Complicated Grief: Diseases and Conditions.* Rochester, MN: Mayo Clinic. Available at www.mayoclinic.org/diseases-conditions/complicated-grief/basics/definition/con-20032765, accessed on 02/25/15.

Meiners, C. (2010) *Cool Down and Work Through Anger.* Minneapolis, MN: Free Spirit.

Ogawa, Y. (2004) 'Childhood trauma and play therapy intervention for traumatized children.' *Journal of Professional Counseling, Practice, Theory, and Research 32,* 1, Education Module 19–29.

Rando, T. (2013) 'On Achieving Clarity Regarding Complicated Grief.' In M. Stroebe, H. Schut, and A. Bout (eds) *Complicated Grief: Scientific Foundations for Health Care Professionals.* New York: Taylor and Francis.

Rubel, B. (2009). *But I Didn't Say Goodbye.* NJ: Griefwork Center, Inc.

van der Kolk, B. (2003) 'The neurobiology of childhood trauma.' *Child and Adolescent Psychiatric Clinics of North America 12,* 2, 293–317.

Watts, G. and Hodson. B (2009). *Hear My Roar: A Story of Family Violence.* Canada: Annick Press.

Weaver, S. (2011) *Worry Busters.* Herndon, VA: Rainbow Reach.

Chapter 3

Serving Underserved Students

THE VIEW FROM THE CLASSROOM

Kyle Schwartz

One American classroom

On any given morning when you walk into room 207 at Doull Elementary in Denver, Colorado, you will see students behaving a little differently than you might expect. You are likely to see a student sitting cross-legged on top of a desk while another student lies flat as a pancake on the rug. The reason for this is simple. Especially when reading, I let students sit wherever and however they want (Figure 3.1). To get in the zone with reading, I have to be comfortable, and I figure kids are no different. This belief is as the center of my classroom. My students are people. While I do have authority in my classroom, the influence I have comes from my expertise and knowledge, not from controlling my students' every action.

So, whether kids are cocooning themselves into a pile of pillows or perfectly postured at a desk, when you enter my classroom you will see third grade students who love to read, children with extraordinary potential and even greater dreams, doing the hard work of learning, often in their second or third language.

Figure 3.1 Classroom

Many of the students in my classroom have experienced idyllic childhoods thus far. Many have never worried about how long they will be able to sleep in the same bed. Some of my students have not been forced to cope with separation from a family member or grieved the loss of a loved one. Most of my students always have had food in the refrigerator. Some have not witnessed or experienced abuse. But, the truth is some have. And that is at the center of my classroom too. My students need support.

Some of my dedicated girls and boys deal with the absence of a parent who was deported or incarcerated. Some are working toward healing after abuse. Sometimes students walk to school in the snow wearing shorts and sandals. Sometimes a student turns in homework that was completed in the backseat of the car they slept in the night before. At times during a lesson, a student nods off, not in defiance but in exhaustion. Once, a boy routinely hid classroom snacks, a pragmatic response to knowing exactly what it feels like to starve. A few of my students have even attempted to harm themselves at school; one even tried to jump out of a second-story window in an effort to cope with overwhelming pain.

Still, there are many days when everything goes right, days when I display student work in the hallway like trophies. On some mornings, families triumphantly deliver carefully constructed models of the solar system to the classroom. On some afternoons, I watch my students nap as a school bus bumps along, exhausted from a field trip touring a museum or trekking through the mountains. On some nights, I crowd into our gymnasium alongside families as we cheer on our basketball team, taking each play way too seriously. Some of my favorite days are when I get to meet with families and tell them the hard work has paid off and their child is making progress.

But there are also days when my students lash out at me in intense rage. There are days when a small frustration erupts into physical fighting. There was once a moment before a lesson when a student gently tapped me on the arm as her eyes conveyed equal amounts of hurt and bravery before whispering, "Can I talk to you about something?" And there was another time when a child disclosed to me the details of sexual abuse that she had suffered. During some school conferences families confide in me about hardships and ask for my support and understanding. A mother once said, "My son is starting to ask why he doesn't have a dad like other kids—what should I tell him?" There have been days in my teaching career when an overwhelmed student ran away from the building. When we found one student, he could not explain his actions. He was not running towards any particular refuge; the act of fleeing appeared to be the only solution to escape feelings he could not quite articulate.

In education there is a catalogue of euphemisms to describe some of my students. Words like: at risk, challenging, free and reduced lunch, low income, underserved. Terms like these lessen the sting of the truth—children lack basic resources and much-needed supports. Children are suffering and our society allows it, and often contributes to it.

While I cultivate empathy for my students, I do not pity them. I pity our city. The word "heartbreaking" has been used to describe some of my students' circumstances. But my students are far from broken. They are strong, resilient, and creative. These students at my school display so much talent. They perform Shakespeare, compose music, and write computer code. My students find solutions, not just to personal problems but also to real-life challenges our world faces. I see my students' brilliance and insight every day. By not fully investing in the education of all children, our community is missing out on so much potential. This scenario is played out in schools and communities all over our country. *My students and the millions of American students that they represent do not deserve pity, they deserve investment.*

Time and time again, I come back to and feel validated by the conclusions made by the researcher and pioneer of the Effective Schools Movement, Ronald Edmonds (1979):

> We can, whenever and wherever we choose, successfully teach all children whose schooling is of interest to us; we already know more than we need to do that; and whether or not we do it must finally depend on how we feel about the fact that we haven't so far. (p.23)

There are a million little ways I reach out to the children in my classroom, but there is one activity that has had a tremendous impact. Thanks to the power of social media, this activity and the voices of my students have been heard all over the world.

In my first year of teaching I began asking students to complete the sentence: I wish my teacher knew… (Figure 3.2). Their answers were representative of the unique personalities and diverse life experiences in my classroom. Some answered with whimsy, saying, "I wish my teacher knew how to play video games." Some children told me about their dreams, saying, "I wish my teacher knew I want to go to college." Other responses were poignant: "I wish my teacher knew I don't have pencils at home to do my homework."

Figure 3.2 I wish my teacher knew…

A few years into this tradition, I posted a picture of one note on Twitter and watched with amazement as teachers from around the world tried the same simple exercise in their classrooms. Soon bloggers and journalists saw notes teachers shared and a powerful dialogue was started. As I explained in my book *I Wish My Teacher Knew: How One Question Can Change Everything for Our Kids* (Schwartz, 2016):

> My goal in posting this little girl's note was to share a simple message with other educators: that students will share their realities with us

if we simply give them an invitation. The real power of the exercise, and why so many people responded to it, has to do with the raw truth of the students' words. When we are willing to really listen, our students might feel safe enough to express their truth. As teachers we need to ask, so that our students will answer. But we also need to listen, so our students are heard. (p.4)

In my own classroom, the "I wish my teacher knew…" lesson has evolved from just collecting the notes to a community-building experience. On my students' insistence, I allowed them to read their notes aloud to the class. We sat in a circle as kids eagerly waited their turn to share if they so chose. To watch this is to witness a community grow. As children one by one read their notes, I could feel the compassion the students had for each other. One year, a boy started to read his note. He only got through the first few words before breaking down in tears and passing the note to another boy to read: "I wish my teacher knew my dad left me." No one laughed or rolled their eyes. The kids sitting next to him put their arms around him and rubbed his back. A chorus of voices echoed around the room saying a frequently used phrase in our classroom: "We got your back."

On one level the "I wish my teacher knew…" lesson informs teachers of the realities students face. It can help a teacher understand what a student is interested in or how best to support a student's needs. On another level, the exercise can be a powerful tool in building a classroom community. In a classroom where trust has been established, students can experience the vulnerability of sharing their life experiences as well as the strength that comes from advocating for their own needs.

TEACHING ME: SCHAI

Schai is a spoken word artist in the Washington DC Metro area and deeply committed to advocating for her community. She credits aspects of her personal identity such as her family structure, her sexuality, and a medical condition for giving her a unique worldview and providing her with a source of strength. However, these personal attributes were only ever viewed in a negative light during her school experience. This is what she wishes her teachers had known about her:

I wish my teachers knew they were my parents away from home.

Even though I have always been passionate about learning, school has never been a safe space for me. Unfair judgments by teachers continually exacerbated the very real challenges I faced. While the schools I attended were all relatively diverse, I still stuck out. When I was one year old, I was adopted from Haiti and moved to my new home in Maryland. It was clear to me my unique family dynamic was not accepted when I overheard teachers whispering about my white mother's failure to manage my hair. When I was in sixth grade, a teacher announced, "That Schai, look how she dresses. She wants to be a boy." I was confused about my sexuality myself and comments like this confirmed I would not find acceptance at school.

As a result of experiences like these, relationships with my teachers were slow to form. I acted out and "got disciplined" a lot. So, when I experienced my first seizure as a sophomore in high school, I only expected minimum support from my teachers. I was wrong. My low expectations weren't even met. After a meeting at the school, my mother informed me I wouldn't be attending school the next day. I was told my condition posed a risk to other students. Thankfully, my mother fought this decision and I was eventually allowed to go back to class, but I returned as a pariah.

Reactions to my return varied. Some pretended nothing had happened. Some teachers actually thought I was using my seizures as a way to get out of class work. Each day was a struggle. The diagnosis of frontal lobe epilepsy was frightening, but it was also humiliating to be so vulnerable in front of my peers. Once, I gave a teacher a prearranged private signal to let her know I felt a seizure coming on. She panicked, called the office, and yelled, "Schai is going to have a seizure… Oh my god, come now!" I felt betrayed.

I can understand how my seizures caused trepidation and uncertainty for my teachers. I myself was terrified every time it happened. Instead of avoiding or fearing me, I wish my teachers had taken the time to educate themselves. I wish they had tried to find out more about my epilepsy and how it was affecting my learning. Even just an expression of support and understanding from a teacher would have meant the world to me.

It would have been easy to give up, to sacrifice my education to find a place where I felt safe and accepted. But, that's not who I am. I'm almost done with college and I found the voice I never had in school. I am dedicated to my craft of spoken word because I know that sharing my truth empowers others.

Realities that students and teachers face

The experiences and realities my students have shared with me are not unique to my classroom. In my school, about 90 percent of students qualify for free or reduced priced lunch from the government, a marker of poverty among school children (Denver Public Schools, 2016). In Denver, a Sunbelt city with a public image of being a modern western metropolis, 68 percent of students live below or very close to the poverty line (Communications Office—Denver Public Schools, 2016). More than half of students nationwide, 51 percent, now qualify for free or reduced priced lunch as reported by the Southern Education Foundation (2015).

All schools share the responsibility of educating our youth, but the job of supporting students who live in poverty is not shared equally, not even close. More than half of American children in our public schools live in low-income households and struggle to have basic needs met. The effect of this injustice and all its implications are compounded by the concentration of poverty in our communities and schools. Students who live below or very near to the federal poverty line tend to go to school together. These schools are deemed "high poverty schools" by the National Center for Education Statistics (NCES) and are defined as schools where more than 75 percent of the students live below or very near the poverty line. Data from the NCES (2016) shows that 24 percent of all public school students attended high poverty schools in 2013. High poverty schools are disproportionately attended by students of color. The NCES also found, "In school year 2012–13, higher percentages of Black, Hispanic, and American Indian/Alaska Native students attended high-poverty public schools than did Pacific Islander students, students of Two or more races, Asian students, and White students" (p. 1). More specifically, 45 percent of all public school students who identify as Hispanic or Black attended high poverty schools, while only 8 percent of their White peers attended the same high poverty schools.

A 2016 article in *The Atlantic* explained the implications of this concentration of poverty, saying:

> Systemic economic and racial isolation looms as a huge obstacle for efforts to make a quality education available to all American students…
> [This] "economic isolation and the concentration of poverty among students of color afflicts not only a few struggling cities, but virtually all cities. (Boschma and Brownstein, 2016, paras. 1, 7)

The article also quoted Professor Sean F. Reardon of Stanford University, who said "We don't have much evidence that we can make major improvements in educational equality solely through school policy alone. Educational policy has to be part of the picture. But we need more than that" (para. 24). Reardon argues that, in order to change educational outcomes, issues like residential and school integration as well as economic parity must also be addressed. I could not agree more.

Like all classrooms, mine is made up of students who are all dealing with the universal challenges of childhood. Kids are learning to develop friendships, build a personal identity, and understand academic concepts. Yet some of my students also have to contend with problems beyond their years. Some are coping with trauma and grief and more experience anxiety and chronic stress. My school, along with so many high poverty schools, is tasked with educating students to a high standard while also ameliorating the effects of our inequitable and unjust society.

American schools reflect the political and social landscape. While teachers are not individually responsible for the disparity in our schools, we are frequently held accountable for it. The political becomes very personal for us. When education budgets are slashed or never fully funded in the first place, it is teachers who are asked to do more with less. When jobs leave our communities or affordable housing is limited, it is our classrooms' doors that revolve to bid farewell to old friends and welcome new students. If social services are underfunded, it is our students who are left at risk. When mental health support is treated as a luxury for the fortunate few, it is the children in our schools who suffer.

What constitutes a good teacher?

Even in our clearly inequitable school system, there is this myth that a "good" teacher can overcome any learning obstacle. This also means that if a certain measure of success is not met, the blame is often assigned to a teacher. When asked "What's the best way to evaluate a teacher?" National Teacher of the Year 2015, Shanna Peeples, answered with this story.

One year, Shanna had two distinct groups of students in her high school English courses in Amarillo, Texas. She taught one class of high school juniors in an Advanced Placement course. One hundred percent of these students passed their graduation test. That same year Shanna also taught a class made up of students who were recent refugees.

None of these students passed the graduation test. "Which is the truth?" she wondered. "Was I the worst teacher? Or the best teacher?" She continues, "Where, what, and who you teach will show similar patterns of 'successful' and 'failing' schools and teachers across your district. Any district" (Peeples, 2016, para. 18).

All of this information is not to argue that failure in high poverty schools is a foregone conclusion. It is not. This is to explain the pressure of being a teacher to students who are subject to economic and racial isolation in school. I also argue that teachers should advocate for equity in our school system. Often, the powers that be in education send messages every day to teachers that make us believe the ultimate goal of a school is to produce measurable student outcomes. They tell us that classroom success is only determined by how big the difference is between a pre-test score and a post-test score. By this one number our merits as an educator will be judged. This makes it seem like any action a teacher takes in their classroom only really counts if it can be proven to immediately boost test scores or decrease undesired behavior. It can make teachers think that taking valuable class time to ask students about their lives or leave the textbooks behind to go on a field trip must be justified by data. Never mind if it is the right thing to do, never mind if it makes a kid feel cared about. *The pressure of unsupported accountability is destructive when it creates an atmosphere where measuring learning is prioritized far above meeting the very real needs of our students.*

To teachers who find themselves in this situation, Peeples offers these words of wisdom:

To bow to the pressures of "teaching to the test" or worrying about "preparing for the test" to the exclusion of authentic literacy learning dishonors and devalues students. Ironically, a singular focus on "achievement" vis-à-vis standardized scores serves to inhibit the very literacy skills we trust incessant test preparation to build. As teachers, it is incumbent upon us to make spaces for our students' voices. We must, in a sense, turn our backs on an inferno that is burning us up with demands and pressures; instead, we must turn toward our students and be open, supportive, and welcoming. (2016, p.23)

I do not argue that all testing should be eliminated. On the contrary, the information gained from assessing my students is among the most powerful forces in my instruction. Nor do I believe that schools exist only to meet the social and emotional needs of children. I am a firm believer in setting rigorous standards as well as communicating student progress with families, communities, and students themselves. However, I also know that children can only learn when they feel safe. It is not a case of choosing which to prioritize—academics or social development. The truth is, each is deeply dependent on the other. It is impossible to comprehend literature without the ability to empathize and understand the characters' motivations and emotions. Learning complex concepts can only be accomplished by student determination. We must nurture children as both intellectual beings and social creatures with human needs. Developing intellect and strengthening character must be done hand in hand.

Given the current climate in education, it is easy to overlook that our pupils are real people who need social and emotional support. If it is needed, I would like to grant teachers permission or, as my principal Jodie Carrigan says, "wave the magic wand that allows teachers to do what is right for kids," even if it doesn't change a single test score, even if what you do can never be proven to impact measurable student outcomes, and even if no one notices. Care for kids. Nurture kids. Discover their interests, pique their curiosities, and push their thinking. Study the systems and forces that impact your school's community. Investigate the barriers that keep your students from reaching their full potential. Uncover and display the resources—the passion, intelligence, and humor—that your students come to school with each day. Give your students your unrelenting empathy and indestructible faith.

How? Relationships.

Relationships that lead to learning

While those outside of education may think that a teacher's role is solely to impart knowledge to their pupils, the truth is that the work of being a teacher is to strengthen relationships with students. This is complex, nuanced work and yet it is intuitive and straightforward. It is both innate and developed over time. Care for kids. There is no one strategy that works best in relationships, just as a lawyer doesn't deploy a singular strategy for every case. Nor is there a step-by-step sequence that ensures results, just as a doctor doesn't prescribe the same treatment to each patient. Every school year is different, and every child is unique. That is the beauty and the challenge of it.

The pace at which relationships develop varies widely in my classroom. While some students seem to bond with me effortlessly, other students approach me with caution as they have already learned the inherent risk involved with trusting a new adult. Patience and consistency are crucial for these students. There are also those students who seem to fly under the radar. It is often done by design. Shrinking from view is a self-protective strategy that can be learnt at a young age. When no one notices you, it is hard to get hurt. A colleague once challenged me to take a sheet of paper and write down all my students' names. The purpose was to note the students I left out. It is these forgotten children who might need my attention the most. Reaching these students is often just a matter of showing steady interest and care.

Forming a relationship with some students is particularly challenging. Students have displayed aggressive behaviors towards me or even hidden behind protective walls of apathy. This is not as an act of disrespect or defiance. If a child is struggling to connect with me, they have likely experienced turbulent relationships with other educators. It is my goal to create conditions where growth can take place and a relationship can form.

The influential psychologist and major contributor to the student-centered learning movement, Carl Rogers, developed the concept of core conditions. His theory suggests that relationships that lead to significant learning form when three traits are present: congruence or genuineness, unconditional positive regard for students, and an empathetic understanding (Rogers, 1995).

Genuineness

First, teachers need to be genuine in order to build relationships. To Rogers, this meant a teacher must bring their authentic self and feelings into the classroom. A teacher is "not a faceless embodiment of a curricular requirement, or a sterile pipe through which knowledge is passed from one generation to the next" (1995, p.287). We need to "enter into relationships with the learners without presenting a front of a façade" (Rogers, 1989, p.271). This means that we accept and display our true feelings for our students. It also means teachers should bring their interests and passions into the classroom as well as share aspects of their own lives with students. If you expect students to share life experiences with you, you should be prepared to reciprocate.

Unconditional positive regard

Additionally, the relationship that Rogers believes leads to significant learning requires the existence of unconditional positive regard. According to Rogers, this is a "warm, positive, and acceptant attitude" (1995, p.62). "It is an atmosphere which simply demonstrates 'I care'; not 'I care for you if you behave thus and so'" (Rogers, 1995, p.283). Especially when children struggle with behavior in school, it is easy for them to believe they are valued only when they are acting appropriately. Unlearning this can be a long process. In my classroom, I find it necessary to be explicit. Some children need to hear that they are truly accepted over and over again. Typically the first words to students in the morning are: "I care about you. Do you believe me?"

Empathetic understanding

Finally, if teachers want to build relationships in their classrooms, they must have an empathetic understanding of our students. This happens when we have "the ability to understand each student's reaction from the inside." This is why it is essential to find out who our students are as people, the barriers they face, and the resources they bring to school each day. Having empathy for our students also requires us to reserve judgment as we make every attempt to understand their worldview (Rogers, 1989).

Building relationships with students is challenging work, but it is work we must do if we are to create the conditions where learning can take place. Our students need to know that their classroom is a place where they are safe and valued if they are to engage in deep learning. When teachers are genuine, display an unconditional positive regard for our students, and are empathetic, they set the stage for powerful classroom communities to form.

TEACHING ME: BRITTNEY

Brittney never had the opportunity to tell her teachers exactly what she wished they knew about her. For most of her educational career, school was a place where Brittney felt labeled by the system and isolated from her peers. This is what she wishes her teacher knew:

> *I wish my teacher knew how much she impacted me every day and how much she still impacts me.*

Like most small towns, my hometown is the kind of place where everybody knows everybody. Which meant on my first day of middle school, everyone already knew two things about me: I have cerebral palsy and my father had just ended his own life. Both facts were common knowledge and yet neither was openly discussed. I don't know if my teachers kept silent due to their own discomfort or as an attempt to save me from embarrassment. Maybe they were just afraid that acknowledging suicide at all would "give kids ideas." Either way, treating my father's death like a secret ended up breeding misunderstanding and pain. I'm sure my classmates were confused why anyone would take their own life. I was too. I believe that sweeping the nature of my father's death under the rug caused me to become a target.

Admittedly, I always had difficulty connecting with my peers, but I suddenly felt even more out of touch with them. A group of students, led by one boy in particular, were especially cruel to me. During recess, this group of kids taunted me with phrases like: "You should kill yourself just like your father." By far the most painful thing to hear was them reference my disability and saying, "Your dad killed himself because of you." Each day my wounds were reopened and my grief was extended. Looking back, I actually have empathy for that little boy. As an adult, I can now recognize that he had experienced childhood trauma himself. Maybe if he had been supported and his hurt had been addressed he would not have inflicted so much pain on me.

My teachers did not seek to help me. I was the victim, and yet I was and made to feel I had brought this bullying on myself. In high school, another student poured ranch dressing on my head at lunch. An administrator responded by suggesting that I had provoked the incident by dying my hair red. Another day, I was shoved into a locker by another student and I texted my mom about it. I was subsequently reprimanded for using a cell phone in school. As you can imagine, this treatment made school unbearable to me. Many days I just stayed home.

I suffered tremendously at school, but mine is a story of hope. In my junior year of high school, Mrs. Baumgardt's English class provided me respite. In her classroom, there was no cruelty from my peers, she simply wouldn't allow it. Feeling safe inside a school was strange but welcomed. She got to know my passions and curiosities, and then she used those to push me academically. She even made an exception for me when she allowed me to write my essay about Harry Potter. I think she knew how much I identified with the boy wizard's experience with loss and search for acceptance. On days when chronic pain kept me out of school, Mrs. Baumgardt and I held virtual book club meetings. She didn't treat me like I was a lost cause, nor did she treat me like I was just like everyone else. The obstacles I faced were acknowledged and met with individualized support. My natural talents were nurtured and she encouraged my writing. It made me feel I had something important to say.

I want teachers to know it's never too late to reach that seemingly unreachable student. One teacher's care can be incredibly healing. I know that there are many kids who are hurting. I hope every child can experience what it is like to have a teacher who acts as their champion. It's the last semester of college now and I'm chasing down my dream to become a professional writer. This would not have happened without the investment one teacher made in me. Thank you, Mrs. Baumgardt.

From my classroom: Everyday actions to build community

We got your back

If you visit our classroom for a few hours you will hear the same short phrase repeated over and over again: "We got your back." It's a powerful little saying that communicates so much in four small words.

Each day I make time for students to share anything they would like with the class. Many classrooms have a version of this, but I call mine CQC for "Celebrations, Questions, or Concerns." As I explain in *I Wish My Teacher Knew* (Schwartz, 2016), the information students share "helps me be a better teacher to each student. I can understand certain sensitivities they might have or a situation that might trigger an emotional reaction" (p.84). When a student tells the class about a difficult situation, there is a need for connection. That is where "We got your back" comes in. A veteran teacher and mentor of mine, Susana Moening, taught me this phrase in my first year of teaching, and it has been a staple in my classroom ever since.

For example, a student once shared with our class that her grandmother had gone into hospital over the weekend. I responded by saying, "That seems really hard. Have you been thinking about that a lot lately?" She said she had indeed been worrying about this. Then, students chimed in with "We got your back!" I asked the class another question: "If she needs support today, who will help her? Who will talk with her at recess and sit next to her at lunch?" A forest of hands shot straight up. "Look," I said. "There are a lot of people who care about you and will support you." This interaction is repeated in my classroom almost daily throughout the school year.

The phrase "We got your back" tells students there is a community in this classroom that is looking out for them and supporting them. Each and every one of us faces challenges, and this makes it clear that no one has to struggle in isolation in our classroom. One of the beautiful little aspects of a "We got your back" type of community is each year the kids start to say it to me. If the computer suddenly stops working in the middle of a lesson, I hear a chorus of "We got your back, Miss." If I tell students that visitors will be in our classroom observing and I need the students to be on their best behavior, inevitably someone will say, "Don't worry Miss, we got your back."

Students supporting students

In my classroom, we are not just a random assortment of eight- and nine-year-olds. We are a community. Creating a community-focused environment requires that I sometimes take a step back and deliberately empower students to help each other even through challenging circumstances.

A perfect example of this concept at work was when Gabe's cat died. When I visited Gabe's house a few weeks before, he proudly showed off the family pet, Mittens. One morning, Gabe's mother sent me an email to let me know that the cat had to be put down. So, when Gabe looked at the clock during a reading lesson and flatly said, "It's 9:17, so she has been dead for two minutes now," I knew exactly what he meant.

Some teachers might think the death of a cat is not an issue worth addressing in class. They are wrong. To a child, the loss of a pet is significant, especially because it is often the first experience with grief. Which means it is an opportunity for children to go through the grieving process with support. I invited Gabe to write about Mittens. I told him he could put down all his thoughts and feelings so he would never forget his pet. At the end of class, Gabe asked if he could share what he wrote with the class. The rest of the class chimed in, saying, "We got your back."

"Mittens, My Wonderful Kitten" by Gabe

I will never forget my cat Mittens. I will never forget how soft and fluffy she was. She was the best cat I ever met. March 15th 2016 was rough, my mom said, "She's really sick." And then she said, "They are going to give her medicine that will put her to sleep but not sleep because she'll be dead." So it was a rough night for me because I did not want to lose my first pet because at first I never knew what being a pet owner was like but now I do know and we only had her from August 2014 to today, March 15th 2016. She was so sweet and her stare was so cute.

Mittens I love you!

A few weeks later Rainah came into class ready to talk. The first thing she said to me was: "When are we doing celebrations and concerns? Because I have one to share." She gave the class a detailed account of her cousin's funeral. She told the class that she didn't know why all these bad things were happening and she broke down in tears. Several students scooted closer to her and patted her back while she cried. I told her that this must be a sad time, but we were all here to support her. Then I asked Gabe if he would help Rainah write about her cousin, just as he had done for Mittens. The two cozied up in a corner of the room. I am not sure what they said to each other, but that was not the point. This was an opportunity for students to support each other. At the end of class, Rainah shared the following writing about her cousin.

"About My Cousin Alfredo/Nico" by Rainah

My cousin Nico was a great man [...] he got leukemia in 2014 [...] before he got leukemia he married my cousin Jasmine [...] that's how Nico became my cousin. My cousin Nico was also a rapper [...] his rapper name was West one. Back to leukemia [...] he was in the hospital for a while... But two weeks later he had passed away into the light. Next Friday it was his funeral and my cousin Jasmine was saying, "It was not fair that her family is going to heaven because her Mom died when she was only 11 months old [...] and her Uncle died when she was 11 years old also when she was pregnant with a Baby Girl she died in her stomach and now she is losing her Husband." I wish the hospital found a cure for Nico because he would still be alive right now and I would be so happy [...] but now it feels like a part of my heart is gone forever and it hurts [...] and if he was alive my cousin Jasmine will still be happy. So that was about my cousin Nico. Nico I still love you and I miss you so much and I love my cousin Jasmine so much. It won't be the same without you. I love you Alfredo. REST IN HEAVEN. I will see you again someday.

This whole episode benefited both students. They were able to tell their community about a personal challenge and feel supported. For Gabe, he not only processed his loss, but his grief had a greater purpose. He now knew how to shepherd someone else through a difficult time. For her part, Rainah was able to pay it forward a few days later when another girl came to school distressed about a fight she had with her mother. Rainah knew just what to do and helped this girl process her feelings. The entire class also benefited. Students saw that death and loss are acceptable topics at school and were witness to a healthy model of bereavement.

As a teacher, I know how to directly support my students in the mists of tragedy. I can sit with each one of them individually and help them process their feelings. Ultimately, that is not my goal. My goal is to create an environment where students are able not just to be the recipient of support but also empowered to be a source of encouragement for others. This happens when relationships and trust are established and teachers intentionally allow for students to take active roles in helping each other.

What a community teaches

Even with every support and resource available, learning is hard. Even under perfect conditions, teaching is hard. This work becomes exponentially more difficult when challenges such as racial and economic isolation, grief and trauma, and inequitable access to the economy are introduced. These factors make the role of each individual classroom even more important. When our classrooms become communities, our students feel safe and valued enough to engage in the hard work of learning.

The question becomes: How can we create space for teachers to do the essential work of forming community-focused learning environments? Amidst the ever-growing demands of the industrial education complex, how do we hold sacred the time it takes to build human connections? The truth is, in this data-obsessed educational climate, it takes courage to value things we can't even measure—skills like integrity, kindness, and empathy.

In the end, it is worth the energy we put into building strong, supportive spaces, because our students will learn what their classroom community teaches them. If their classroom community cares more about the product than the process, they learn that they are only worth what they can produce. If their classroom community turns learning into a competitive sport, they will learn that their neighbors' failures amplify their success. If their classroom community sacrifices human connection in service of an obsession with data, they learn that all that they are can be distilled down into a number. On the contrary, if our students learn in a community that values connectedness, collaboration, and compassion, they will learn that they can achieve more when they support each other. That is a lesson our students will take with them far beyond our classroom doors.

References

Boschma, J. and Brownstein, R. (2016) 'The concentration of poverty in American schools.' *The Atlantic*, February 29. Available at www.theatlantic.com/education/archive/2016/02/concentration-poverty-american-schools/471414, accessed on 03/24/17.

Communications Office—Denver Public Schools (2016) *Facts and Figures*. Available at http://communications.dpsk12.org/facts.html, accessed on 08/20/16.

Denver Public Schools (2016) *Doull Elementary School Spotlight Summary Scorecard*. Available at http://spf.dpsk12.org/documents/2016/227_2016SPF_Stoplight_Summary_Trad_Doull_Elementary_School_EN.pdf, accessed on 05/04/17.

Edmonds, R. (1979) 'Effective schools for the urban poor.' *Educational Leadership 37*, 1, 15–24. Available at www.ascd.org/ASCD/pdf/journals/ed_lead/el_197910_edmonds.pdf, accessed on 03/24/17.

National Center for Education Statistics (2016) *Concentration of Public School Students Eligible for Free and Reduced-Price Lunch*. Available at http://nces.ed.gov/programs/coe/pdf/coe_clb.pdf, accessed on 03/24/17.

Peeples, S. (2016) 'Testing the teacher' [Web log post]. Available at www.shannapeeples.com/?p=1128, accessed on 03/24/17.

Rogers, C. (1989) *On Becoming a Person: A Therapist's View of Psychotherapy*. New York: Houghton Mifflin Publishing Company.

Rogers, C. (1995) *A Way of Being*. New York: Houghton Mifflin Publishing Company.

Schwartz, K. (2016) *I Wish My Teacher Knew: How One Question Can Change Everything for Our Kids*. Boston, MA: Da Capo Press.

Southern Education Foundation (2015) *A New Majority Research Bulletin: Low Income Students Now a Majority in the Nation's Public Schools*. Available at www.southerneducation.org/getattachment/4ac62e27-5260-47a5-9d02-14896ec3a531/A-New-Majority-2015-Update-Low-Income-Students-Now.aspx, accessed on 03/24/17.

Chapter 4

Viewing Underserved Populations of Children and Youth through a Trauma-Sensitive Lens

Susan Craig

The landmark study of Adverse Childhood Experiences (ACE; Felitti *et al.*, 1998), as well as research on children's neurological development (National Scientific Center on the Developing Child, 2005, 2006, 2007, 2012), document the relationship between early trauma and anomalies in children's neurological development. Regardless of their source, traumatic experiences alter the architecture of children's brains in ways that threaten their ability to achieve academic and social mastery. Left unattended, this affects the health, well-being, and capacity to learn, not only of children, but adults as well (Karr-Morse and Wiley, 2012).

The news, however, is not all bad. Brain development turns out to be a very dynamic process that retains a certain plasticity throughout the human life span. This ability to change offers hope that the effects of early trauma can be reversed later in life (National Child Traumatic Stress Network (NCTSN), 2009). Schools are well positioned to help children achieve the resilience they need to move beyond their traumatic pasts. An important first step is to recognize the high cost of trauma and the pervasiveness of its symptoms. Only then will the healing begin.

The high cost of trauma

The word "traumatic" is often used to describe extraordinary events, such as the recent terrorist attacks in Paris and Brussels, the Sandy Hook Elementary School shooting, and the massacre in Orlando, Florida, in 2016. This usage is inaccurate, however. *Events are not traumatic in and of themselves; they become traumatic when they exceed a person's capacity to cope.* In other words, trauma depends not only on the event, but also the resources available to help a person manage the situation and restore a sense of safety. Children depend on their caregivers to protect them from harm. In the absence of protective relationships with adults, children are especially vulnerable to developing symptoms of complex trauma. This affects children's learning and behavior in consistent and predictable ways.

A deep-seated distrust of authority figures, coupled with a hypersensitivity to perceptions of danger or threat, seriously compromise children's ability to learn. The greater number of different types of trauma children are exposed to, the greater the number of developmental domains affected, thus causing multiple symptoms. Trauma's impact is most pervasive during the first decade of life. Early experiences set the stage for lifelong unfocused responses to stress because trauma interferes with neurobiological development (van der Kolk, 2005) and the development of core self-regulatory capacities (Ford and Russo, 2006). Children's capacity to integrate sensory, emotional, and cognitive information in new situations is compromised by their brain's response to traumatic events in the past.

The prevalence of childhood trauma

The rate of childhood trauma in the United States is so high that it is considered by many to be a public health epidemic (Oehlberg, 2012). The NCTSN estimates that one in four children experiences at least one traumatic event by the time they are 16 (NCTSN, 2009). Data from the ACE study (Felitti *et al.* 1998) suggests that the rate is even higher. Using a cut-off score of four or more on the ACE Questionnaire, researchers find that one in three children have scores suggesting an early trauma history.

These numbers are shocking. It can be argued that they go a long way to explain why so many children and youth struggle to achieve academic and social mastery.

Some early childhood trauma occurs as a result of accidents, medical procedures, community violence, and bullying (Levine and Kline, 2006). The stress of living in chronic poverty, explained by Dr. Ruby Payne (see Chapter 5), is also traumatic for children when the hassle of daily life limits their caregivers' ability to shelter them from adversity (Lieberman and Osofsky, 2009).

The most widespread source of childhood trauma, however, is child maltreatment. State agencies across the country estimated that there were 702,000 victims of child maltreatment in 2014 (U.S. Department of Health and Human Services, Administration on Children, Youth and Families, Children's Bureau, 2016). Parents or primary caregivers are almost always responsible for this type of trauma (van der Kolk, 2005). As a result, these experiences are often unseen or unrecognized by outsiders. Many victims are not identified as needing help until they come to the attention of social services or the courts due to their involvement in high-risk behaviors such as substance abuse or delinquency (Dierkhising *et al.*, 2013 ; SAMSHA, 2008).

The effects of early childhood trauma on neurobiological development and self-regulation

Early childhood trauma affects the architecture and chemistry of the brain in ways that threaten to compromise children's awareness of both the self and others, as well as language, memory, and attention. In addition, the continuous hyper-vigilance associated with trauma disrupts the neural circuitry between the reptilian brain and neocortex in a manner that compromises children's executive functioning and problem-solving abilities.

Awareness of self and others

Early trauma inhibits the cognitive processes through which children become self-aware. In typical development children engage in what's referred to as "serve and return" interactions that nurture the establishment of preference and perspective. Serve and return activities occur quite naturally within secure attachment relationships. A baby rolls a ball to a caregiver and the caregiver rolls it back. Or a child asks a question and the caregiver responds and perhaps extends the communication by asking another question. Repeated frequently enough, these reciprocal exchanges teach children that they can affect their environment by initiating an action and waiting for a response. Eventually they learn to adjust or regulate their emotional reactions and behavior to meet personal goals.

Serve and return activities form the basis for intentional thought, anticipatory set, and role-taking ability. As such they increase children's awareness of both themselves and others. They learn that others in their environment also have thoughts and feelings that may not be consistent with their own.

Children with early trauma histories often miss out on the serve and return interactions needed to develop an awareness of self and others. Neglect or maltreatment by caregivers robs them of the self-awareness characteristic of children raised in more predictable, secure relationships. These children feel powerless to get their needs met, or to anticipate the reactions of others toward them. They seldom initiate interactions with others, often appearing disinterested in what is going on around them. This passivity and apparent lack of motivation has detrimental effects on their participation in constructionist classrooms where students are expected to take an active role in their learning. The following example underscores the impact of early trauma on a student named Juan.

Juan is eight years old and in third grade. It takes Juan forever to get started on his work. Instead, he wants to sharpen his pencil, sign up for a bathroom pass, or wander around the room checking out what the other students are doing. I thought the problem was a lack of motivation. But the school psychologist explained that the behaviors were probably due to the neglect Juan experienced as a toddler. The situation at home is still pretty inconsistent, so he never really knows what to expect from his mother. What he does know is that a behavior that is fine one day may get him severely reprimanded on another, depending on her mood. So he's learned to stay under the wire, and avoid initiating anything around her.

The psychologist recommended that Juan be given a list of the assignments he needed to complete during each period, as well as some control over the order he worked on each one. She also suggested regular check-ins to monitor his progress and support his efforts. The added structure is helping Juan get something done. I think it's because he knows what to expect throughout the day.

Language, memory, and attention

Early trauma threatens all aspects of children's language development. Language-rich caregiving relationships provide children with opportunities to learn the vocabulary they need to use words to organize their experiences and mediate their emotions.

Initially, parents and other primary caregivers use their own language to label and interpret events for the young children in their care. In this way, they shape children's first assumptions about themselves and the world around them. The inner dialog that results from these early language experiences becomes an important tool children use to reflect on their experiences, monitor their behavior, and plan for the future.

The absence of caregivers who are capable of engaging children in interactive play and conversation limits the vocabulary they have to express themselves. Attachment relationships characterized by unpredictable routines and inconsistent attention compromise children's ability to initiate conversations, take turns, or attend to non-verbal aspects of communication. When caregivers neglect to label steps in everyday activities, children fail to learn how to use language to think sequentially or monitor their behavior.

These language deficits contribute to the difficulties traumatized children have with memory and attention. All memories start with sensory input that the brain sorts, discarding what it judges to be irrelevant (Gazzaniga, 1998). The sensory input that remains is quickly organized into perceptual patterns that are interpreted on the basis of prior knowledge and what the brain has come to expect. The brain constantly scans the environment for stimuli that fit earlier formed patterns. It is primed to attend to familiar stimuli and ignore others. Socially, this means children attend best to expectations of themselves and others that are consistent with non-verbal memories of their interactions with primary caregivers.

Academically, children whose memories of primary caregivers include talking about ideas and predicting outcomes for future events are quick to attend to the critical elements of classroom discussions. Conversely, children whose early language experiences are compromised have a harder time discriminating between important and unimportant stimuli in the learning environment. They often miss the point of instruction because they attend to irrelevant stimuli. This leads to frustration and an inability to complete tasks in an efficient and independent manner. The following scenario depicts a five-year-old boy whose father was incarcerated, and the impact of this life event.

Tyrone's father is serving a ten-year prison term for assault. His mom is raising him alone. She works hard to create a good home for Tyrone. She wants him to succeed in school and have a better life than she does. But some of her child-rearing practices may be undermining her goals for him.

Tyrone attends his local Head Start program. His teacher, Ms. Jackson, is helping his mother rethink her belief in the adage "Children should be seen and not heard." At a recent conference, she explained that children learn to think and monitor their behavior in language-rich environments. She tells her that children who are not exposed to language at home enter school with 30 million fewer vocabulary words than their peers (Colka, 2014).

That struck a nerve with Tyrone's mom. She decided to change her ways. She started following Ms. Jackson's recommendations about playing word games with Tyrone, and singing to him when they are in the car or taking a walk. The shift toward more language at home combined with language-rich experiences at school are helping Tyrone reach the literacy goals Ms. Jackson sets for him. Tyrone's behavior is also improving, as he becomes better equipped to use words to get his needs met.

Neural circuitry between the reptilian brain and the neocortex

The brain develops in a sequential way from the bottom up and from the inside out. Its development is use-dependent, meaning that brain development is heavily influenced by the child's environment and life experiences. A nurturing environment in which children's needs are met in a responsive, predictable manner facilitates the formation of strong neural connections between the reptilian (lower) brain and the neocortex. These strong connective pathways are the required neural structures for self-regulation. In their absence, the ability of the prefrontal cortex to monitor the survival instincts of the reptilian brain is seriously compromised.

Childhood trauma threatens the formation of strong neural connections between the reptilian brain and neocortex. Patterns of insecure attachment and chronic adversity heighten the reactivity of the reptilian brain, while at the same time weakening its connectivity to the neocortex. The resulting dysregulation has negative effects on children's level of arousal and a heightened sensitivity to perceptions of threat of danger. Their inability to maintain a tolerable level of arousal or contain their fear and anxiety are the root of many of the self-defeating, defiant behaviors that interfere with academic achievement or social mastery. The following case study of a ten-year-old girl exemplifies the immigration issues faced by students (see Chapter 6).

RIMA: A CASE STUDY

Rima and her family are recent immigrants from Syria. She's endured the perils of war, living in a refugee camp, and settling in a country that is dramatically different from her own. She's proven herself to be quite resilient, and manages to approach the challenges in her new life with a mixture of curiosity and self-confidence. Most of the time she does quite well until something in the environment triggers a past trauma. Loud, sharp noises are a common trigger. She's been known to scream and run for cover at the sound of the fire alarm. Crowded conditions like a packed stairwell or crowded elevator can cause Rima to panic. So can getting lost. On a recent field trip to a museum, Rima's teacher found her crying outside a restroom. She'd lost track of her classmates and was afraid she'd been left alone.

The school social worker is helping Rima understand her strong reactions to what she refers to as "trauma triggers." She explains that loud noises, crowds, and a fear of being lost trigger her brain's "fight, flight, or freeze" mode to give her the energy she needs to ward off threats and survive. This reaction was advantageous when she was in real danger, but since the dangers are gone, it's counterproductive.

Together, Rima and her counselor work out a plan to slow down Rima's reaction to the triggers. When she feels the urge to "fight, flee, or freeze," she will count to ten. This will give her time to check the accuracy of her panicky feelings and decide whether she needs to react to them or ignore them. The social worker tells Rima she's learning to use a "cognitive brake" to evaluate her situation. She assures her that with enough practice she'll do it automatically. She'll know how to use her neocortex to control her emotions and move on with her life!

The school's role

The argument is sometimes made that schools are first and foremost about academic mastery. It is the job of parents and other family members to ensure that children arrive at school ready to learn. Such a reductionist statement ignores the complexity of the learning process, which always involves an interaction between children's internal world and the environment in which they find themselves.

In 2005, Massachusetts Advocates for Children (Cole *et al.*, 2005) introduced a framework for mitigating the effects of trauma on children's performance in school. They coined the term *trauma-sensitive schools* to describe the type of educational environment traumatized children need to succeed. Since then several states, including Washington, Pennsylvania, California, and Wisconsin, have joined with Massachusetts to draw national attention to this problem and the need to address it in future efforts at educational reform (Craig, 2016).

The vision of a trauma-sensitive school

Trauma-sensitive schools are inclusive school communities characterized by what Carl Rogers referred to as unconditional positive regard. One of the most devastating effects of childhood trauma is the paralyzing sense of isolation that accompanies it. Traumatized children are lonely children. They are alone in their shame, alone in their belief that they are unlovable, and alone in their efforts to contain very frightening feelings that cause them to behave in unpredictable ways. Trauma-sensitive schools embrace these children and help build their capacity to connect with others.

Trauma-sensitive schools are neighborhood schools that follow the principles of universal curriculum design. Based on prevalence data, staff assume that a percentage of enrolled children have trauma histories. And they act accordingly, by building trauma-informed practices into everyday instructional routines throughout the school.

Support is provided using a flexible system of tiered interventions. Like *Positive Behavior Intervention Support* (Sugai *et al.*, 2000), the first tier consists of universal supports that are sufficient to meet the emotional and cognitive needs of most children. But there may be days or weeks when these supports are not enough for some children to continue to succeed. More targeted interventions may be needed to help a child survive a crisis or other short-term problem. The effects of these interventions are monitored closely, and changed when appropriate. This ensures that they are short-lived, with the goal of an eventual return to everyday activities and routines.

Components of the model

The trauma-sensitive school framework is flexible, meaning it can be adjusted to meet the needs of the local school community. There are, however, several model components that need to be included.

Staff training and supervision

Educators cannot be expected to respond to children in a trauma-sensitive manner if they are not provided with state-of-the-art training on how trauma affects neural development. The goal is not to turn teachers into social workers or school psychologists. Rather, it is to give them the insights needed to prepare for occurrences of trauma-related behaviors. Only then will they be able to respond in a manner that promotes resilience and rehabilitation.

Instruction that supports neural development

The ability of magnetic resonance imaging to map the brain provides educators with a framework for designing instruction that works with the brain's plasticity to support children's neural development. These enriching experiences begin with the teacher's ability to engage children in positive and creative ways, and extend to the physical aspects and emotional tone of the classroom.

The neurodevelopmental framework used in trauma-sensitive schools challenges teachers to rethink their choice of instructional activities and projects. These are assessed in terms of their potential for helping children acquire specific neurodevelopmental goals. For example, does a particular activity support Rima's goal of improving the circuitry between her reptilian brain and neocortex? Does participation in a group project help Tyrone increase his vocabulary and make it easier for him to express himself?

Neural networks are strengthened when children are encouraged to do something with what they are learning—talk to a peer about it, write a song about the main ideas, build a model, or debate alternative views about a topic. This type of active engagement facilitates storage in long-term memory, helping "glue" new information onto existing neural structures, thereby increasing children's dendrite mass. As a result they become more efficient at seeing connections between new information and prior knowledge.

Classroom management

Classroom management in a trauma-sensitive school is first and foremost developmentally appropriate. Framed primarily around the principles of positive behavioral support, social-emotional learning, and collaborative problem solving, it avoids behavioral expectations that are beyond a child's developmental capacity. This may seem obvious, but it's important to recognize that children of color, especially boys, are often assumed to be older than they actually are, and may be reprimanded for behaviors that go unnoticed among chronologically same-aged peers.

Teachers in trauma-sensitive schools anticipate trauma-related behaviors and put necessary accommodations in place before they are needed. Social-emotional growth is emphasized, as well as the consistency and teamwork that underscores the collaborative problem-solving model.

Traumatized children are frequently socially inept, often in a manner that makes other children uncomfortable. Teaching them common social behaviors—how to make a play bid, how to ask a question, how to join an ongoing activity—helps them fit in more easily during recess and social activities. They are also taught about emotions and how to separate who they are from what they feel. They learn to pair colors, music, and facial expressions with different emotions, and how to use affirmations to ward off feelings of negativity.

Discipline

The nature of early childhood trauma requires discipline codes in trauma-sensitive schools that focus on self-discipline rather than compliance. Teachers team up with children to garner the strength necessary to resist the insidious urge to hold onto past traumas through compulsive reenactments. Herein lies the most serious effect of early trauma—the inability to let it go, to give up the need to make it right, and to move on. Trauma stops time. Traumatized children cannot imagine a future because they are stuck in the past. Staff members in a trauma-sensitive school help students acquire the courage to think ahead. Collaborative problem solving with teachers helps them understand that relationships are bigger than momentary disconnections or misunderstandings. They can be fixed or repaired. Staff members do not abandon students when they misbehave. Rather, they stand by them and help them make amends.

This type of restorative discipline is the hallmark of a trauma-sensitive school. It heals in a manner that no amount of punishment or coercion can, by reminding children that they are not alone. It is a view of discipline that is quite different from the behaviorist model, which sees children's misbehavior as essentially volitional and recommends using contingency reinforcements (rewards and punishments) to foster compliance. Trauma-driven behaviors are not volitional, and they do not fade as a result of contingency reinforcement.

Policies

Policies in trauma-sensitive schools are intended to safeguard children's safety and confidentiality. They go a few steps further than traditional schools in helping families to access necessary mental health care services. School staff members are assigned to negotiate social service systems with families. This is especially helpful when children require short-term placements in hospitals or residential treatment centers. Staff members work with families to set up transition goals that help children return to school with as little disruption as possible.

Policies about safety planning are particularly important in trauma-sensitive schools given the high likelihood of children living in families marred by domestic violence. These policies include ascertaining which families have court orders preventing contact or the exchange of information, as well as protocols that keep children's personal information out of the hands of perpetrators. Policies about removing identifying contact information from documents before releasing them to a noncustodial parent are strictly adhered to. Such policies ensure the safety of staff and of staff affected by violence.

Collaboration with community agencies

Trauma-sensitive schools are committed to seeing children within the broader contexts of their family and community. This involves forming collaborative partnerships with other key players. Protocols should be in place for creating good working relationships with community resources. Some schools find community partnerships so beneficial that they appoint a staff member as a liaison to community leaders (see Chapter 6).

The benefits of community outreach and improved communication include greater opportunities to share resources, improved access to mental health services for underserved, traumatized students, and the creation of a seamless service delivery to children that avoids further re-traumatization.

The training required to create and sustain trauma-sensitive interventions for children does not occur in a day. It is multifaceted and costly. The time and energy to do it right is more easily arrived at when multiple agencies pool their talent, their money, and their leadership to properly prepare and support staff working with traumatized children and their families.

The issue of resource sharing can and should inform efforts to meet the need of school personnel for trauma-informed, collegial supervision. Schools are unique among helping communities in their failure to protect their employees from the dangers of vicarious traumatization and compassion fatigue. Working with traumatized children takes its toll. Teachers need structured opportunities to relieve stress and recover their enthusiasm and sense of purpose. Partnerships with mental health professionals trained to fill this role are essential to the long-term retention of teachers in a trauma-sensitive school.

Past traumas and current adversities take a toll on the mental health of many students in underserved populations. Trauma-sensitive school policies include protocols that create formal collaborative relationships with community mental health agencies. These partnerships increase opportunities for prevention and treatment programs, and provide schools with readily available referral services. Research shows that students and their families are far more likely to keep recommended therapy appointments when they meet counselors at the school. This enables trusted teachers or administrators to provide a "warm hand off" to the family by introducing them to the person they will work with at the referring agency.

Collaboration across agencies creates a safety net for children to address concerns that extend beyond the school day: before and after school child care programs, public health clinics, social services for family emergencies, and a system for preserving data that is important to children's futures. This is essential when dealing with transient, underserved populations, many of whom are often enrolled in several different schools. While they earn partial credits in each school, this information is often lost. They are then forced to repeat courses or even semesters, thereby delaying graduation. These experiences are re-traumatizing, and often disincline children to continue to keep trying.

A few more practical suggestions

- Understand your own trauma background—your emotional baggage may come into play in the classroom.

- Recognize that children will often instinctively set up a dynamic with teachers that is akin to their parental relationships, so they may act from the beginning to set up rejection.

- Neutral, fair teachers are best for traumatized children. It can be tempting for teachers to try to bond with them, but often such a bond will be more than the children can handle.

- Understand that traumatized children often lack core concepts; they have a misplaced sense of cause and effect, and think they can't do anything right.

- Give children in a meltdown time to recover by letting them draw, listen to music, or journal; don't try to talk to them about the behavior until they calm down.

- Spend a few minutes helping children regulate in the beginning of class.

- Manage "double struggle"—you can't de-escalate the behavior of a child who is out of control if you are out of control, so if a child's behavior starts to get to you, take a break.

- Pay attention to your tone and facial expressions; traumatized children often interpret a lack of emotional affect as negative and are very sensitive to a harsh voice.

- Pay attention to the volume in the classroom; silent classrooms can be very difficult for children who have been abused. Develop a written or pictorial depiction of classroom expectations (even for older children).

- Use role-playing to help children acquire the perspective-taking skills needed for inferential comprehension and empathy.

Conclusion

"A teacher affects eternity; he can never tell where his influence stops."

Henry Adams

Trauma-sensitive schools are committed to infusing trauma-informed practices into the culture of public schools. Administrative leadership encourages staff to view the needs of underserved populations of students through a trauma-sensitive lens. Close collaboration enables staff to create a blend of services, supports, and opportunities that is attuned to individual needs. Emphasis is placed on helping students move beyond past traumas and reach their greatest potential.

Trauma-sensitive schools do not replace learning with discipline. Rather, they rely on positive relationships and neurologically based instruction to nurture children's inherent capacity for self-regulation, and increase their capacity for academic achievement and social mastery.

Achieving these goals helps children with early trauma histories move beyond adversity. Experiences of compassion and respect give students a second chance to achieve happiness and productivity, and make meaningful contributions to their world.

References

Adams, H. (2014). *The Education of Henry Adams*. 2014. Createspace Independent Publishing Platform.

Cole, S., O'Brien, J.G., Gadd, M.G., Ristuccia, J., Wallace, D.L., and Gregory, M. (2005) *Helping Traumatized Children Learn: Supportive School Environments for Children Traumatized by Family Violence*. Boston, MA: Massachusetts Advocates for Children and Harvard Law School, Trauma and Learning Policy Institute.

Colka, L.J. (2014) 'Children's vocabulary skills are linked to their economic backgrounds.' *Teaching Young Children 7*, 3, 26–28.

Craig, S.E. (2016) *Trauma-Sensitive Schools: Learning Communities Transforming Children's Lives, K-5*. New York: Teachers College Press.

Dierkhising, C.B., Ko, S.J., Woods-Jaeger, B., Briggs, E.C., Lee, R., and Pynoos, R.S. (2013) 'Trauma histories among justice involved youth: Findings of the National Child Traumatic Stress Network.' *European Journal of Psychotraumatology 4*. Available at www.tandfonline.com/doi/full/10.3402/ejpt.v4i0.20274, accessed on 03/24/17.

Felitti, V.J., Anda, R.F., Nordenberg, D., Williamson, D.F. *et al.* (1998) 'Relationship of child abuse and household dysfunction to many of the leading causes of deaths in adults: The Adverse Childhood Experiences (ACE) study.' *American Journal of Preventative Medicine 14*, 245–258.

Ford, J.D. and Russo, E. (2006) 'Trauma focused, present centered, emotional self-regulation approach to treatment for post-traumatic stress and addiction: Training adaptive recovery group education and therapy (TARGET).' *American Journal of Psychotherapy 60*, 355–555.

Gazzaniga, M. (1998) *The Mind's Past*. Berkeley, CA: University of California Press.

Karr-Morse, R. and Wiley, M.S. (2012) *Scared Sick: The Role of Childhood Trauma in Adult Disease.* Philadelphia, PA: Basic Books.

Levine, P. and Kline, M. (2006) *Trauma through a Child's Eyes: Awakening the Ordinary Miracle of Healing.* Berkeley, CA: North Atlantic Books.

Lieberman, A.F. and Osofsky, J.D. (2009) 'Poverty, trauma, and infant mental health.' *Zero to Three 2*, 54–58.

National Child Traumatic Stress Network (2009) *Child Welfare Trauma Toolkit: Comprehensive Guide. 2nd Edition.* Los Angeles, CA, and Durham, NC: National Center for Child Traumatic Stress.

National Scientific Center on the Developing Child (2005) *Excessive Stress Disrupts the Architecture of the Developing Brain (Working Paper No. 3).* Available at www.developingchild.harvard.edu/index.php/resources/reportsandworkingpapers/workingpapers/wp3, accessed on 05/02/17.

National Scientific Center on the Developing Child (2006) *Early Exposure to Toxic Substances Damages Brain Architecture (Working Paper No. 4).* Available at www.developingchild.harvard.edu/index.php/resources/reportsandworkingpapers/workingpapers/wp4, accessed on 05/02/17.

National Scientific Center on the Developing Child (2007) *The Timing and Quality of Early Life Experiences Combine to Shape Brain Architecture (Working Paper No. 5).* Available at www.developingchild.harvard.edu/index.php/resources/reportsandworkingpapers/workingpapers/wp5, accessed on 05/02/17.

National Scientific Center on the Developing Child (2012) *The Science of Neglect: The Persistent Absence of Responsive Care Disrupts the Developing Brain (Working Paper No. 12).* Available at www.developingchild.harvard.edu/index.php/resources/reportsandworkingpapers/workingpapers/wp12, accessed on 05/02/17.

Oehlberg, B. (2012) *Ending the Shame: Transforming Public Education so It Works for All Students.* Pittsburg, PA: RoseDog Books.

Substance Abuse and Mental Health Services Administration. (2007). *Results from the 2006 National Survey on Drug Use and Health: National Findings.* Rockville, MD: Department of Health and Human Services.

Sugai, G., Horner, R.H., Dunlap, G., Hieneman, M. *et al.* (2000) 'Applying positive behavior support and functional behavioral assessment in schools.' *Journal of Positive Behavior Interventions 2*, 131–143.

U.S. Department of Health and Human Services, Administration for Children and Families, Administration on Children, Youth and Families, Children's Bureau (2016) *Child Maltreatment 2014.* Available at www.acf.hhs.gov/programs/cb/research-data-technology/statistics-research/child-maltreatment, accessed on 03/24/17.

van der Kolk, B.A. (2005) 'Developmental trauma disorder.' *Psychiatric Annals 35*, 401–408.

Part II

THE CHALLENGE

Supporting Underserved Student Populations

"There can be no keener revelation of a society's soul than the way it treats its children."

Nelson Mandela[1]

---

1   Speech at the launch of the Nelson Mandela Children's Fund, May 1995.

Chapter 5

Children and Poverty

HELPING THEM LEARN

Ruby K. Payne

Introduction

What is it about poverty that significantly impacts students'
opportunities to learn? And equally important, what can we do
about it?

Poverty affects children more profoundly than any other demographic
group in the United States. A 2014 Children's Defense Fund report
titled *The State of America's Children* indicates: "In 2012 children
were 60% more likely to be poor than adults ages 18–64 and nearly
2½ times more likely to be poor than seniors" (p.22).

What does or does not happen at home, both before and after
school, has a major impact on the ability of students from poverty to
learn. As we'll see in this chapter, myriad factors (including grief and
loss) impinge upon students from poverty and their learning potential.

For example, a student's home environment impacts learning, as
we see in Chapter 3 with Kyle Schwartz's innovative lesson, "I Wish
My Teacher Knew." One message clearly explains that a student
wished his teacher knew he didn't have a pencil to do his homework
(Figure 5.1).

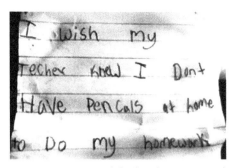

Figure 5.1 No pencil (Kyle Schwartz, 2016)

Two key strategies for educators and others in combating poverty are developing relationships of mutual respect, and building resources.

Regarding relationships, educators can make a big difference to students' self-esteem and learning by recognizing the grief and loss issues involved with poverty and the impact those issues have on students. It's no small feat, of course, to form mutually respectful relationships with large numbers of children in a busy school week. But such relationships are vital to the learning process for all students—especially those from poverty.

As for resources, let us now look at nine resources and the vital role they play in helping people from poverty, including students, begin to rise above the culture of survival.

The importance of resources

Poverty is an environmental condition rooted in one's socioeconomic class and is about the resources to which one does or does not have access. Resources, it must be noted, are about far more than money.

In *A Framework for Understanding Poverty: A Cognitive Approach*, poverty is defined as "the extent to which an individual does without resources" (Payne, 2013, p.7). The more of nine resources you have, the more abundance you have. The fewer resources you have, the more you live at a survival level. As resources become fewer, the environment in which you live becomes less stable and more unpredictable. The greater the level of instability, the harder it is to plan. The absence or presence of any one of those nine resources can create instability or stability. As noted next, money is only one of the nine resources. The following issues involving resources can greatly impact learning:

- *Financial:* Having the money to purchase goods and services.

- *Emotional:* Being able to choose and control emotional responses, particularly to negative situations, without engaging in self-destructive behavior. This is an internal resource and shows itself through stamina, perseverance, and choices.

- *Mental/cognitive:* Having the mental abilities and acquired skills (reading, writing, computing) to deal effectively with daily life.

- *Spiritual:* Believing in divine purpose and guidance.

- *Physical:* Having physical health and mobility.

- *Support systems:* Having friends, family, and backup resources available to access in times of need. These are external resources.

- *Relationships/role models:* Having frequent access to individual(s) who are appropriate, who are nurturing, and who do not engage in self-destructive behavior.

- *Knowledge of hidden rules:* Knowing the unspoken cues and habits of different groups.

- *Language/formal register:* Being able to competently use the vocabulary and sentence structure of work and school.

Lack of resources affects learning

First, one of the ways that poverty significantly impacts students' opportunities to learn is how they spend their time. One way that everyone in the world is alike is that each of us has 24 hours a day. Period. Unless you need only two hours of sleep a night, time constrains each of us. *How you spend your time is a key determining factor in what you know.*

But when students are forced to figure out each day where/how to get food, how to stay safe, how to get sleep, etc., it limits what girls and boys get to learn in an academic world. In a knowledge-based economy, being educated is critical for making a living and remaining table.

Second, when your environment is unstable and unpredictable, and just about every day there is a crisis, you learn not to plan. Yet to negotiate school and work, young people have to plan. At the University of California,

Berkeley, the researchers used EEGs to compare the brains of nine- and ten-year-olds from poverty with the brains of wealthy children.

Lead researcher Mark Kishiyama described what was found in the brains of low-income children: "It is similar to a pattern that's seen in patients with strokes that have had lesions in their prefrontal cortex [which deals with executive function]... It suggests that in these kids, prefrontal function is reduced or disrupted in some way" (Toppo, 2008, para. 1).

Third, if you have been in generational poverty (two generations or more), research shows that you have significantly less language (Risley and Hart, 1995), with one exception: if you come from a very religious household. Academic achievement and IQ tests are heavily dependent upon vocabulary, as is the world of work. In fact, a study done in Australia followed 8,556 women from their first clinic visit for pregnancy to the child's fifth year, and then again at age 14. The study found that the occupational status of the child's maternal grandfather independently predicted the child's verbal comprehension levels at age five and non-verbal reasoning scores at age 14 (Najman *et al.*, 2004).

Fourth, learning is double-coded—both emotionally and cognitively. Emotional coding has to do with the nature of the relationships, and cognitive concerns vocabulary, processes, disciplines, and patterns. Because of generational poverty's excessive amounts of death, trauma, sometimes abuse, violence, dysfunction of some households, and frequent moves, the emotional crises that many students have are often left unaddressed, thereby significantly interfering with learning (see Chapter 2).

In the book *The Growth of the Mind and the Endangered Origins of Intelligence* (1997), Stanley Greenspan and Beryl Benderly say all learning is double-coded, both mentally and emotionally.

It's very important to understand the emotional underpinnings of learning. All learning that "sticks" has an emotional component, and virtually all learning starts with significant relationships. The primary motivator for the development of each of the following six stages is a significant relationship. These developmental stages in the learning process occur when relationships are supportive and nurturing. Schools and educators can provide such relationships, and make that difference for underprivileged students to feel hopeful, positive about themselves, and willing to be open to learning. The six stages are described in Table 5.1.

Table 5.1 Developmental learning stages

Stage	Explanation
1. Ability to attend	To pay attention to the sensory data in the environment. The earliest sensory data—touch, taste, sound, smell, sight—result from the interplay of relationships.
2. Ability to engage	To experience feelings—joy, pleasure, anger, emotional warmth, disappointment, assertiveness, etc. Intimacy and relating begin at this stage.
3. Ability to be intentional	To create and direct desire. To use non-verbals with purpose and intention. For example, I (as an infant) want you to hold me, so I hold up my arms, and you pick me up.
4. Ability to form complex interactive patterns	To connect and use one's own intentional signals in interaction with another to negotiate and receive security, acceptance, and approval.
5. Ability to create images, symbols, and ideas	To give abstract mental constructs emotional meaning and significance. This is the basis of reasoning and emotion-based coping strategies. When images, symbols, and ideas don't have emotional investment, they tend to be fragmented.
6. Ability to connect images, symbols, and ideas	To develop the infrastructure and architecture of the mind. To "image" one's own feelings and desires and to understand emotional signals from others.

Research-Based Strategies (Payne, 2010, p.233). Reprinted with permission.

In discussing the six stages, one overriding reality must be remembered—emotion organizes experience and behavior.

Stage 1: Ability to attend

At the very beginning of learning, the infant must sort out what the sensations he/she experiences are and what they mean. Those earliest sensations almost always come through relationships. Someone is holding the child. Someone is feeding the child. The child must stay calm enough to notice the sensations he/she is experiencing. The child must find patterns in the sensations. From these patterns come security and order. From security and order comes the ability to regulate the mind.

Stage 2: Ability to engage

When young children can attend to their surroundings and actions of the people who are their caregivers, they become engaged. The caregivers smile, and they smile. In short, the children mirror the expressions of the caregivers. Greenspan and Benderly (1997) describe this well:

> Without some degree of this ecstatic wooing by at least one adult who adores her, a child may never know the powerful intoxication of human closeness, never abandon herself to the magnetic pull of human relationships… Whether because her nervous system is unable to sustain the sensations of early love or her caregiver is unable to convey them, such a child is at risk of becoming self-absorbed or an unfeeling, self-centered, aggressive individual who can inflict injury without qualm or remorse. (p.51)

Stage 3: Ability to be intentional

At this preverbal stage, a purposeful exchange of signals and responses is used to elicit what the child desires. In this stage the child learns to distinguish between you and me—that is, between self and other. Boundaries are established. When responses are inappropriate, the child becomes disorganized and subsequently loses interest. For example, if a person is talking to someone with a "poker face," eventually the conversation becomes fragmented; the speaker loses interest and gives up. But when interactions become purposeful, "willful reciprocity" occurs, which also signals a higher developmental level of the central nervous system. Desires or wishes are tied to actions, not ideas. Desires or wishes also are linked to subjective needs, not objective ones.

Stage 4: Ability to form complex interactive patterns

At this stage, purpose and interaction become the focus. The child learns to communicate across space—that is, I am not touching my caregiver. She is in the next room, but I know she is there. This gives a strong sense of emotional security. Imitation is a part of this stage. The child mimics what the adult does. Also at this stage, a child's emotions are attached to patterns of response. Attitudes and values start here. Meaning is established from patterns of desire, expectation, and intention.

Stage 5: Ability to create images, symbols, and ideas

Here the child experiences himself/herself in images, not just in feelings, physical sensations, and behavior. To be able to negotiate school and work, a person must be able to use abstract representational systems. The easiest way to explain this to students is to take a picture of them and ask them if the picture is them. They will say yes. Then I ask them if the picture is breathing. They will say no. And then I will ask them how it can be them if it is not breathing. They will say, "It looks like me. It represents me." And I will tell them yes, *and that is what school is about.* The numbers are not the things; they *represent* the things. The letters represent sounds. Words represent ideas. Blueprints represent buildings. This is a key understanding students need to have in order to negotiate the world of work and school. It's important to note that children who haven't mastered the previous stages tend to operate in a concrete, rote manner. At this point in time, individuals can try out behaviors and actions inside their head without actually doing them.

Stage 6: Ability to connect images, symbols, and ideas

At this stage, the individual connects the images, symbols, and ideas that were developed in Stage 5 to architecture in which abstractions are emotionally embedded and interwoven. The individual is able to view emotions abstractly and work through them both at a feeling level and a cognitive one. Sorting occurs both cognitively and through emotion.

Fifth, the nature of academic learning is in abstract representational systems. In order to survive in school, a learner must be able to negotiate the abstract representational world, which is the paper world or the world as represented on a computer screen. This takes a different skill set because of the requirement that sensory information be represented on paper or the screen. For example, an apple in three dimensions does not look like a two-dimensional drawing of an apple. The drawing only represents the apple. Words represent a feeling, but they are not the feeling. A photo represents a person, but it is not the person. Numbers represent an amount, but they are not the actual item being counted.

The paper world is how information and understandings are conveyed in formal schooling. Words, symbols, etc. are used to convey the meaning. Paper doesn't have non-verbals, emotions, or human interaction. Paper depends on a shared understanding of vocabulary in order to communicate. If you grew up in a household where there were very few books, calendars, clocks, etc., the concept of information on paper is difficult. It has to be learned.

Because schools and the work setting operate at Stages 5 and 6, many individuals have to learn about the abstract (Payne, 2008). The following case study of Kevin sheds light on this journey of poverty and academic success.

A CASE STUDY ON POVERTY: KEVIN

Kevin is a senior in a rural high school. He is tall, slender, good-looking, and smart. When he was 14 he started working two jobs because his mother and father were separated due to domestic violence and drug use. He and his mother moved to a property, and Kevin helped his mother pay the bills. Because he was too young to qualify for a loan, his parents co-signed for him to buy a car (he got a hardship license). He had only two payments left to pay off the car when his father took the car and traded it in for a truck. The payments for the truck were $20 a month higher and the debt on the truck was now over $10,000. When Kevin was 15, his mother went back to the father and they moved again.

Kevin's mother had been 18 when she married his father, who was 40 years old at the time. When his mother was 36, both his mother and father lost their jobs, resulting in Kevin's wage becoming the family's main source of income. Although Kevin had saved for college, his parents begged him to use that money to pay bills, promising they would eventually repay him for college. Kevin agreed, using his money to pay family bills. While in high school, Kevin's older stepbrother Joseph suffered a traumatic accident when his then girlfriend ran over him with her car, never fully recovering from head injuries. His younger stepbrother Alex dropped out of high school and began selling and making meth. His dad was arrested several times for driving under the influence. Each time his father was released from jail after a couple of weeks.

During his junior year of high school, Kevin spent time with his dad's brother, Uncle Frank, who was a very successful interior decorator in a large city. Uncle Frank wanted Kevin to go into business with him. He bought him a used BMW and put the title in Kevin's name. A month after he gave him the car, his uncle told him he expected Kevin to have sex with him. After all, he had given him a car. Kevin told Uncle Frank, "No way," and sold the car.

Second semester of his senior year, when Kevin wanted to go to college, his parents informed him, first, that there would be no money from them and, second, the truck would be given to his older brother who had been in and out of jail for numerous offenses. At that time, only his mother was working, and his father and brother were making meth. At home, there was periodic domestic violence, as well as a great deal of alcohol and meth use by both the father and brother. Kevin's grandmother and mother were his key relationships and provided much encouragement and hope for him.

Kevin excelled at "bridging social capital." In other words, he was very good at making friends with people who were different from himself or his mother and father. One of his contacts offered to help him with college, but it would require a move to another state. Kevin jumped at the opportunity and left. But when he got to the new place, he found that he would awaken in the night with panic attacks—not because he missed his family (he did miss his mother), but because all the emotional grief that had been stored up in him over the years had begun to surface. Goldman explains in Chapter 2 that young people often process grief and trauma when they finally feel safe enough to do so. Kevin's contact signposted him to a counselor to help process these emerging thoughts and feelings.

The high school that Kevin attended was small—approximately 100 students in the graduating class. The high school principal was fired halfway through Kevin's senior year but was retained as principal for that year. The high school was in chaos. Kevin needed to request a transcript multiple times before he got one. Of the students in Kevin's high school, 19 percent took Advanced Placement exams, and the pass rate was just 8 percent. Thirty-eight percent of the students scored at mastery level or above on state assessments in reading; the math score was 47 percent. When Kevin graduated from high school, he had a high-B average—and when he enrolled in community college, he had to take two remedial math courses.

Debriefing the case study

One of the issues that often occurs in poverty is the almost constant instability and unpredictability. The second issue is that, when resources are scarce, the child usually suffers. Grief is compounded from multiple issues and sources: changing allegiances of the adults, moving from one place to another to live, broken promises and abusive environments, time taken from child and adolescent development to take care of the adults or young children, death and violence, inadequate educational opportunities, etc. How many of these characteristics and factors were part of Kevin's life?

Safety and belonging—the roots of emotional stability

All emotional wellness at its essence is rooted in two things: safety and belonging. These form the very basis of well-being, and they begin in infancy. Safety and belonging are developed in the context of a relationship. As Yale University professor James P. Comer (1995) stated, "No significant learning occurs without a significant relationship."

When individuals feel safe and that they belong, the chemicals produced by the brain actually change. "Unpredictability in the environment requires immediate physiological responses (allostasis) to promote adaptation" (Schamberg, 2008, p.9). In the Adverse Childhood Experience (ACE) study, ten questions regarding adverse childhood experiences were used—physical and sexual abuse, physical and emotional neglect, household dysfunction (incarceration, mental illness, addiction), etc. For each yes answer, the individual was given one point. "Parents and other caregivers who are able to form close, nurturing relationships with their children can foster resilience in them that protects them from many of the worst effects of a harsh early environment…the effect is biochemical" (Tough, 2012, p.28).

Because there are so many losses in poverty (death, mobility, violence, gangs, prison) and because of the lack of resources to provide counseling for grief, as well as the stigma in poverty for being "weak," then the grief compounds, and learning is significantly diminished.

In Chapter 6, Las Americas Newcomer School represents a state-of-the-art model for providing the loving, nurturing relationships that meet the needs of students discussed in this chapter. This school serves as an inspirational paradigm for what a school system can create in order to enhance learning and self-esteem with young people who may be experiencing poverty, or isolation from familiar language, family, and culture. The following are examples of projects at the Las Americas Newcomers School that promote well-being.

The first project is a book drive that offered students needed resources that they may not have otherwise been able to afford or access. Another project was a student and family school celebration with partnered organizations in order to adopt every family for a Christmas event. Educators researched the needs of these children and families and provided boxes of toys, gifts, and important supplies with a generosity of spirit.

The simple mental model below (Figure 5.2) is a way to teach students about the impact of grief on their life.

Emotional issues at each transition

If the transition was self-initiated, abrupt, or done by someone else, then the emotional issues will be different. Often if the separations come frequently, the emotional issues do not get processed but rather accumulate (Figure 5.2).

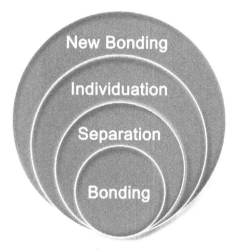

Figure 5.2 Emotional issues at transition (Payne and O'Neill-Baker, 2015, p.88). Reprinted with permission.

This figure represents the natural changes that occur over and over again in a person's life. As an infant, we bond to a caregiver. Then we get to the "terrible twos," and we say NO! We are starting the process of separation, which moves us on to individuation. Girls and boys might ask, "What do I like about myself with this person, how am I different, which pieces do I want to keep of myself?" Then we move on to new bonding. At each white line, we have emotional work to do. And if we have a caring, nurturing adult in our life, we can usually make these transitions in an emotionally well manner because we've been able to be safe and belong.

If you are in poverty, there are multiple situations forced upon you that create grief for you. Because resources are so thin, you seldom get the help you need to address the grief. It becomes compounded and, eventually, learning is negatively impacted. Kevin in our earlier case study had to fight through the negative impacts of his parents, his older stepbrother, and his uncle to places of individuation (saying no to his uncle, saying yes to a move) and new bonding (the counselor at the new high school). Many students from poverty struggle to have the kind of inner resolve and resilience that Kevin showed. Yet even Kevin, as evidenced by his nocturnal panic attacks and counseling sessions, had difficulty processing all the pain and grief from his past.

Recommendations for educators
Stay out of the triangle—this establishes boundaries
In an article titled "Fairy Tales and Script Drama Analysis" (1968), Stephen Karpman describes his Drama Triangle or Cycle of Victimhood (Figure 5.3)[1] and explains that many of us tend to play different roles in our relationships.

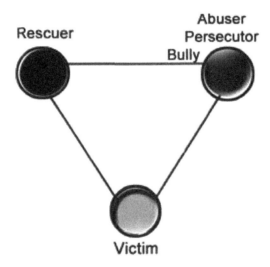

Figure 5.3 The triangle

The same person can take all three roles in different situations. In one setting the person is a bully, in another setting the person is a rescuer, and in a third setting the person is a victim. Once you are in the triangle, you will eventually take on all three roles—and boundaries disappear because ownership isn't taken by anyone. To stay out of the triangle, you can ask questions.

The following is an example of ways to use questions to avoid the triangle: When my son was in second grade, he came home from school and told me he was "bored." I asked him, "Whose problem

---

1   Adapted from "Fairy Tales and Script Drama Analysis" (1968), by S. Karpman.

is that?" He said, "The teacher's." He was presenting himself as a victim and asking me to go to school and "rescue" him. So I asked him, "Is the teacher bored?" He said, "No, I am." So I said, "Then it isn't the teacher's problem. It's your problem. Since it's your problem, how can you solve it?"

Had I gone to the school and "bullied" the teacher in order to "rescue" my son who was a "victim," chances would have been very good that the teacher would've felt like a "victim" and gone to the principal to be "rescued." The principal likely would have called me and "bullied" me for being so insensitive to the teacher and blaming the teacher for my son's problems. Then I would have felt like a "victim," told my husband so that he would "rescue" me, and gone to school to "bully" the principal. The cycle would continue.

In other words, once a person is in the triangle, he/she can eventually be expected to take on all three roles. Most importantly, the problem won't get solved, and vital boundaries will disappear. The best way to stay out of the triangle is to ask questions and clarify the issues—so that the problem can be resolved.

Develop a relationship of mutual respect with the student

What does that mean? It does not mean that you are the student's friend. It does mean that you provide high expectations, insistence, and support; for example: "I know you can do it. I care about you. I will show you how to do it. I expect you to do it."

Ensure that your classroom has safety and belonging

If classrooms are chaotic, disorganized, and unpredictable, the school situation has just replicated the instability of the external environment. Allostatic load increases for the student, and learning correspondingly decreases. Learning occurs when you are safe enough to focus *on* the learning. Good classroom management helps eliminate the stress factors and creates a predictable and orderly place to learn.

Create a resource list to open dialogue and provide support

It is important for educators to have readily available books and organizations that are helpful for students who are experiencing these life issues. Books can serve as a vehicle for group communication or a catalyst for dialogue as a "teachable moment" when a spontaneous discussion arises. An inspiring example of resilience is the book for young children, *Something Beautiful* by Sharon Wyeth (2002), about a girl who searches and finds beauty in a poverty-stricken neighborhood after her teacher writes the word *beautiful* on the blackboard at school. Other children's resources include: Boelts (2009), *Those Shoes*; Bromley (2010), *The Lunch Thief*; Carmi (2006), *A Circle of Friends*; Grimes (2010), *Almost Zero: A Dyamonde Daniel Book*; Gunning (2004), *A Shelter in Our Car*; Landowne (2005), *Sé La Vi: That is Life*; and McDonald (2010), *Chill Wind*.

Community and national organizations can provide added help for students, families, and educators. They can often provide food, clothing, and health care beneficial to the student.[2]

Insist that each student has a future story

A future story allows you to stay focused on your learning in spite of chaos and lack of order. There are at least a couple of ways to obtain that future story. The first is outlined below.

Future Story   Name:
You are ten years older than you are now. You are the star of a movie. What are you doing? Who is with you?
Circle any of these that are in your future story: children, job, career, marriage/partnership, health, wealth, travel, living in a city, town, rural area, another country, vehicles, hobbies, sports, music, movies, college, technical school, military, church/religion, Internet, video games, friends, family, other.
Coming back to the present, for which of these reasons do you want to graduate from high school?
Keep track of money, I will know I am getting paid correctly, so I can go on to college or military or technical school, to get a better job, to take care of my parents or siblings, to afford my hobbies, to pay for my vehicle, to take care of my children, other.

2   The following organizations can provide support for those experiencing difficult circumstances: Children's Defense Fund (www.childrensdefense.org), Child Trends (www.childtrends.org), U.S. Department of Education (https://www.2.ed.gov/parents/read/resources/edpicks.jhtml), and WIC (Women, Infants, and Children Food and Nutrition) (www.fns.usda.gov/wic/women-infants-and-children-wic).

| What do you enjoy doing and would do even if you did not get paid for it? What do you need to do so you can do that and get paid for doing it? |
| Who are the friends and adults who will help you achieve your future story? |
| *Write out your future story and include how education will help you get it.* |
| Signature: DATE: |

Source: *Research-Based Strategies* (Payne, 2010, p.180). Reprinted with permission.

Additional information on the key issues/strategies can be found in *Under-Resourced Learners* (Payne, 2008) and *Research-Based Strategies* (Payne, 2010).

Another way to get a future story is to ask students to take a piece of paper and divide it into nine squares. They then think about what they want to be like when they are 25, and go on the Internet and choose one picture for each square. Some example questions to help with this exercise: what kind of car will you be driving, what will your house look like, what will your college diploma say, what will you look like when you go to work, what kind of work will you do, what will be your personal relationships, what is a hobby you will have?

Provide validating experiences for students

What are validating experiences? These are experiences with adults or circumstances in your life—childhood, adolescence, adulthood—that validate you in an emotionally playful, affectionately delightful, and genuine way. They allow you to see yourself as an authentic human being. It is emotionally grounding for you, and these experiences help you enjoy being *you*.

An example: Tony was a very bright freshman in high school and came from a high-poverty area along the river. He and others from that neighborhood were called "river rats." I finally realized that he was deliberately failing my class. One day I took Tony aside and said, "Help me understand why you are failing my class on purpose." He said, "I'm dumb." I told him that wasn't true, so his second reason was that he forgot the answers. Again, I told him that wasn't true—that I knew he knew.

Tony then responded, "You're crazy if you think I can get an A in here." I asked him why he couldn't have an A. He told me that he would then have no friends. I asked him how many friends a B would cost him. He told me that he still wouldn't have any respect. So I questioned him how many friends a C would cost him, and he said that he could do that. After our conversation he did start learning, and we agreed he would not get above a C in any of his courses. This experience may not have paved his way to college, but it did validate him as a human being.

Analyze the resources of your students to target your interventions

When you analyze the resources of your students—and base your interventions on existing resources—then the interventions can actually work. The key factor: An intervention will not work if the person does not have the resources to use it.

When my son was in high school, a friend of his from middle school, Chris, became homeless. We invited him to live with our family—as it turned out, for seven months. Chris had very few resources when he came to our home—except for mental brightness and physical strength. Chris initially also was quite angry because his mother had brought a new boyfriend into their house. So Chris moved in with us. When you have a student who is really smart but has few emotional resources, then it becomes critical that you work with his/her thinking.

Chris agreed to develop a future story, which originally was to get a degree in video-gaming design. Later Chris was successful in achieving a BS degree and is now certified as a teacher. A future story is a spiritual resource. He developed a plan around it and was able to use that to keep his lack of emotional resources from derailing him. In the process, he also *developed* his emotional resources.

Conclusion

Expanding the school environment to include the needs of each and every student is imperative. One of the most difficult parts of working with children and students from poverty is knowing the grief and scarcity the student is in, yet being unable to change that reality for most students. Each of us, however, has the potential to be an incredible role model. Every day we can show these students another way to navigate the world. And it usually starts by establishing a relationship of mutual respect, which costs no money.

I used to say something along these lines to students: "I respect you so much for your strength and courage to face your challenges. I cannot change your reality. But I can provide the tools, skills, and knowledge you will need so that you can choose to live in a new and different way as an adult."

The power of an adult who works lovingly, respectfully, and persistently with children and adolescents cannot be underestimated. Schools such as Las Americas Newcomer School under the leadership of Principal Marie Moreno (see Chapter 6) shine as an example of what can be done by a group of dedicated and caring educators, providing not only loving support and caring, but also meeting physical needs, and offering cultural understandings and health resources, to empower all students, in any life situation, to achieve success in school.

References

Boelts, M. (2009) *Those Shoes*. Madison, WI: Demco Media.

Bromley, A. (2010) *The Lunch Thief*. Gardiner, ME: Tilbury House Publishers.

Carmi, G. (2006) *A Circle of Friends*. New York: Star Bright Books.

Children's Defense Fund Report (2014) *The State of America's Children*. Available at www.childrensdefense.org/library/state-of-americas-children, accessed on 03/27/17.

Comer, J.P. (1995) Lecture given at Education Service Center, Region IV, Houston, TX.

Greenspan, S.I. and Benderly, B.L. (1997) *The Growth of the Mind and the Endangered Origins of Intelligence*. Reading, MA: Addison-Wesley.

Grimes, N. (2010) *Almost Zero: A Dyamonde Daniel Book*. New York: Putnam Juvenile.

Gunning, M. (2004) *A Shelter in Our Car*. New York: Children's Book Press.

Karpman, S. (1968) 'Fairy tales and script drama analysis.' *Transactional Analysis Bulletin 7*, 26, 39–43.

Landowne, Y. (2005) *Sé La Vi: That is Life*. El Paso, TX: Cinco Puntos Press.

McDonald, J. (2010) *Chill Wind*. New York: Farrar, Straus and Giroux.

Najman, J.M., Aird, R., Bor, W., O'Callaghan, M., Williams, G., and Shuttlewood, G. (2004) 'The generational transmission of socioeconomic inequalities in child cognitive development and emotional health.' *Social Science and Medicine 58*, 1147–1158.

Payne, R.K. (2008) *Under-Resourced Learners: 8 Strategies to Boost Student Achievement*. Highlands, TX: aha! Process.

Payne, R.K. (2010) *Research-Based Strategies: Narrowing the Achievement Gap for Under-Resourced Students, 2nd Edition*. Highlands, TX: aha! Process.

Payne, R.K. (2013) *A Framework for Understanding Poverty: A Cognitive Approach, 5th Edition*. Highlands, TX: aha! Process.

Payne, R.K. and O'Neill-Baker, E. (2015) *How Much of Yourself Do You Own?* Highlands, TX: aha! Process.

Risley, T. and Hart, B. (1995) *Meaningful Differences in the Everyday Experience of Young American Children*. Baltimore, MD: Brookes Publishing Co.

Schamberg, M. (2008) *The Cost of Living in Poverty: Long-Term Effects of Allostatic Load on Working Memory*. Available at http://ecommons.library.cornell.edu/bitstream/1813/10814/1/Schamberg%20-%20Pov%2c%20Load%2c%20Working%20Mem.pdf, accessed on 05/02/17.

Toppo, G. (2008) 'Study: Poverty dramatically affects children's brains.' *USA Today*, December 10. Available at http://usatoday30.usatoday.com/news/health/2008-12-07-childrens-brains_N.htm, accessed on 03/27/17.

Tough, P. (2012) *How Children Succeed: Grit, Curiosity, and the Hidden Power of Character.* Boston, MA: Houghton Mifflin Harcourt.

Wyeth, S. (2002) *Something Beautiful.* New York: Dragonfly Publishers.

Chapter 6

Immigration Issues in School

A CHALLENGE TO LEARNING AND LIVING

Marie Moreno

Education is the most important indicator for a person's success in America. We no longer live in the days where agriculture and working the fields will bring the wages needed to raise a family and live with a middle-class income. The world, however, has also changed. We can no longer educate our children of tomorrow with the strategies used from the 20th century. We have more and more children attending our schools that need educational and social services. It is these services that schools need to provide for their students to ensure their success.

In the United States, 4.7 million students are English Language Learners (ELLs) (IDRA, 2015, p.8). The states with the highest percentage of ELLs are Alaska, California, Colorado, Hawaii, Nevada, New Mexico, Oregon, and Texas. In Texas alone, there are 860,000 ELLs in our schools with 200,000 students registered in middle and high schools (IDRA, 2015, p.8). America has been known for being a humanitarian country providing aid for immigrants and refugees from around the globe. It is also known as the land of opportunity—many Mexicans and Central Americans enter this country for a better life. Just recently, thousands of children from Guatemala, Honduras, and El Salvador made the dangerous trek through Mexico in search of their parents. Sonia Nazario documented this trek from Central America by writing a book about Enrique and the dangerous journey through Mexico to find his mother living in the United States (*Enrique's Journey*; Nazario, 2006). These parents left their children behind years ago and never returned. Now, these resilient children are in our public schools.

But is this country prepared to educate these students that have not been disciplined in high standards and college readiness?

We can complain about the situation but it does not solve the problem. These children will continue to enter our schools. It is up to our teachers, administrators, districts, board members, and politicians to change the way we educate our students to ensure that they get the support they need to thrive and make dreams come true. It is the new workforce of tomorrow—a future that is forever changing. As principal of Las Americas Newcomer School, I have joined a dedicated faculty in approaching learning and living for many disenfranchised immigrant students in our schools by creating a working model and effective paradigm for an educational shift to meet their unique needs.

Understanding the plight of refugee immigrants

Our first step as educators was to become educated in the extent and history of immigration in our country. It is crucial in developing a heartfelt program that works practically with girls and boys who have experienced profound life issues. Thousands of refugees are allowed into the United States every year. It is projected that this number will rise to over 100,000 refugees (*FoxNews*, 2015). Refugee camps are located in many countries across the globe including Nepal, Bhutan, the Democratic Republic of the Congo, Turkey, Syria, Iraq, Afghanistan, Eritrea, and Ethiopia.

In order for educators to provide the "right" instruction for these children, we must take a closer look. One must understand the uniqueness of every child. You will find that these children have been given a wide variety of educational opportunities. Some attended schools their entire lives and for whatever reason (e.g., war, government) fled their country for safety. Other families have lived in refugee camps so long that their school-aged children were born there. These refugee camps are inadequately funded and have little support for families. For example, families can wait days—even weeks—before food and fresh water is brought to the camp for everyone. Education varies as well. There are camps in which "school" is provided, but one must ask if it is rigorous enough to be compared to the high stakes, college-readiness that is expected by the United States, and does it provide activities to bring out the very best in students? Or does it do neither? Depending on particular refugee camps, there may be absolutely no opportunities for school—leaving students even further behind. Then you have countries that only educate males, leaving female children to look after the family.

For years, the United States has had immigrants cross its southern border as families and children seek the American dream. Many unaccompanied minors come from Guatemala, Honduras, and El Salvador. In recent times, children have been making this journey alone; these children experience situations that many adults will never face in their lives. Imagine yourself making this journey—alone. You have gangs, thieves, rapists, hunger, and safety all working against you. Children, at times, face deportation from Mexico back to their country, not once but many, many times, as they hope to make it to the United States. Only when school systems can fully comprehend the enormous number of loss and grief issues experienced by these young people can they begin to create a comprehensive approach that incorporates a traumatic past with a welcoming present, and a hopeful future.

Why is background so important?

Educators usually assess for student knowledge. Are they ready for the grade level they are currently enrolled in? Are they prepared with the knowledge and skills for the upcoming grade level? Are there educational gaps that could impact their future learning? When working with refugee and immigrant students, those questions are just not enough. They don't even scratch the surface. Although these questions may seem important, there are other factors that must be considered to help a student learn English.

Stephen Krashen, a University of Southern California professor emeritus and educational researcher, coined the term "Affective Filter" (Bilash, 2009). It refers to a theoretical construct in second language acquisition that explains the emotional variables associated with the success or failure of acquiring a second language. It is a psychological filter that can either facilitate or hinder a student learning English. Students with a high affective filter experience stress, lack of self-confidence, or anxiety that can affect their ability to learn. However, a student with a low affective filter will increase their risk-taking behavior and show greater gains in their overall education. The student's environment will determine if this filter is raised or lowered. As educators, we must keep this filter in mind. An example of one of our students, Jose, and the background and traumatic events he brings with him to Las Americas Newcomer School, is given below.

Jose, a 12-year-old boy from El Salvador, a country with one of the highest murder rates in the world, is one of thousands of children who have made the dangerous journey from Latin America in search of a brighter future. He, along with his brother and aunt, fled Central America because of all of the violence. It is not a safe place. Guns and violence are evident in the streets every day. Playing outside, going to the park, or strolling through the town is uncommon. The MS-13 (Mara Salvatrucha) gang rules the streets and kills innocent people daily. He wanted to reunite with his mother who now lives in Houston, Texas. Because Jose's mother is undocumented herself, she was unable to go to El Salvador to get her son, knowing first-hand how dangerous this journey can be because she too made that journey, years ago. Knowing the danger, this mother still felt it was the right thing to remove her son from the daily violence and provide Jose with a better life in the United States. Jose left behind a younger brother, grandmother, and aunts and uncles. Jose spoke no English when he first arrived in Houston. Oftentimes, he is quiet, reserved, and sad. Family separation is hard for many students to understand and cope with. He is just one of a growing number of immigrant and refugee students finding a new home in America.

Jose, like many other Central American children, was reunited with his parents for the first time in years. Jose's parents traveled north—leaving Jose with his grandparents when he was only five years old. They could no longer afford to take care of the children. With no employment or means to uphold the household, seeking a better life in the United States was the only solution. These are decisions that children don't understand. Many of them ask, "Why did they leave me?" "Did they not love me?" These are questions that many 9- to 15-year-old children have that require years of therapy or counseling to fully understand.

Maslow's *Hierarchy of Needs* is a great example of how to approach education for our students that have experienced years of grief and trauma. Children bring with them lots of "adult" experiences that need to be addressed so they can thrive and be successful. Maslow creates a pyramid with self-actualization at the top, followed by self-esteem, belonging, love, safety, and physiological needs at the foundation (Maslow, 2013).

The physiological foundation (food, water, shelter, warmth) of the pyramid is key and very important for a child's success. Houston Independent School District, along with many other districts, is now providing free breakfast for all students as part of a federal grant. Safety is another growing concern. Children fleeing from war-torn countries or unsafe environments seek safety and security in a protected place without violence. No more fear of drug cartels storming through their neighborhoods or bombs being thrown from unstable governments going through civil war. Each tier describes an important factor to be addressed to ensure students' needs are met (Maslow, 2013).

Meeting the needs of grieving and traumatized students

Las Americas Newcomer School in Houston, Texas, has provided that safe and secure environment needed to work with students who have suffered from loss, grief, and trauma. It has all the essential elements that are demonstrated in Maslow's Hierarchy of Needs. This school has been featured on PBS NewsHour and in the *Houston Chronicle*, the *Dallas Morning News*, and the *Los Angeles Times*. It's a special place that provides a stepping-stone for all children.

There are children from all over the world representing up to 32 countries at times. Students are from Angola, Honduras, Guatemala, El Salvador, Costa Rica, Colombia, Mexico, Iraq, Nepal, Afghanistan, Miramar, Somalia, and the Democratic Republic of the Congo. Nearly 30 languages and dialects are spoken amongst the students; however, English is one that they are all beginning to learn.

Arriving in America not knowing English or American culture takes time. Providing a school that allows students the time needed to adjust, to learn the language, and to acclimatize is essential. It needs an environment that takes into account the challenges they have faced, and programs that will allow them to cope and grieve, as well as supporting them as they adjust to a new country. And so Las Americas is that stepping-stone for students that have lived in the United States for less than one year and have very limited or no English skills. Many of the children enrolling have never set foot in a traditional school. They are unfamiliar with sitting down at a desk on a chair for long periods of time or do not know how to hold a pen or pencil. These are basic fundamental needs to be addressed before the journey to learning English begins.

A paradigm shift in teaching: Holding unconditional love with high expectations

Creating a school to reach the most-at-risk children requires specialized training for teachers. Teachers must show *unconditional love while still holding high expectations*. With high-stakes testing and state accountability, one must take into account a child's prior knowledge. What knowledge do they have? Do they have gaps in their education? Were they schooled? The basic understanding of English is essential to learning the more challenging content. Jim Cummins, a University of Toronto professor, introduced the acronyms BICS (Basic Interpersonal Communication Skills) and CALP (Cognitive Academic Language Proficiency) (see Street and Hornberger, 2008).

Grouping by language proficiency: At Las Americas, students are grouped by language proficiency—not by grade level. Students in lower proficiency levels are working on their BICS, while those with higher proficiency are working on their CALP. Another way of looking at this can easily be summed up as learning to read versus reading to learn. When students are grouped in this manner, their affective filter is lowered.

Intensified language learning: Consider an eighth grader who does not know his alphabet sitting in a classroom where most of the students are learning/reading about the water cycle. It is very difficult for this student to engage and participate with the rest of the students. Whereas, at Las Americas, regardless of age, all students who need to are learning the alphabet together. Students receive up to five hours of English a day to intensify their English acquisition. Students move through eight levels of English at their own pace, allowing students to better understand difficult content. The school has seen student progress increase year after year. Everything is strategic. The classroom setup is a non-negotiable.

Workstations for support: Students work in workstations in every classroom. It is designed to ensure students in the lower proficiencies get the support they need. Students who speak common languages are seated together so that teachers can use native language support, like bilingual dictionaries, or gestures, to assist them. In the higher proficiencies, teachers do the opposite. To allow students to help each other, students are placed in groups by their different languages. The only common language amongst them is English.

Classroom setup is essential. Figure 6.1 illustrates how students are strategically placed with the different learning modalities. There are listening, speaking, and writing activities in different workstations. Students rotate through each of the workstations to ensure students are engaged in a variety of activities. The room setup is a non-negotiable. It ensures teachers are able to facilitate student learning at multiple levels. In a reading class, for example, a teacher could have up to five different workbooks for each of the student groups to ensure work is set at the right level for the students.

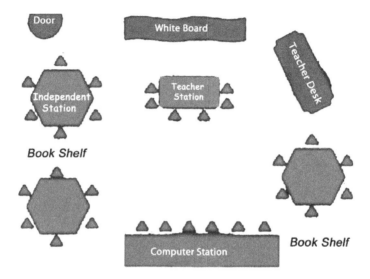

Figure 6.1 Classroom set up with learning modules

Social workers: The school has invested in social workers to assist students who have experienced trauma. Nearly every student at Las Americas has experienced some form of trauma that can affect their daily lives. Examples would be everything from "I want to hurt myself," to "I can't go on," to "Well, it's really hard, I'm sad, but I will be OK." There are other factors that children face. They don't know who they are. The refugee kids, children from overseas, may not ever have had an identity. The Central American children are angry about their identity due to the fact that they had to leave their home due to poor living conditions or they are angry that their home/country was not safe. Others are angry that their family is now separated—some here in the United States and others there in their home country.

Investing in resources: Being sensitive and respectful to every child is important. Ensuring that teachers have the resources and the information needed to educate all students is a must. Investing in dictionaries and other materials that translate words from English to the child's native tongue and vice versa is essential.

Demonstrating caring: It's also important to show students and their families that schools care and understand their background. As principal of Las Americas, I have traveled to Israeli schools designed to assist refugees from around the world, provided professional development to teachers in Jinja, Uganda, in strategies in learning English, and most recently been to Guatemala to learn more about their diverse cultures and languages. In Guatemala, I discovered a book written in K'iche', a Mayan language that a Las Americas student, Moises, had learned, along with Spanish, growing up there. It made a world of difference to Moises to know his principal took the time to research and understand his roots and heritage. He felt better, and that's when the learning began.

Internet use: Although traveling to countries is the most ideal way to learn, the Internet is also a resourceful tool to gather information. When students know that educators have taken the time to research, understand, and gather background information about their home country, they tend to embrace their fears and open their hearts and minds to the challenges that lie ahead.

Another type of technology that can be useful is smartphones and apps. When working with multiple languages, having the ability to translate and understand students is essential. Take, for example, two students that speak different languages having a conflict. How do you facilitate that conversation? How do you make the student feel safe and understood? How do you correct any misunderstandings? Apps now have the ability to take a student's concern in one language, translate it to English, and help facilitate any misunderstandings.

Teacher awareness of traumatic grief: Oftentimes, disputes and other outbursts are a sign of the deep emotional issues many students arrive with. These are signs that teachers must be aware of (see Chapter 1). There are essential programs needed to help students cope with feelings that have been masked for years. It could be the trauma they faced getting to the United States. It could be that when the teacher is discussing a lesson a memory of family, fear, or loss is triggered and suddenly they are angry, crying, or just sitting with a silent stare. Many teachers, who are untrained, see this type of behavior as being defiant, when in reality, the students are crying out for help. These programs are designed to help students use coping skills, peer mediation, and self-identity. It is the essentials they need that were not given to them previously because they were too busy being the "young adults."

Interventions for immigrant students

Interventions for these immigrant students center on the traumatic past they incurred, the unfamiliar present they are living in, and the uncertain future they imagine. They help to normalize unconscionable circumstances and overwhelming feelings of isolation, sadness, rage, and fear. One can comprehend the depth of adversity incorporated in the "young adult" life by looking closely into the lives of specific children.

Jose, age 14, and Maria, age 8, are two children who lived in El Salvador with their 75-year-old grandmother. Their mom left both children to go to the United States when Maria was six months old, unable to care for her children due to the tragic death of her husband who was killed by gangs. She tried to find work to help raise her children, struggling to feed them and provide an education, by frequently sending money to El Salvador. For eight years, her children essentially raised themselves. Separated from their mom, there was little discipline and guidance through their childhood and adolescence.

Both Jose and Maria helped around the house by working in the fields and aiding in supporting the household. Family members warned their mother that the gangs were trying to recruit them and they were in danger. Female gang members are usually used for sex and become servants to the male leaders. Their mom had been living in Houston for almost eight years now. She had since found a boyfriend and was six months pregnant with another son. Her children made the journey alone with other people from El Salvador. A "Coyote" (a person who helps smuggle illegal aliens into the United States) was to accompany them but abandoned them in Tamaulipas, Mexico. The kids jumped on trains and rode on buses to the Mexico/U.S. border. They nearly lost each other several times and almost did not make it crossing the river (as they swam across using a raft). They were quickly captured by Immigration and were placed in a shelter for six weeks before their release to their mother.

Student groups for coping skills

When these children arrived in our schools, they needed support to help them cope with the years of neglect and lack of supervision. Schools must intervene and provide the support needed to build the foundation for success. Student groups are created to discuss coping strategies and provide students with therapy to help manage their feelings. After all, they have experienced grief and loss at many levels. Leaving behind the only thing they have known, their country, for something much more important—their safety. They must feel that they are not alone. Others feel the same; others made the journey—and hearing each other's stories helps them cope and grieve. Oftentimes, we will see children crying as they begin to be aware that this too shall pass. They become stronger and more resilient.

Closet of Hope

Jose and Maria also received gently used clothing from the *Closet of Hope*. It is a special place within the school where gently used and/or new clothing is donated to the school for children and their families at no cost. Maria, when she enrolled, wore shoes that were too small for her feet. The only clothes that made the dangerous journey were the clothes the children wore. They had no coats, sweaters, hats, or gloves for the cold temperatures they were going to experience in Texas. Many of the items found in the closet are donated from suburban, affluent high schools along with churches, colleges, and other organizations. Many families also donate to the closet by providing clothing that no longer fit their children and thus provide help to our new families just arriving into the country. You never know what you can find in the *Closet of Hope*. Donations have now expanded to kitchenware, accessories, bedding, and small appliances.

Other helpful techniques include validating the past and cultural heritage through storytelling, letter writing, drawing, and poetry, sharing information and activities that help students and families acclimatize to America, doing activities that focus on the present through a book campaign for students, and journaling on what America is and what future it holds.

Telling stories: Sharing the past

Storytelling is an important component of healing. Often, sharing one's life journey helps students feel less alone and more cared for. Providing that opportunity in school through a lesson or homework assignment gives children the opportunity to share with others and normalize difficult life experiences. The following is an example of a student sharing their story of coming to America. The story helps to promote discussion, release feelings, normalize events, and create safety. Arsema tells the story of her journey from Eritrea, and expresses her gratefulness to the school.

First of all, my name is Arsema. I am from Eritrea. I live in America now. I am a student in Las Americas Newcomer School and I am 14 years old. Even though I used to know English language, Las Americas really did help me and still helping out with my English [...] not only English [but] with my grades too. When I first come to America, I knew English language but each word I say I thought it was wrong or make no sense. But when I come to Las Americas and learn with students like me where English is their second language and not really knowing the American system... really helped me to have a confiden[ce] [i]n my English skills because it is much better for me to talk in English with people like me instead of people who are used to it and know everything about it. Second thing that Las Americas Middle School helped me is since I am in grade 8, I am going to high school for grade 9 next year.

So Las Americas is helping me to prepare for high school because high school is gonna be totally different. There are a lot of programs that help you who you are supposed to be when you go to high school. The good thing in Las Americas Middle School is the teacher and everybody else. They are so friendly, helpful. I am so glad I come to this school because if I see back to my country, we don't play with our teachers. They really have strange face on their students. You don't even feel confidence and happily to ask questions about school. Las Americas Middle School's teachers are totally different than that. Those teachers' door is wide open for their students that they [make] time for their students. Las Americas Middle School let me know whole lots of people and different cultures. I knew what America is and what about it in Las Americas Middle School. The first day of school was really hard for me.

When I got to the school, it was different than I expected it to be. Everybody smile and everybody friendly and I felt more comfortable. Each day I go to school, I learn or get at least two word[s] in a week [...] my

English skills usually add something to it or change something good and knowing English and improving it. Everything is because of Las Americas Middle School. [Lastly], I wanted to say thanks to Las Americas Middle School. To all the teachers and principal, thank you for your hard work and letting me see my English language skills improving every day. Thank you so much [...] and with all your hard work I am ready to go to high school and go through it without any fear.

The love and compassion she felt from her school enabled her to move forward in high school without fear. Her heartfelt appreciation of Las Americas Middle School was extended with a huge thank you for improving her language skills every day, and having an open-door policy of inclusion and acceptance.

Children commonly describe their joy at being safe in school and their sadness at leaving their home and sometimes family members. Many students share that their journey of coming to America often includes leaving a troubled past comprised of danger, violence, poverty, and criminals—as well as the anguish of saying goodbye to loved ones. These young people are often comforted when placed in a safe school with new friends. Although their stories provide insights into the threats families are facing in their country, the process of acclimatizing to America creates another layer of anxiety. It is important to help bridge those gaps and provide that support. Las Americas Newcomer School depends on external organizations to support families and introduce them to traditions they may have never experienced.

Learning about America

Thanksgiving is a tradition that families in America are accustomed to celebrating. Every year, children and families at Las Americas are introduced to these traditions by having parent meetings, classroom assignments, and homework sent out to help our newly arrived immigrants with the traditions of America. St. Luke's Methodist Church provides a traditional meal, which includes turkey, stuffing, and apple pie, for all families at the school. It is building tradition in a new country they have chosen to call their new home.

The school also partners with other organizations to sponsor and adopt every family for Christmas celebrations. Because there are a number of religions and beliefs, it is important to have families understand and respect each other's faith. Families are interviewed to gather information to determine what they need. Items such as personal hygiene products, bath towels, pillows, and other household goods are often needed. Many of the children share the only bath towel they have.

A huge celebration takes place the day before students leave for winter break. Boxes and boxes of toys, gifts, bedding, and other supplies pack the school cafeteria where many of the sponsors meet their adopted families and share tears of joy for their generosity.

Sharing information

It is important to consistently share information with families. Examples can include a resource fair, free adult English as a Second Language (ESL) classes, information about school readiness, expectations, and a variety of "how to" meetings, including:

- how to read my child's report card
- how to read my child's transcript
- how to graduate from high school—what credits are
- how to get involved—what parent involvement is.

Let's face it, many of our new families do not know how to get involved in their child's education. They were never expected to and they never had to. In America, it is engraved in parents to visit their child's school and become involved. Our immigrant families need to be trained on all of that.

Cultural sharing

Pride in one's heritage, and owning it as part of one's identity, creates self-esteem and empowerment. This sharing of a myriad of varied cultures and heritages has become an integral part of creating inclusion in diversity at our school. Figure 6.2 is an example of Paulina's artwork. She is from Mexico. She draws to ease her mind and remember her home. She still has family there. She doesn't know if she will ever see them again.

Figure 6.2 Elephant

Telling about past and present

One of the first activities we complete at school is "Where I'm From." It's an opportunity for students to learn from each other and provide background for their teacher. It also establishes self-identity and helps them celebrate their differences. This activity is modified by the teacher to differentiate between ages and language proficiency. It allows them to revisit the past and explain their present, creating a positive link between the past and present for the students.

Poems about America

Another activity we do at Las Americas is poetry writing. Children were asked to express their feelings about America (Figure 6.3). Some felt it had lots of money, they liked the flag, or it had good parks, great food, and opportunity. These poems are very hopeful and help to imprint a successful future.

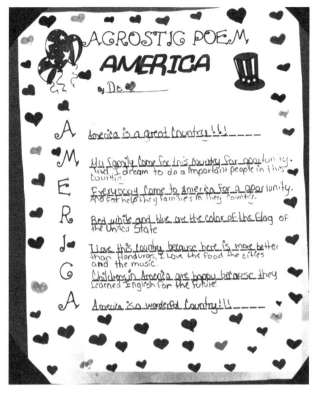

Figure 6.3 America

A book drive

Reading is an integral part of learning language, leading to greater cultural assimilation and success at school. A book drive was held for students by the school. Children could make choices about what they would like to read. Many girls and boys showed their appreciation for resources they might not have been able to access or afford by displaying signs of thanks and showing off their books.

Building self-esteem

Often children aren't aware that they may possess many natural attributes of resilience. This particular intervention helped students to identify the attribute of choice of attitude and how changing their perspective can actually change their day.

Another activity is called "The Attitude Tree." Students place words that reflect their attitude about being in America. One student wrote, "I'm thankful to be in the United States away from war in my country."

Lucy is "going to do [her] best to be a nurse to help others." Other kids explained they are grateful to finally reunite with their long-lost parents and pursue their dreams.

A SUCCESS STORY: MAGNIFIQUE

Magnifique was a student at Las Americas. She was born on May 14, 1995 in a refugee camp called Musuhura in Tanzania, Africa. She lived with her mother and grandmother. Her story demonstrates the impact a school system can make when it includes compassion, understanding, dedication, and acknowledgment of trauma and suffering in the curriculum in order to enhance learning.

The key to the future is the past

When Magnifique was about three years old, the camp was destroyed. The people found refuge in another refugee camp for nine years before Magnifique's entire life would change. This was her chance for a new beginning—an opportunity to come to the United States. For 12 years, Magnifique only knew life in a refugee camp. There was no electricity, running water, kitchen, or bathroom in the house. The family used petroleum and candles to light the house, which was made of bamboo and mud. Grass and soil were used to coat the roof to keep the rooms cool during the hot summer months. Schooling was important. She attended Nelson Mandela Elementary School while living in the refugee camp.

To understand why this family became refugees in America, you must understand the history of Burundi. It gained its independence from Belgium in 1962. In 1972, one of two occurrences of genocide resulted in massive killings in the country. Magnifique's grandparents and mother fled the country and settled in Rwanda and later Tanzania. While living in Tanzania, they attempted to return to Burundi; however, after more than 30 years, other people had already occupied the land they once owned.

The International Organization for Migration (IOM), a leading inter-governmental organization in the field of migration, helped Magnifique's family complete the application and they went through three interviews before being accepted and relocated to the United States. The family of four (Magnifique, mother, father, and younger sister) traveled on several planes before they arrived at their final destination—Houston, Texas. It was the first time the family had been on a plane. She recalls that when she arrived at Houston Airport their caseworker from the Alliance for Multicultural Community Services welcomed them. He escorted the family to their new apartment and helped the family enroll in school. Having an apartment was foreign to Magnifique. Electricity, running water, a stove, and a refrigerator were also new to the family.

The first day of school

The first day of school was exciting—she remembers her first day (Figure 6.4). She was greeted by a warm, welcoming staff. She was introduced to several other students who also spoke Kirundi. The "Buddy System" matches new students with current students to escort them to class and show students the systems and routines that everyone follows at school.

Figure 6.4 First day

This transition for her was very supportive. She was scared, nervous, and anxious. As she entered the classrooms, the teachers and staff made her feel comfortable.

She recalls her teachers saying "urakoze," meaning thank you in Kirundi. This is one of many strategies teachers at Las Americas use to welcome students. Key words and phrases are given to all teachers in a variety of languages to help students feel at ease.

PAIR: Helping refugee students acclimate

For three years, Magnifique attended school at Las Americas. She participated in PAIR (Partnership for the Advancement and Immersion of Refugees), an afterschool program to help acclimate young students to this new country. She is grateful for all the support, patience, and unconditional love she received from all her teachers. Their willingness to do whatever it took made her feel empowered. She had plenty of questions and she knew that teachers were open to answering each and every one of them. Many students ask the question "why?" for just about everything. She was no exception. But not once did a teacher close that door. It's important to provide those answers. These adolescent children are like sponges—everything is new to them.

At Las Americas, teachers introduced Magnifique to a school library and exposed her to a variety of genres of book. It was the first time she needed to take a state exam for promotion. She knew that if she did not pass the state exams, her chances of success were slim. After her third year in America, she made a perfect score on her eighth grade math test. She owed her success to the teachers. But was her success due to the teachers or Magnifique's drive to succeed? Actually, she says it's both. You need intrinsic motivation, parent support, and the support of teachers. Ensuring a smooth transition to high school is also necessary. Las Americas provides all students with a school tour of the high school and a bridge in the form of an eighth grade summer school program.

High school

In high school, things were hard. It was a bigger school, but the counselors and teachers also showed compassion. After Magnifique's freshman year, she had a 3.9 grade point average (GPA). She became much more involved in school in the second semester of her sophomore year. She was inducted into the National Honor Society. She attended workshops to help write essays and was supported by her college counselor in completing college applications. She was also a yearbook staff member. Her senior counselor nominated her for the POSSE Foundation fellowship program. This program awards high school seniors a full tuition free scholarship. Magnifique was one of 61 out of the 800 applicants awarded. She now attends Texas A&M University.

Success and resilience

Magnifique is currently in her fifth semester. She has recently changed her major to focus on Nonprofit Business Management. She hopes one day to return to Burundi and Rwanda to help other families that live there. She hopes one day she can change their lives by providing them with opportunities she was given. She dreams of establishing an educational nonprofit in Burundi and Rwanda that will fundraise money to support underprivileged students to continue their secondary school education.

Recommendations for educators

Short-term and long-term strategies: Susan Craig, in *Reaching and Teaching Children Who Hurt: Strategies for Your Classroom* (2008), provides strategies that are available to support teachers in identifying student behaviors that are the effects of trauma. Short-term solutions include behavior/classroom management to include modeling appropriate behavior and inappropriate behavior, assigning students with meaningful "helper" tasks in areas that they excel, and implementing an organized classroom stretch/break to help break up the long hours spent in classrooms. Long-term strategies would focus on connecting with other students, classroom set up, and building social and emotional capacity among the students.

School discipline: In Ruby Payne's *A Framework for Understanding Poverty: A Cognitive Approach* (2013), she describes how educators tend to mistake the role of punishment for a changed behavior (see also Chapter 5). When students misbehave, they usually acquire some type of consequence to change behavior; however, that usually happens to middle-class children. Students living in poverty require more of a structured-type conference where the student, parent, and teacher come together to discuss and clarify expectations. It is these expectations that schools must teach their families. It is from this resource that our school's behavior contract was created. Before a student can be disciplined, they must first understand the behavior that caused them to receive a consequence in the first place. Simply providing students with a book of rules, code of conduct, or any other policy is unproductive.

Student contract: Students can be suspended from school, given detention, or given other teacher consequences, often without knowing what they did wrong. With a student contract, students are given an explanation of the infraction and the student writes that infraction in his or her own words. Then they own it and they understand it. Teachers then provide students with examples of what they can do to ensure that infraction is not repeated. This type of dialogue between the teacher, student, and parent is necessary so that the family understands rules and consequences in a much more fundamental manner.

Systems and routines: Schools need to be consistent and as fundamental as possible. Students need to feel safe and form healthy relationships with school personnel. Screaming, yelling, and other behaviors can trigger a student to regress and form barriers that would harm a student's success. Providing positive rewards for students and peers fosters self-confidence and reassurance by creating a system that builds knowledge without overwhelming them with everything they need to know. This requires time and patience. It can take years to overcome the trauma they have faced.

Learn the history and background of students: Educators need to understand a child's history and background to better support them. This can occur by simply having a conversation with the student and understanding their journey—their story about how they arrived in America. Young children, however, are less able to articulate their story. Using images and other graphics on the Internet can help students describe and help educators better understand how poverty, losing a loved one, or other barriers have affected their lives. It provides insight and awareness that cannot be overlooked. It is something that students need to discuss, and it is helpful for them to know that grieving can be part of the learning process.

Interventions for grief and loss: It is essential for schools to address ways children and adolescents can cope with grief and loss. Having counselors and social workers work with children to help them grieve, express themselves, and help them understand and establish their identity is important. There are different techniques to accomplish this. Students can dialogue with one another about how their stories are similar and discuss it in a group setting; write letters describing how they feel; draw artwork to describe how they feel and discuss it with their peers; or share their cultures and beliefs with one another to better understand each other.

Provide resources for discussion and teachable moments. The following are a few of the many resources available for students to help them identify with the immigration issues they have faced in their lives. Examples of resources about immigration are *The Name Jar* (Choi, 2001), *Growing Up Rita* (De Gusman, 2011), *Mexican Immigrants in America* (Hanel, 2009), *The Fifth Sun* (Lagasse, 2004), *Orange Peel's Pocket* (Lewis, 2010), *Gervelie's Journey* (Robinson and Young, 2010), *Escape From Saigon* (Warren, 2008), and *All the Way to America* (Yaccarino, 2011).

Conclusion

As schools explore ways to respond to refugees, the federal government has also provided guidance. In November 2014, President Obama created the Interagency White House Task Force on New Americans to identify and support state and local efforts to welcome and integrate newcomers into communities. The White House Task Force released a strategic action plan in April 2015 that prioritized expanding educational opportunities for immigrants and refugees. The U.S. Department of Education has since led a series of webinars to share key research and best practices for the integration of these students into schools. The sessions focused on ideas for creating welcoming school environments, engaging families, supporting dual-language learning, ensuring early learning opportunities, and more. These efforts are modest, but steps in the right direction.

It's easy to get swept away by divisive rhetoric and political grandstanding. But real people's lives hang in the balance, and it's likely that more refugees will be coming to America, where many will enter American schools. For these newcomer children, school provides a unique stepping stone for integration into American life. On November 19, 2015, PBS dedicated a program to creating understanding about the challenges educators face in educating young people who are refugees with little or no English language skills. The show highlighted Las Americas Newcomer School for its ability to teach the ABCs and the basics of life in a new country (PBS Newshour, 2015):

> Coming in with not knowing the language, not knowing the culture, it just takes them [students] at least a year or two just to kind of acclimate, kind of understand what's going on, understand the language, how does this all work, this education in America work? And so it just provides them that stepping-stone. (Moreno; PBS Newshour, 2015)

That stepping stone can help restore stability in these individuals' lives. So, while it won't drive the next 24-hour news cycle like provocative demagoguery, policymakers and educators should carefully consider how to design intentional supports for refugee students' socio-emotional, linguistic, and academic needs.

References

Bilash, O. (2009) *Best of Bilash – Improving Second Language Education*. Available at www.educ.ualberta.ca/staff/olenka.bilash/best%20of%20bilash/krashen.html, accessed on 03/27/17.

Choi, Y. (2001) *The Name Jar*. New York: Dragonfly Books.

Craig, S.E. (2008) *Reaching and Teaching Children Who Hurt: Strategies for Your Classroom*. Baltimore, MD: Paul H. Brookes Publishing Co.

De Gusman, M. (2011) *Growing Up Rita*. Seattle, WA: Createspace.

FoxNews (2015) Kerry says US will take 85,000 refugees next year; 100,000 in '17.' *FoxNews*, September 21. Available at www.foxnews.com/politics/2015/09/21/kerry-says-us-will-take-85000-refugees-next-year-100000-in-17.html, accessed on 05/02/17.

Hanel, R. (2009) *Mexican Immigrants in America*. Chicago, IL: Capstone Press.

IDRA (Intercultural Development Research Association) (2015) *New Research on Securing Educational Equity and Excellence for English Language Learners in Texas Secondary Schools*. IDRA Jose A. Cardenas School Finance Fellows Program. Symposium Proceedings, February 2. Center for Mexican American Studies and Research, Our Lady of the Lake University.

Lagasse, M.H. (2004) *The Fifth Sun*. Chicago, IL: Curbstone Books.

Lewis, R.A. (2010) *Orange Peel's Pocket*. Sapna Online.com: Harry A. Abrams.

Maslow, A.H. (2013) *Motivation and Personality*. New York: Harper and Row.

Nazario, S. (2006) *Enrique's Journey*. New York: Random House Publishing.

Obama, President Barack (2014) The White House Task Force on New Americans. Presidential Memorandum—Creating Welcoming Communities and Fully Integrating Immigrants, November 21. Available at www.whitehouse.gov/the-press-office/2014/11/21/presidential-memorandum-creating-welcoming-communities-and-fully-integra, accessed on 03/01/16.

Payne, R.K. (2013) *A Framework for Understanding Poverty: A Cognitive Approach*. Highlands, TX: aha! Process, Inc.

PBS Newshour (2015) 'For young newcomers, school offers a stepping stone to life in America. April Brown Commentator. Marie, Moreno, Las Americas Newcomer School.' November 19. Available at www.pbs.org/newshour/bb/for-young-newcomers-school-offers-a-stepping-stone-to-life-in-america, accessed on 03/27/17.

Robinson, A. and Young, A. (2010) *Gervelie's Journey*. London: Francis Lincoln Children's Books.

Street, B. and Hornberger, N.H. (eds) (2008) *Encyclopedia of Language and Education, 2nd Edition. Volume 2: Literacy*. New York: Springer Science + Business Media LLC.

U.S. Department of Education (2014) *White House Task Force on New Americans Educational and Linguistic Integration Webinar Series*. OELA (Office of English Language Acquisition). Available at http://www2.ed.gov/about/offices/list/oela/webinars/new-americans/index.html, accessed on 02/29/16.

Warren, A. (2008) *Escape From Saigon*. New York: Square Fish Publishers.

The White House Task Force on New Americans (2015) *Strengthening Communities by Welcoming All Residents*. Available at https://obamawhitehouse.archives.gov/sites/default/files/image/tfna_progress_report_final_12_15_15.pdf, accessed on 05/02/17.

Yaccarino, D. (2011) *All the Way to America*. New York: Dragonfly Books.

Chapter 7

Addressing Weight Stigma and Body Dissatisfaction

IMPACT ON STUDENT HEALTH AND WELL-BEING

Kathy Kater

Background

Children and teens today grow up in a sea of fear-based messages pushing a very narrow range of prescribed, acceptable weights. Whether it's the "thin ideal" for appearance, a "normal" body mass index (BMI) for health, or, for a smaller group, a precise size for a competitive sport or arts performance, pressures to have the "right body" are so pervasive, the criteria for "success" so dichotomous (thin/ fat, right/wrong, good/bad), and the stigmatizing effect of "failing" so unforgiving, it is rare when any child escapes weight insecurity. Yet these standards are not realistic for many, if not most, of our students. This fosters anxiety, self-judgment, self-consciousness, and distraction from important developmental tasks, imposing a detrimental effect on their ability to learn and live well. As you will see in this chapter, this harm is just the tip of the iceberg.

Once limited primarily to girls driven by mass media pressures to achieve the "right" (thin) look, anxiety about weight has now become increasingly common for boys as well. Even more troublesome, added pressures arising from "obesity prevention" campaigns have provoked fear of fatness in children at ever-younger ages. Studies report 40–60 percent of elementary school girls (ages 6–12) of all sizes and shapes are worried about their weight, and teachers often report hearing girls and boys in kindergarten, and even preschool, asking, "Am I fat?" Those who are heavy, or even merely chubby, learn to believe early on that their bodies are *wrong*, and the reason is their fault. Not a passing phase, these concerns reliably endure into adulthood (Smolak, 2011).

Messages supporting this belief are delivered from multiple, well-meaning sources, including parents, family physicians, and teachers who are "concerned about (the child's) weight," but also from not-so-well-intentioned peers. In fact, students who are seen as fat are up to 65 times more likely to be bullied than any other children, regardless of gender, race, socioeconomic status, social skills, and academic achievement (Lumeng *et al.*, 2010) *The harsh truth is, many kids with visible fatness grow up to believe their bodies have already betrayed them, and that the negative judgments and bullying they experience are somehow deserved.*

With the stigma of fatness so cruel, even students who meet prescribed weight standards routinely worry that, without enough vigilance, they might gain weight and thereby lose the positive attributions that are granted to those who are lean. The result is that, among clearly non-overweight girls, more than one in three are "dieting" (eating to lose weight) as a prophylactic measure at any given time (Wertheim, Paxton, and Blaney, 2009). One beautiful and lean by any standard eighth grade student told me, "Being thin in my school is so important, if I don't lose 10 pounds by next fall, I might as well not even go to high school!" What none of these young dieters, and few of their parents, know is that restrictive eating is actually one of the most common causes of overeating and weight gain over time. As you'll read later, by dieting, many young people are stepping into a predictable cycle of pathological eating, yoyo dieting, and long-term weight gain, not loss.

Finally, thin or heavy children who are biologically vulnerable to eating disorders are at a high risk of being triggered by today's widespread belief that the only acceptable and healthy body is fat free. While the number of students who may develop an eating disorder is relatively small, it's critical to note that these have the highest mortality rate of all the psychiatric disorders (Arcelus *et al.*, 2011). While most weight concerns will not lead to such a dangerous and debilitating end, weight control behaviors, such as skipping meals, fasting, eliminating entire food groups, smoking cigarettes, vomiting, and taking laxatives, clearly interfere with energy, focused attention, and self-confidence.

Body angst is a serious distraction from major developmental tasks and ability to learn. Whether they face covert, overt, or even imaginary judgment, kids who are worried about their sizes and shapes cannot help but disconnect from who they are, as they scrutinize their images critically from the outside-in—comparing their bodies as objects, internalizing the stigma that is or could be thrust upon them, and judging their acceptability based on this. Anyone who has experienced self-consciousness even for a few minutes, for any reason, knows that for a child to feel this virtually every time he or she walks down the school hallway, or is on the playground, is devastating. This kind of trauma can grossly interfere with everyday tasks, focus, and the mental space needed to learn. As Goldman discussed in Chapter 1, adolescence is already difficult in regard to this. But now, at a time when they should be looking inward to develop their own strong voices, kids at ever younger ages are experiencing additional, unprecedented pressures to measure themselves according to the number on a scale.

Weight stigma: The controversy

In a little more than a decade, concerns about medical risks associated with rising rates of obesity across the population have massively trumped worry about the effect of body image woes, resulting in a new, increasingly forceful, weight-focused approach to health and well-being. While few would purposefully endorse widespread angst about weight, many feel that, with health at stake, increased stigma (shame associated with fatness) may be a price that must be paid. And paid it is. Since 1998 when then U.S. Surgeon General Koop declared a "war on obesity," there has been a 66 percent rise in weight stigma across the United States (Puhl and Heuer, 2009). Once considered a consequence exclusively of the fashion industry, weight bias and the negative, moral judgment it spawns is now fueled more by public health campaigns than by the covers of magazines and "ideal" appearance icons.

Given this transformative shift, it's essential to ask if this weight-focused approach to health is working. Is "war on obesity" motivating children and adults to prioritize a lifestyle that is more health-enhancing? Does a heightened focus on controlling weight predict better eating, more physical activity, improved health, and lower rates of obesity?

The answer, provided even by those who are most invested, is "no," it is not and does not. Fear of fatness and weight stigma is significantly up, but outcome data does not at all show that children or adults are eating better or becoming more active as a result. Nor is the nation overall leaner or healthier since this campaign began. Students are paying the high price of increased bias and stigma, but with no positive return. But rather than questioning whether pressures to "prevent obesity" might be part of the problem, conventional wisdom seems to be that people are just not trying hard enough. Fortunately, new and emerging research, prompted by deep concerns regarding the harmful effects of weight bias and stigma, is shedding new light on this.

A growing body of long-term data (3 to 5 years) is confirming what many clinicians, such as myself, have learned from decades of intense work with patients struggling, often since childhood, with weight concerns. The crux of the matter is that exposure to environmental and social pressures to be lean, with an emphasis on personal responsibility for weight control, leads children and teens to feel critical and unhappy with virtually any visible fatness. What follows is a huge drop in body security and trust as children internalize self-blame for their weight (Gapinski, Brownell, and LaFrance, 2013). Rather than motivating healthy choices, as some would hope, worry about weight completely sabotages all imagined benefits of "weight control." Regardless of their actual weight status, children who are dissatisfied with their bodies are more likely to suffer poor physical health and socio-emotional well-being compared to children who are satisfied. They are less likely to feel energetic or enjoy physical activity, and they are more likely to have low self-worth, not enjoy many activities, and to report poor quality peer relationships (Daraganova, 2013).

Significant research now shows that, rather than improving self-care, feeling fat or fear of fat and poor body image specifically predict poorer and disordered eating and fitness choices, diminished health, and weight gain (not loss) (Neumark-Sztainer et al., 2006a). Following the lead of their elders and the media, children who are worried about weight regularly turn to "dieting" for weight loss (Davison and Birch, 2001; Neumark et al., 2011). Girls who diet frequently are 12 times as likely to binge and add pounds over time as girls who don't diet (Neumark-Sztainer, 2005). In summary, studies now show that kids who diet are more than twice as likely to have gained weight after five years compared to non-dieters (Neumark-Sztainer et al., 2006b) and are at a higher risk for additional weight gain and obesity in adulthood (this is not due to dieters being heavier at the start) (Stice et al., 2005).

Because many teachers are themselves good students of the "diet mentality," a bit more explanation could be helpful here. One large study, including 14,000 adults followed for up to 22 years, revealed that merely *thinking* of oneself as needing to lose weight is highly associated with over-eating and future weight gain (Robinson, Hunger, and Daly, 2015). This makes sense when we learn that mere exposure to messages containing weight bias (fat is bad, thin is good) is highly stressful, leading more than 75 percent of people who *perceive* themselves as fat to cope by eating *more* low nutrient food and exercising *less* (Puhl and Heuer, 2010). Anyone concerned about the health and well-being of our kids should recognize that simply identifying with "needing to lose weight" predicts less healthy choices, even for those who are not "overweight" at the start. Clearly "feeling fat," which is common, not only for those who are larger, but for many "normal" weight girls and boys, is not benign.

In summary, rather than a price that must be paid to motivate improved eating and more physical activity, worry and angst about meeting prescribed weight standards are actually harmful. Not only do they diminish self-confidence and esteem, they fail as an incentive for improving health-enhancing behaviors while reinforcing behaviors leading to poorer health and added fatness (Goldberg and Puhl, 2013). Instead of helping, fear and disdain of fatness makes it a lot *harder* for kids to make self-caring, healthy eating, and positive fitness choices, making it harder to focus and learn in school.

For those of us who have grown up with the weight-focused paradigm (most parents, teachers, parents, and medical practitioners today), this information is often difficult to grasp. But with some consideration, it makes absolute sense. In what arena aside from weight do we expect fear and negative self-judgment to be sustainable, long-term, positive motivators? Teachers know better than anyone that extrinsic motivation (to make the grade) is not as effective for learning as a drive that is intrinsic, and so they readily support students in making their best effort, regardless of the outcome. Clearly comparing a child who finds math or physical education challenging to one for whom these come easily is a formula for a defeated child. Similarly, when kids with diverse body sizes and shapes are routinely compared against weight standards that are not realistic, we can expect them to feel demoralized. Why would they want to tune in, stay connected to, listen to, care for, and be motivated to take good care of a body they have been taught to objectify, judge, dislike, mistrust, or, at the least, fear is not good enough—to say nothing of a body that has, in many cases, been bullied or overtly shamed? Personal best, it seems, is never good enough when it comes to weight.

A more hopeful way

Einstein observed, "You cannot solve problems with the same thinking that created them." Nowhere is this more apropos than in the arena of weight concerns. He also noted that peace cannot be achieved by hatred, but only by acceptance, understanding, and love. We must consider this in light of national campaigns that have literally urged a "war on obesity." The resulting message, upon which the conventional approach to weight is based, is that fatness, of virtually any amount, is very bad, deserving even of hatred. At the same time we have learned that when bodies are viewed as "bad," many new, seriously harmful, self-perpetuating problems emerge. Unfortunately, proponents of the conventional approach to weight remain blind to this.

Einstein's premise suggests that instead of a question that produces bad feelings and stigma about higher weights, a *new approach* is needed, one that helps without harming. Let's consider a new paradigm question like this one: *Regardless of size and shape, what can we teach children to help them stay connected to, listen to, care for, and to be motivated to take care of their bodies?*

In contrast to *How can we prevent fatness?*—a weight-focused approach—this question is the essence of a health-focused approach. With the latter, educators, parents, and other caring professionals can help counteract the prevalent messages that push kids to compare their bodies to unrealistic, externally prescribed standards. With less self-criticism and more positive body esteem, children naturally *want* to care for and take care of the bodies they were born with. This conclusion is borne out by the important research of Kristen Neff. To paraphrase Neff, she points out that self-criticism asks if you're good enough, while self-compassion asks what's good for you, tapping into our inner desire to be healthy and happy. If we care about ourselves, we'll do what we need to do in order to learn and grow. Valuing ourselves in a deep way makes us *want* to abandon unhelpful ways in order to make choices that lead to well-being in the long term (Neff, 2011).

Isn't the best possible outcome a generation of kids who have learned to stay connected to, care for, and who want to take care of their diverse bodies? Few could argue that a well-fed, physically active and fit generation of diverse-sized children is not preferable to the status quo.

But what about the dangers of obesity? What about the need for "healthy weight?"

Educators, parents, medical providers, and public health systems have a responsibility to teach kids an approach to self-care that will help them to be healthy. The approach suggested here—teaching young people to embrace health-enhancing behaviors without regard to size—begs the question, *"Should we simply disregard the health risks associated with fatter bodies?"* If size diversity is accepted, how do we define a "healthy weight" and guide children toward this goal? Before answering, it's important to look at how the conventional, weight-focused approach to health defines a "healthy weight," and to see how this definition blindly disregards several critical factors.

First, the conventional approach to weight recommends "weight control" as part of the formula, as if weight is something a person can choose to do or not do, like drinking enough water, not smoking, going to bed at a reasonable hour, or buckling a seatbelt. In fact, "obesity prevention" campaigns have sometimes been modeled after those that successfully reduced smoking, including the purposeful introduction of stigma (i.e., portraying fatness as unattractive). But suggesting that weight is a behavior—something a person could "quit" if only they tried—defies reality.

Weight, of course, is not a behavior at all; it is an outcome. Furthermore, it results from a host of powerful, complex factors, only some of which we are free to choose or control. Other potent factors, such our genetic contribution (which accounts for 60% to 70% of the influence; NIH, 1998), socio-cultural determinants (favorable or unfavorable) (Mikkonen and Rafael, 2010), and even the unique bacteria a person carries in their gut (Turnbaugh *et al.*, 2006), are not in our power to regulate. While it's true that we can influence weight, just as we can blood pressure, cholesterol, or blood sugar, the key word is *influence*. With the latter three, it is widely understood that even our best efforts may not lower the numbers. In contrast, total personal and moral responsibility is assigned to people for their weight. Most of the negative judgment and stigma attached to higher weights stems from the belief that everyone can "do something" to achieve a "normal" weight if they just try—making them fair game for criticism and judgment, and making stigma about fatness defensible.

Second, conventional approaches to weight define a "healthy weight" specifically as one that falls within a narrow weight range that is labeled "normal" (a BMI of 18.5 to 24.9). Given this definition, a slim child's weight is considered "healthy" even if their eating and/or fitness habits are atrocious, disordered, or unsustainable. Indeed, eating and fitness habits are rarely questioned for those who are not fat. Instead, there is an assumption of good self-care and good health, or what we call "thin privilege." In contrast, *even if a child's or adult's eating and fitness habits are impeccable*, if their BMI falls into the "overweight" range (25 to 29.9), they are categorically denied "healthy weight" status. This is all the more true if a BMI is 30 or above (classified as "obese"). *Even if a higher weight person is in perfect health, and has lifestyle habits that are above reproach, a judgment is made that their weight is "unhealthy" and should be reduced.* This perspective clearly discounts the many complex contributors to weight. If a fatter child is doing everything "right," their body is still "wrong." This demoralizing formula is the essence of weight stigma. Educators can easily understand the negative effect of this on a child's spirit and motivation to grow, learn, and look forward to life.

To be clear, any rapid loss or gain of weight warrants assessment of the possible contributing causes. The point is that assumptions made on the basis of a high or low weight alone tells us nothing at all about the health or lifestyle habits of a child or adult. We would do well to heed this statement from the President's Council on Physical Fitness and Health Research Digest (2000): "Active obese individuals actually have lower morbidity and mortality than normal weight individuals who are sedentary…the health risks of obesity are largely controlled if a person is physically active and physically fit." Many studies before and since 2000 have reaffirmed that fatter individuals who are fit are actually a lower risk for health problems than many thinner people who are not fit (Blair *et al.*, 1996). Despite this, messages continue to assert that a "normal" BMI is, in fact, "normal," that is, realistically attainable and best for all, leaving the next generation to suffer the ill effects of weight stigma and body dissatisfaction, as well as the poorer eating and fitness habits that predictably follow.

As an alternative, when we shift the focus from weight to promotion of health-enhancing behaviors, regardless of size, "healthy weight" can be defined as an outcome of behaviors and principles that support overall health and well-being. With this perspective, weight itself is *not* the goal. Instead, we see that *weight happens*. It may well be *influenced* by lifestyle—and health will most certainly be influenced—but it is accepted that weight is not within our power to "control" over the long term through healthy, sustainable means.[1] Even with identical eating and fitness choices, different people will be different weights. When health and well-being are the goal, weight is considered to be as healthy as it's going to be when a person engages, over time, in sustainable, life-enhancing choices (eating well, staying active, managing sleep and stress, etc.). In addition, other influences, such as physical, economic, social, spiritual, and emotional needs, should be taken into account.

It warrants clarification that a health-focused approach is not pro-fat or anti-thin. It is simply weight-neutral. This paradigm respects the fact that weights resulting from positive, sustainable self-care will vary significantly, and that weight bias and stigma are highly destructive forces. With promotion of health-enhancing behaviors instead of size, all kids can succeed. Nor, to be clear, is this approach "soft" on the need to promote health-enhancing choices. In fact, when weight outcomes are no longer the goal of eating and fitness choices, much more space opens up in which to seriously urge all kids (and their families) to satisfy hunger with enough of the foods their bodies need and get plenty of enjoyable movement every day, regardless of size or weight. Let's turn now to a model that serves as a basis for this approach with students.

A new model for educators: Promoting health instead of size

The Model for Promoting Health Instead of Size (see Figure 7.1) was developed as the basis for the *Healthy Bodies: Teaching Kids What They Need to Know* curriculum guide (Kater, 2012). This model includes facts, concepts, and perspectives that children need to learn today in order to be resilient in the face of unrealistic and stigmatizing messages about their weights. It also provides guidance aimed at cutting through the many confusing and harmful messages they hear about how to avoid fatness. In line with best practices for learning, the model proposes teaching students what is empirically true and useful in support of their

---

1   It is possible to force weight up or down through extraordinary means, but such means are almost always unsustainable. When limited to sustainable eating and fitness behaviors, the degree of long-term control children and adults have over weight will be limited.

health and well-being. This stands in stark contrast to conventional, weight-focused models, that regularly emphasize what to avoid (e.g., too many calories, too much sugar and junk food, too much sedentary time, and, ultimately, a weight that is "too high").

Conceptual Building Blocks	Foundation	Desired Outcome	Goal
BIOLOGICAL FACTS: Developmental change is inevitable Weight gain is normal during puberty and other developmental stages of life. Fat does not by itself define "overweight". The greatest determinant for weight is genetic. Eating and fitness habits play a part and absolutely effect health, but genes strictly limit the degree to which weight can be controlled through healthy means. Restricted eating for weight loss or control [dieting] has predictable long term consequences that are counterproductive to sustained weight loss. It interferes with normal hunger regulation and is likely to result in weight gain over time.	Recognize and respect basic biology. Understand what is not in our control regarding size, shape, weight, and hunger.	Accept the Innate body "This is the body I was born to have."	Healthy Body Image
WHAT TO DO: Balance attriention to all aspects of identity. Looks and weight are only one part. Satisfy hunger regularly with a good variety of wholesome food in a predictable and reliable manner. Satisfy the body's need for enjoyable, vigorous, physical activity every day. Choose role models that reflect a realistic standard of diverse sizes and shapes.	Emphasize what can be influenced or chosen.	Enjoy eating for health, energy, and hunger satisfaction. Create a physically active lifestyle for fitness, endurance, fun, recreation and stress relief	Prevention of Poor and Disordered Eating Well-Fed Fit and Strong Bodies at Every Size
SEEK OUT: Historical perspective on today's unrealistic body image and weight related attitudes. Critical thinking skills in regard to media and other messages that negatively affect body image attitudes and mating behaviors. Support in resisting unhealthy norms about weight, dieting, low nutrient food choices, and a too-sedentary lifestyle.	Develop social and cultural resiliency.	Develop autonomy, self esteem, confidence, and the abiliuty for critical thinking.	

Figure 7.1 Model for Promoting Health Instead of Size (Kater, 2012, p.11). Permission to reprint freely for educational purposes.

As you can see, the model is divided into three tiers. Concepts in the top tier address the biological limits to control of body size and shape through healthy means. These are factors "built in" to each of our unique bodies that are not in our power to choose, change, or control. Young people are taught to be curious about their body's innate predisposition, and to accept and care for the diverse bodies they were born to have. Concepts in the middle tier identify behaviors that enhance health and well-being, the same for everyone, regardless of size or weight. Girls and boys are taught to invest in these behaviors, not for the purpose of "controlling weight," as many fear-based messages urge, but because they value this life and want to take care of it. Concepts in the lower tier address the fact that children need to be prepared for and resilient in the face of continuing pressures that promote weight bias and stigma, as well as the normalization of poor and unbalanced eating and movement habits.

Developing the model

The Model for Promoting Health Instead of Size is based on identification of four prevalent cultural myths that form the seedbed out of which most body image, eating, fitness, and weight-related concerns are spawned. Most of us, including today's educators, parents, and healthcare providers, learned in our own formative years to believe in and to take these myths for granted. Unless prompted, we rarely question them. But when viewed in light of scientific evidence, these myths are revealed for what they are—seriously flawed, and therefore "toxic" to health and well-being. Science also provides us with the known facts, presented by the model in the form of universal health promotion lessons, or "antidotes," that children should learn to help them avoid problems with body dissatisfaction, and the poor eating and fitness habits that routinely follow.

I'm confident teachers will agree that our mission is to universally help *all* students, whether they are fatter, thinner, or in between, to develop a stake in *caring for and taking care of their bodies*. Hopefully it's now clear that this requires a shift away from weight-focused outcomes, toward a more realistic, achievable objective—one that excludes no one. The new goal would be to help each child to invest in their personal best health and well-being, with acceptance of the diverse bodies that result from good care. Teaching this new paradigm requires modification of our conventional, myth-loaded ways of thinking and talking about weight, which can be challenging. Understanding the four toxic myths and their antidotes will help you with the new perspectives, facts, and some of the corrective language you will need for this. The following section introduces these. Readers who want more information and direction may want to refer to the *Healthy Bodies: Teaching Kids What They Need to Know* curriculum guide (Kater, 2012), in which each antidote is the basis for one of ten scripted lessons.

The four toxic myths and their antidotes

Myth 1—based on the body as an object to be compared to external standards. There is a "right" size to be. Striving to achieve the "thin ideal" for appearance and a "normal" BMI for health should be everyone's goal. How we look and what we weigh is more important than how we actually take care of our bodies.

How this myth works: Mass marketing of the lean body "ideal" and public health promotion of a "normal" BMI as if these are superior, essential, and achievable by everyone affects almost everyone today. Promoting the notion that there is a "right" (slim) weight range literally requires people to compare and objectify their bodies, while encouraging widespread fear and disdain of fatness, weight stigma, body dissatisfaction, and disconnection from internal body cues that are perfectly attuned to what bodies need to be well. Many adults, let alone children, do not realize that *anxiety* about weight is a new social construct (not a given), originally manufactured and widely "sold" by the 1960s fashion industry. More recently it has been dramatically fueled, however inadvertently, by "obesity prevention" campaigns. Rather than helping, this fear triggers extrinsic motivation to "make weight," making it harder to tune in, listen to, and take care of our body's needs.

Three "antidotes" challenge this myth. Their aim is to help students resist messages pushing them to compare their bodies to externally prescribed standards for size, shape, and weight—standards that may be unrealistic for many, if not most.

1. Provide students with an historical perspective on today's "right/ wrong" body size messaging. This dichotomous way of judging bodies did not always exist, and it has proven to be harmful. History and science show that when people compare themselves

against external standards that may not be right for them, it leads to self-criticism. This, in turn, predicts poorer long-term success outcomes. The next generation should learn there is no "right" or "normal" size to be—only their own personal best body. (*Note:* Myth 2 antidotes teach that bodies are biologically predisposed to express a wide range of sizes and shapes.)

2. Help young people develop media literacy and critical thinking about advertisements and public health messages that (however inadvertently) promote today's "right size/wrong size" mentality.

3. Encourage and guide kids to develop a strong sense of identity based on *inner* qualities, not on appearance or the number on a scale. How they look and what they weigh is only one small part of who they are.

Myth 2—based on denial of biological diversity: Anyone can be slim if they work at it. Fatter people (inevitably) eat too much and/or are inactive. Fat is bad/wrong and unhealthy.

How this myth works: For a "normal" BMI or the "thin ideal" to be widely embraced as the "right" weight for all, the facts of biological diversity have to be disregarded or denied. This myth teaches children that fatter people "must be doing something wrong" (over-eating and/or being too sedentary) and, thus, weight bias freely develops. In turn, weight stigma emerges, leading to rampant body criticism, and anxiety about the need to control weight. In fact, science has documented many complex contributors to weight that are not in our power to control— even the very best eating and fitness habits result in a wide range of sizes and shapes. Less than half of post-pubescent white females and even fewer women of color have the genetic predisposition for a slim body or "normal" BMI.

Children can easily grasp that only *behaviors* can be controlled, and weight is *not* a behavior. With elementary lessons on genetic influence, students understand that people who eat well and maintain an active lifestyle will have diverse weight outcomes that are "normal" for them, ranging from thin to fat. They realize that we cannot assume someone is taking good care of themselves, or not taking good care of themselves, based on weight or appearance alone.

Four "antidotes" challenge this myth. Their goal is to arm students with the scientific facts of innate size diversity.

1. Teach pre-pubescent children that they will soon be growing in diverse ways that will not affect only their height, but weight and shape as well. Anticipating these biologically "wired" changes as inevitable, and something that everyone experiences, can reduce worry. Differences in growth and development are not good or bad, or right or wrong, but simply normal variations. Teasing someone about body differences is hurtful, and it is not OK.

2. Inform and discuss with children the normal, expected changes in outward appearance that occur with puberty. Over a period of several years, most boys and girls gain weight and fill out. For example, the addition of up to 20 percent of their weight in fat is normal for girls, and should *not* be interpreted as "getting fat" (negative connotation implied).

3. Educate kids about the biological basis for size diversity. Along with many other inherited characteristics and traits, all bodies are genetically predisposed to range from taller to shorter and fatter to thinner.

4. Help children understand that the internal weight regulatory system *limits* the extent of long-term control that is possible over weight through healthy means. Many complex factors influence fatness/slimness. It is presumptuous and prejudicial to judge an individual's lifestyle behaviors by his or her appearance or BMI. Eating and activity habits can influence weight, but this is limited by each person's genetic make-up.

Myth 3—based on denial of the reliable and predictable results of externally prescribed hunger regulation: "Dieting" is an effective weight-loss strategy.

How this myth works: When a prescribed size is mandated, a means to reach it is needed. Because restricted eating results in weight loss in the short run, this is routinely used as evidence to support the belief that anyone could be slim(mer) if he or she uses weight-loss diets and exercise (see Myth 2). In fact, long-term outcomes show that individuals who complete weight-loss programs lose an average of 10 percent of their body weight, but gain two-thirds of it back within one year and virtually all of it within three years. Half to two-thirds of all dieters regain *more* weight than they initially lose, creating an unrealistic sense of failure, and adding to the rising rates of fatness across the population (Mann and Tomiyama, 2007).

Many people, including medical providers, continue to blame a dieter's lack of willpower rather than reconcile with the clear evidence showing that dieting for weight loss is intrinsically flawed. Fortunately, even young children realize that when hunger is not satisfied, it will become like a caged lion, waiting to get free, and then eating all that was previously forbidden. The following reliable and predictable outcomes for even moderate restrictions in food intake have been well documented since 1950: increased obsession and preoccupation with food, difficulty concentrating, ravenous hunger, irritability and/or depression, as well as uncontrolled compulsive or binge eating when diet restrictions are lifted (Keyes *et al.*, 1950).

Suggesting to children that they should eat less than hunger dictates teaches them that they cannot trust and should not listen to internal hunger cues, and that they must rely on external rules if they want to be healthy and acceptable in the eyes of others. Such a plan creates an adversarial relationship with the body, and is a set-up for failure.

One potent "antidote" challenges this myth. The goal is to reinforce what students already know instinctually: eating less than what the body needs to satisfy hunger for the purpose of weight loss is a set-up to fail.

1. Teach students the well-documented facts about the counterproductive effects of "dieting" for weight loss. It is likely that weight will be lost at first, but only by fighting against nature. In the end, science shows that most weight lost is regained, and frequently with added pounds.

Myth 4—based on discounting the value of health in its own right; complacency about health-enhancing choices if they don't result in the desired weight. Eat, drink, and be merry; healthy choices (just for health's sake) are not worth the effort.

How this myth works: The promise of a reduced size or "normal" BMI as the prize for a healthy lifestyle is unrealistic and a recipe for complacency in regard to healthy habits for health's sake. As previously noted, even with the best of lifestyles, bodies will be diverse. When people improve their lifestyle habits, but still do not reach their goal weight, they feel demoralized, and give up—returning to former habits, or worse. Good self-care requires an investment of time and energy. When the primary objective is weight loss, the almost laughable conclusion is: "I did all this, and all I get is health!?"

Similarly, when the purpose of healthy habits is "weight control," those who are naturally low weight are often complacent as well. How many lean teens dismiss poor eating and fitness habits by asking, "What difference does it make? I'm not fat!" The promise of a slim physique or "normal" BMI as the reward for a healthy lifestyle has backfired, leading many to give up on healthy habits that don't deliver on the implied promise, or that seem not to be needed by those who already have this "prize."

Maintaining a healthy lifestyle takes a strong intention, inspiration, and motivation, and an investment of time and effort. If the primary purpose is to "control weight," we can expect what we've gotten: young people growing less healthy and in many cases fatter on feelings of failure or complacency. Instead, students can be taught that *health and well-being*—not size or shape—are more important rewards. With a size-neutral approach and body respect, nutritional health and physical fitness are achievable for every student, regardless of size.

Three "antidotes" challenge this myth. The overall message should teach kids to systematically embrace health as a value rather than size as a goal. Valuing themselves and their health in a deep way will help them *want* to make choices that lead to their personal best.

1. Model and teach eating competency. Teach kids to understand that different foods have different qualities with different purposes. It's important to satisfy hunger with foods the body needs at regular meals and snack times—*not* because they "should," but because they care about their bodies and want to take care of them. Help kids enjoy "just for fun" foods without conflict, confident that their nutrition needs are taken care of.

2. Model and teach embodiment. Teach kids to listen to their body's need for plenty of physical activity every day—not because they "should," but because they care about their bodies and they want to take care of them. Urge kids to find the kind of movement their body enjoys. *It's not the same for everyone.*

3. Actively intervene to help students reject comparisons to external size and appearance standards that are not right for them. Discuss how the story of the *Ugly Duckling* would have ended if the swan had stayed with the ducks—unrealistically comparing itself to them indefinitely. This happens to too many kids. Urge kids to seek role models that inspire them to feel good about themselves.

Awareness of these myths and their antidotes can allow educators, parents, healthcare providers, and other adults to teach young people the truth about weight, health, and well-being. Empowering boys and girls to resist pressures promoting weight bias and stigma will enhance their body- and self-esteem, and in turn their ability to learn. Teachers should examine their school culture and ask themselves whether they are teaching their students to:

- maintain a caring, mindful connection to their bodies from the inside-out

- develop an identity based on who they are rather than how they look

- reject weight bias and stigma, and respect the genetic diversity of body size and shape

- understand how appearance changes with puberty

- defend against unhealthy cultural pressures regarding looks, weight, food, and dieting

- choose positive role models that support their deeper values

- actively embrace health and vitality through positive eating and physical activity

- support each other in having a healthy body image, eating well, and staying fit

- use problem-oriented coping skills.

The *Healthy Bodies: Teaching Kids What They Need to Know* curriculum guide (Kater, 2012) presents engaging methods of teaching these concepts, with lessons scripted for grades 4–6 that are easily adaptable for any age. *Healthy Bodies* has demonstrated positive results in outcome studies with students in grades 4–6 (Kater, Rohwer, and Levine, 2000; Kater, Rohwer, and Londre, 2002; Niide *et al.*, 2013), and is included in the *Bodywise Packet for Educators* provided by the U.S. Department of Health and Human Services' Office of Women's Health (1999).[2]

Closing thoughts

It's important to note that the "antidotes" for the four toxic myths strive to be holistic and internally consistent, strictly avoiding recommendations that are unrealistic for many, unsustainable for most, or triggering of other problems. The goals and the means to reach them—healthy body image attitudes, balanced eating and fitness choices, and diverse, personal best weight outcomes—are universal; that is, they are attainable by all who have sufficient access to food and safety. As such, the model is non-discriminatory, simple enough to be taught both to young children and teens, and useful for educators in the prevention and reversal of problems. Rather than promoting fear by warning students about scary outcomes to avoid, or delivering "rules"—for example, regarding "good" or "bad" foods—concepts teach students to stay *connected to* (tune in and listen deeply to), *care for* (be motivated to respond to what is needed), and use their wise minds and compassionate hearts to *take care of* their bodies through mindful eating and embodied movement.

Last, but not least, given the prevalence of weight concerns among kids today, it goes without saying that—both inside and outside of the classroom—educators are presented with many opportunities to respond to student's "fat talk" and confusion about weight. All teachers can serve as agents of change by knowing how to respond to these concerns with factual information and wise, realistic perspectives in a caring, supportive way. The approach should always begin with empathy—realizing that student misinformation and unrealistic views are completely understandable in light of the prevalent myths about body image and weight they have learned. A familiar Chinese proverb

---

2   See www.bodyimagehealth.org for more information, including free downloads, colorful posters, and other printable handouts.

states: "A culture is formed by the stories its children are told." Students today will benefit greatly when teachers are prepared to acknowledge harmful cultural beliefs based on weight bias and stigma, and to present students with corrective antidotes.

Situations and suggested responses

Situation: You overhear adolescent girls engaging in "fat talk"—for example, "I'm so fat!"

Possible response:

- Oh girls, I know you hear so many messages suggesting any amount of fat is bad, and that everyone can and should be thin. But that's just not reality! Bodies are born to be all different sizes and shapes—not only taller and shorter, but fatter and thinner too. What's important is that we *care for* and *take care of* our diverse bodies. You might ask yourself, "Am I eating all the foods my body needs most days?" If not, maybe you want to try harder to do this. Do you have fun ways to get your heart pumping most days? If not, then your body would be so happy if you did! But if you are already caring for yourselves in these ways, then your bodies are probably already the sizes and shapes that are right for each of you.

Situation: At the start of the school year a middle school student confides in you, "I really want to try out for a part in the spring musical, but I know I have to lose weight first."

Possible response:

- I wonder why you think that... Because, bodies are really born to be all different sizes and shapes, from thin to fat. How much fatness do you think might be right for you? [Opening the door to talk about 1) genetic diversity, 2) added fat in puberty, 3) the counterproductive results of dieting for weight loss, and 4) the importance of eating well, staying active, and accepting the size and shape that results.] Before you dive into trying to lose weight, I wonder if we could first take a look at whether you are eating enough of the foods your body needs to be strong and healthy?

Situation: You hear grade school students talking about the teacher's "Biggest Loser" contest. They mention that the band teacher drinks Diet Coke instead of going to lunch.

Possible response:

- You know a lot of people—even many adults—still believe that going on a diet or skipping meals or extreme exercise is a good way to lose weight. I know the *Biggest Loser* TV show makes this look like it works. But that's too bad, because, in fact, it usually doesn't turn out very well in the long run. A person can lose weight by dieting for a while, but hunger is so much more powerful! It's like a lion—if you put it in a cage, when it gets out, it is going to eat everything in sight! That's what happens when people diet. They drop pounds for a while, but in the end, most people eat so much more just to make up for having "caged" their hunger! Did you know that 80 to 95 percent of weight that is lost by dieting is regained— often along with even more pounds! In fact, it was recently reported that's what's happened to most of the *Biggest Loser* contestants. Better to work with Mother Nature, and always satisfy hunger with the foods our bodies need. That's really the only way we can be sure our weight is right for us.

References

Arcelus, J., Mitchell, A.J., Wales, J., and Nielsen, S. (2011) 'Mortality rates in patients with anorexia nervosa and other eating disorders.' *Archives of General Psychiatry 68*, 7, 724–731.

Blair, S.N., Kampert, J.B., Kohl, H.W. 3rd, Barlow, C.E. *et al.* (1996) 'Influences of cardiorespiratory fitness and other precursors on cardiovascular disease and all-cause mortality in men and women.' *Journal of the American Medical Association 276*, 3, 205–210.

Daraganova, G. (2013) 'Body Image of Primary School Children.' In *The Longitudinal Study of Australian Children Annual Statistical Report 2013.*

Davison, K.K. and Birch, L.L. (2001) 'Weight status, parent reaction, and self-concept in five-year-old girls.' *Pediatrics 107*, 46–53.

Gapinski, K.D., Brownell, K.D., and LaFrance, M. (2003) 'Body objectification and "fat talk": Effects on emotion, motivation and cognitive performance.' *Sex Roles 48*, 377–388.

Goldberg, D. and Puhl, R. (2013) 'Obesity stigma: A failed and ethically dubious strategy.' *Hastings Center Report 43*, 3, 5–6.

Kater, K. (2012) *Healthy Bodies: Teaching Kids What They Need to Know* (curriculum guide). St. Paul, MN: Body Image Health.

Kater, K., Rohwer, J., and Levine, M.P. (2000) 'An elementary school project for developing healthy body image and reducing risk factors for unhealthy and disordered eating.' *Eating Disorders: Journal of Treatment and Prevention 8*, 1,3–16.

Kater, K., Rohwer, J., and Londre, K. (2002) 'Evaluation of an upper elementary school program to prevent body image, eating and weight concerns.' *Journal of School Health 72*, 5, 199–204.

Keyes, A., Brozek, J., Henschel, A., Mickelsen, O., and Taylor, H.L. (1950) *The Biology of Human Starvation* (2 volumes). Minneapolis, MN: University of Minnesota Press.

Lumeng, J.C., Forrest, P., Appugliese, D., Kaciroti, N., Corwyn, R. *et al.* (2010) 'Weight status as a predictor of being bullied in third through sixth grades.' *Pediatrics 125*, 6, 1300–1307.

Mann, T. and Tomiyama, A.J. (2007) 'Medicare's search for effective obesity treatment: Diets are not the answer.' *American Psychologist*, April.

Mikkonen, J. and Rafael, D. (2010) *Social Determinants of Health: The Canadian Facts.* Toronto: York University School of Health Policy and Management.

Neff, K. (2011) *Self-Compassion.* New York: HarperCollins.

Neumark, D., Neumark-Sztainer, D., Wall, M., Larson, N., Eisenberg, M., and Loth, K. (2011) 'Dieting and disordered eating behaviors from adolescence to young adulthood: Findings from a 10-year longitudinal study.' *Journal of the American Dietetic Association 111*, 7, 1004–1011.

Neumark-Sztainer, D. (2005) *I'm, Like, SO Fat!* New York: Guilford.

Neumark-Sztainer, D., Paxton, S.J., Hannan, P.I., Haines, J. and Story, M. (2006a) 'Does body satisfaction matter? Five-year longitudinal associations between body satisfaction and health behaviors in adolescent females and males.' *Journal of Adolescent Health 392*, 244–251.

Neumark-Sztainer, D., Wall, M., Guo, J., Story, M., Haines, J., and Eisenberg, M. (2006b) 'Obesity, disordered eating, and eating disorders in a longitudinal study of adolescents: How do dieters fare 5 years later?' *Journal of the American Dietetic Association 106*, 559–568.

NIH (1998) *NIH Clinical Guidelines on the Identification, Evaluation, and Treatment of Overweight and Obesity in Adults: The Evidence Report.* Rockville, MD: National Institutes of Health, National Heart, Lung, and Blood Institute.

Niide, T., Davis, J., Tse, A. and Harrigan, R.L. (2013) 'Evaluating the impact of a school-based prevention program on self-esteem, body image, and risky dieting attitudes and behaviors among Kaua'I youth.' *Hawaii Journal of Medicine and Public Health 72*, 8, 273–278.

President's Council on Physical Fitness and Health Research Digest (2000) Series 3, No. 12, December.

Puhl, R. and Heuer, C. (2009) 'The stigma of obesity: A review and update.' *Obesity (Silver Spring) 17*, 5, 941–964.

Puhl, R. and Heuer, C. (2010) 'Obesity stigma: Important considerations for public health.' *American Journal of Public Health 100*, 1019–1028.

Robinson, E., Hunger, J.M., and Daly, M. (2015) 'Perceived weight status and risk of weight gain across life in US and UK adults.' *International Journal of Obesity 39*, 12, 1721–1726.

Smolak, L. (2011) 'Body Image Development in Childhood.' In T. Cash and L. Smolak (eds) *Body Image: A Handbook of Science, Practice, and Prevention, 2nd Edition.* New York: Guilford.

Stice, E., Presnell, K., Shaw, H. and Rohde, P. (2005) 'Psychological and behavioral risk factors for obesity onset in adolescent girls: A prospective study.' *Journal of Consulting and Clinical Psychology 73*, 2, 195–202.

Turnbaugh, P.J., Ley, R.E., Mahowald, M.A., Magrin, V., Mardis, E.R., *et al.* (2006) 'An obesity-associated gut microbiome with increased capacity for energy harvest.' *Nature 444*, 1027–1031.

U.S. Department of Health and Human Services' Office of Women's Health (1999) *Bodywise Packet for Educators.* Washington, DC: U.S. Department of Health and Human Services' Office of Women's Health.

Wertheim, E., Paxton, S., and Blaney, S. (2009) 'Body Image in Girls.' In L. Smolak and J.K. Thompson (eds) *Body Image, Eating Disorders, and Obesity in Youth: Assessment, Prevention, and Treatment, 2nd Edition.* Washington, DC: American Psychological Association.

Chapter 8

Children with Incarcerated Family Members

EDUCATORS CAN HELP

Amalia Cortina and Sandra Trutt

About 195,000 children in California experience life without a mother or father, because mom or dad is serving time in prison (Simmons, 2000). "Seven million, or one in ten of the nation's children, have a parent under criminal justice supervision—in jail or prison, or probation, or on parole" (San Francisco Children of Incarcerated Parents Partnership, 2016). Too many children in our schools feel the loss of self-esteem due to the stigma of parental incarceration, and the pain of separation from a loved one. These challenges can impact learning potential and performance.

Children of imprisoned parents suffer as well as their parents. Many times they lose contact with parents, or visit them very rarely. They are more likely to drop out of school, engage in delinquency, and subsequently be incarcerated themselves (Dallaire, 2007). More mothers are being incarcerated, and evidence indicates this can be more damaging to children. The increase of imprisoned parents can have a great impact on families and communities (Goldman, 2014). The Sentencing Project (2009), states that children

> have been observed to suffer a variety of adverse outcomes that are consistent with the research on the effects of insecure attachment... and that more than half of children with incarcerated parents have had school problems such as poor grades and instances of aggression. (Parke and Clarke-Stewart, 2001, p.11)

There are many barriers preventing children from having contact with their parents. They include collect calling rates from prisons, the remote prison locations hundreds of miles from where their families live, poverty and the resulting inaccessibility of reliable transportation, and confusing prison visiting policies and regulations. Fortunately, visitation programs, such as *Get on the Bus*, are cost-effective interventions that eliminate the barriers to contact, and normalize child–parent interaction. These interventions help to ameliorate the negative impacts of parental incarceration on children, and build self-esteem.

The primary purpose of *Get on the Bus* is to alleviate the suffering caused by this separation and to strengthen the bond between the child and parent (Figure 8.1), aiding children's learning and growth in school. It serves as a model of what communities can do to bond families during incarceration, decrease shame and stigma, and enhance a child's ability to learn and grow.

Figure 8.1 Bonding

Get on the Bus

Get on the Bus is a program of the Center for Restorative Justice Works, a nonprofit organization that began in 2000 in California sponsored by the Archdiocese of Los Angeles. The effort began with one bus from the Southern California area to Central California Women's Facility in Chowchilla, California, bringing 17 children to visit 9 mothers. The program has expanded its outreach to visit 11 women's and men's prisons in California. In 2015, *Get on the Bus* provided 46 buses that brought 1,044 children to visit 474 mothers and fathers (Center for Restorative Justice Works, 2015). Children and their caregivers go to pre-arranged pick-up spots near where they live, usually a church, to catch the bus. Each bus makes various stops picking up more families along the way. Usually only children and their caregivers are involved.

Get on the Bus's administration contacts a prison facility to set up and arrange family visits for a four-hour period. Visits usually occur on Saturdays from 10 a.m. to 2 p.m., but occasionally the visit is on Friday during school hours. The invitation to the inside parent to have a family visit begins with the prison officials. They give applications to those parents, who have children less than 18 years of age, who are allowed a visit. We contact the families to see if the children want to participate. We generally do not work with schools, nor are children or teachers involved in arranging visitations. In our experience children are too ashamed to mention their situation to teachers or classmates. Kyle Schwartz in Chapter 3 discovered one of her third grade students' parents was in prison. Jim Sporleder in Chapter 15 shared a similar example of this discovery with a kindergartener. Both students could have easily been referred to a community resource like *Get on the Bus* once a teacher or principal becomes aware of the situation.

One goal of *Get on the Bus* is to aid in reducing the shame and stigma students feel by normalizing the prison experience. Hopefully it will inspire school systems to create peer support groups within their schools for children who have incarcerated family members and provide community resources. Our contacts are primarily with family members. Since the opportunity for a visit begins in the prison, with inmates being selected by the officers, only those deemed appropriate are given the application form. Unfortunately, schools cannot be directly part of the selection process. The visits occur during several weeks around Mother's Day and Father's Day each year. Visitor requirements are listed at the California Department of Corrections website.[1]

Preparing for the *Get on the Bus* trips requires teams to coordinate the buses, train hundreds of volunteers, and process paperwork and the clearances required for every visitor, even infants, without which the visitors would not be allowed on the prison grounds. An adult who provides supervision must accompany children. The task employs an array of networks, parishes, schools, volunteers, prison administrators, social workers, and counselors, that come together to ensure that more than 1,000 children each year find their way into their mother's or father's arms.

---

1   www.cdcr.ca.gov

Volunteer bus teams coordinate family visits, supplies, logistics, and supervision related to transportation and activities on the bus rides. Volunteer prison event teams coordinate the on-site supplies, food, crafts and activities, and family photos, and interface with prison staff. The program staff members coordinate community outreach, volunteer recruitment and training, program planning, strategic relationships with prison leadership and the California Department of Corrections and Rehabilitation, media relations, vetting of new prison sites, communications, and contracting with bus companies.

A look at the day

The following is a picture of what a *Get on the Bus* trip experience looks like. Families meet at a central location, usually on church grounds, very early in the morning, possibly 2 a.m., for a long trip. *Get on the Bus* volunteers welcome the families and give the children a backpack filled with snacks, paper, pencil, crayons, books, chapstick, and other things to make the long journey comfortable.

Caregivers also receive a bag of goodies. A volunteer checks the paperwork of the caregiver and children to be sure that all is in order. During the trip there is usually a stop for breakfast, often an in-kind donation by a local restaurant. After that there is conversation among the participants and a joyful, expectant atmosphere on the bus, joking, laughing, and telling stories.

On arriving at the prison, the families go through a check-in with the prison officials, where their documents are presented. Their possessions are checked or scanned as they are at airports. Then everyone is led to the meeting area in small groups, often the lunchroom, which has been decorated with streamers, Happy Mother's Day or Father's Day signs, and tablecloths by the inside parents who will be getting visits. The room looks cheerful; a party is about to take place.

The best part, of course, is when the children come in and run to their parents' arms, hugging and kissing, smiling and laughing, happy to see and touch their mom or dad. After greeting, hugging, and kissing (Figure 8.2), the children can select games to play with their family. There are puzzles, coloring sheets, board games, and crafts (Figure 8.3).

Figure 8.2 Hugs and kisses

Figure 8.3 Crafts

Get on the Bus has negotiated a four-hour time period for the family visits, usually on a Saturday from 10 a.m. to 2 p.m. Children get their picture taken with their mom or dad and take it home to remember the day.

> *We talked and ate and played games together. This is one of the best days of my life! (11-year-old)*

Around noon, lunch courtesy of *Get on the Bus* is served, pizza or submarine sandwiches, etc., sides, and a drink. The families eat together at a table just as they used to. It is a happy time of conversation, getting caught up with news, asking about school, having a friendly meal, and sharing time together. This continues until near 2 p.m., when a guard announces that they have five minutes to say their goodbyes and prepare to leave. Immediately, the mood changes; frowns and tears appear on sad faces. Even teenagers become red in the face with emotion, having to leave mom or dad behind.

The bus trip back is quieter, more thoughtful. Each child has been given a letter to them written ahead of time by their parent, plus a teddy bear, which is said to be from the parent, as well. Children read and reread their letters, look at their pictures just taken, and then tuck them into their backpacks to save for later. Josh, a 16-year-old, explained he was deeply touched by the gifts he took home. He was surprised and delighted by them.

The best part of the trip is that I got to see my mom. It's been two years. (12-year-old)

Benefits of parental contact

Get on the Bus provides many benefits to children and their incarcerated parents. Regular contact fosters a healthy relationship, keeping the connection intact during the many years of separation. Seeing, touching, sitting on mom or dad's lap, and making eye contact with their loved one is paramount to a child's happiness. It reminds them that the parent is real and loves them still. But another important part is that children see that they are not alone—lots of other kids are in the same situation. It makes their circumstances more bearable, seeing others handle the same predicament; it helps to normalize incarceration for the children.

During the year, there are occasions for the families of the incarcerated to meet together. A summer picnic and a December holiday party are planned for families to meet and get acquainted with each other, and just have fun. There is an advantage to seeing other youngsters and their families who are working out their problems, coping with the situation, too.

The following research states that facilitating contact between children and their parents inside can reduce the strain of separation and increase the likelihood of successful reunification. The Messina, Calhoun, and Braithwaite (2015) study reported: "While the majority of the women are able to maintain contact with their children through phone calls and letters, many reported that being able to see and physically touch their children has the most positive impact on their physiological well-being."

Connection with their children plays a big role in how women adjust to prison life, whereas those who do not receive visits appear to experience more negative emotions and engage in more problematic behavior. Similar to the incarcerated mothers, the one thing that caregivers and children really look forward to is being able to see each other in person and being able to physically touch each other (Messina *et al.*, 2015). A parent, after release, accorded her good relationship to her son to visits, saying, "My son was able to visit me, touch me, talk to me. I would entertain him during visiting hours and tell him I loved him."

I got to see and hug my daddy! I love him and miss him. (Five-year-old)

Maintaining a strong connection between parent and child (Figure 8.4) is beneficial for positive reunification after release of the parents. A good relationship with a parent behind bars helps the child deal with his/her separation issues and fosters their resilience in handling the situation as well as possible.

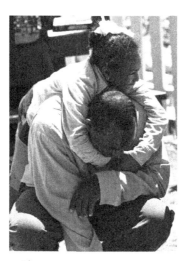

Figure 8.4 A strong connection

What children need

School-age children require special attention to get through the trauma of separation from their incarcerated mom or dad. Educators can support these young people by reassuring them that their mom or dad is still there, that they really exist and, most of all, still love them. The bond between parent and child needs constant reinforcement. Girls and boys need reassurance over and over again throughout the many years of separation that they are loved.

A loving connection to the parent should be fostered in as many ways as possible. Nena Messina and colleagues (2015) performed a three-year study to examine incarcerated parents and their children. The following conclusions stand out.

Frequent contact with the parent in prison is important. Contact with the missing parent by a combination of letters, phone calls, and visits, *more than* once or twice a month, is necessary to assuage the feelings of abandonment suffered by the child. In the Messina *et al.* study, children had significantly less behavioral, mental, or physical problems with frequent association with their parent (2015). The missing parent should continue the parenting role, in absentia, for as long as the separation lasts.

The child should be kept in her/his regular school, if possible. A larger percentage of children who were forced to change schools due to relocating to a new home had behavioral problems compared to children who did not change schools (Messina *et al.*, 2015). Arrangements for the child should take into consideration the comfort offered by remaining in her or his school with friends. Having suffered the loss of a missing parent, it is comforting to know that other areas of life remain the same. Keeping the child's life as normal as possible means less to grieve over, less change to adjust to. Children going into foster care suffer multiple losses besides losing mom or dad. These may include going to a new school, losing old friends, having a new place to live, losing a loving caregiver, separation from siblings, and living in a home with strangers. This is a heavy load on a child already going through the grieving process. The child needs to be encouraged to talk about their feelings of anxiety and sadness.

After being reunited with her parent, Sara, a 15-year-old, wrote that one of her most important outcomes was arriving at a point in life where she no longer repressed her feelings or needed to pretend not to be hurt by all that she had gone through. Sara recognized the wounds that had been left behind—wounds that needed healing.

Financial assistance for the caregiver helps the child. Financial assistance relieves some of the money problems in the newly configured family. A greater percentage of caregivers reporting receipt of financial aid also reported a greater frequency of child–mother contact. Eighty-one percent of caregivers receiving financial aid were able to facilitate calls and letters and more frequent visits between children and mothers several times a month (Messina *et al.*, 2015). Child social welfare services and members of the criminal justice system should inform families of available aid and provide assistance in applying for financial help. Unfortunately, since financial aid comes from the State of California, school fundraisers would not be appropriate.

Acknowledgment of grief

Incarceration represents a crucial childhood loss, the loss of the idealized family. The secondary losses of self-esteem, safety and protection, and daily routines follow. In addition, the child is likely going through many phases of grief from separating from a loved one. Kids having witnessed a parent being arrested and removed from the house by police may be suffering from traumatic grief.

Educators need to be vigilant and maintain a loss inventory (see Chapter 1) to create this awareness of potential grief and trauma involving incarceration. Once aware, teachers can be educated on the signs of traumatic grief (see Chapter 2), and realize that many behaviors are pain-based and represent a child's cry for help. Some useful resources for educators include *My Daddy Is in Jail* (Bender, 2003), *The Kissing Hand* (Penn, 2006), *Wish You Were Here* (Spanne, McCarthy, and Longshine, 2010), *An Inmate's Daughter* (Walker, 2010), and *Visiting Day* (Woodson, 2002). These books can be used to create a teachable moment for classroom groups or individuals by highlighting and normalizing children's feelings, and providing words to use to discuss incarceration. Kids are encouraged in a discussion by asking questions that require more than a yes or no answer.

Feelings of loss, sadness, anger, and isolation can be validated. Caring adults can encourage girls and boys to draw pictures of their loved one and write about their feelings.

Letter writing and journaling are effective methods of communicating. Figure 8.5 is an example of the way children can use writing and drawing after a visit. Teachers can use the arts as a tool for exploring and releasing emotions.

Figure 8.5 Letter writing

Children can choose special pictures and keep mementos to remind them of the missing parent. Girls and boys receive a letter and teddy bear from their parent after the *Get on the Bus* visit. They become enduring linking objects that connect these kids to their family members and remind them of their visit and love. They help to create a safe space for expression of difficult feelings.

Acting out grief

There is a good reason why the child may be acting out in school through aggression, bullying, or even becoming the class clown. When a child witnesses a parent being taken away, life instantly turns upside down. Jack, age 7, cried and cried as he watched the police handcuff his mom, forcing her to go with them. "Where is Mommy going? When will I see her? Can I go with her?" he pleaded with his dad. Jack was inconsolably sad. That sadness turned into anger and inattention at school. His teacher, Mrs. Jones, began to observe a lack of concentration, hyperactivity, and fighting on the playground. Dad informed her of Mom's incarceration, as she had not been aware. She began to talk to Jack about Mom, give him special time, and allowed him to call his father if he felt upset in the classroom. Jack felt cared for and his behaviors improved. Goldman, in Chapter 1, expands on the practical techniques to help children with these special situations.

Missing their mom or dad, or maybe siblings, and sometimes living in a new place, can be disconcerting, to say the least, for students with incarcerated family members. If we add to those challenges the shame and humiliation of having a parent in prison, we can understand why many youngsters feel disenfranchised and choose not to talk about the situation to friends or teachers. They may present a façade and appear to carry on. All of that distress can be simmering inside and needs to be expressed. It helped Jack that Mrs. Jones was a safe person in school to talk with.

Creating meaningful dialogue

We can empower our young people by advocating for their rights after many have been abruptly ripped from a parent or sibling, often left with so many questions and so few answers. One intervention is presenting the following Bill of Rights for children of incarcerated parents. By creating a meaningful dialogue around them, we can help to give a voice to countless girls and boys who feel voiceless and invisible.

Children of Incarcerated Parents Bill of Rights

I have the right to be kept safe and informed
at the time of my parent's arrest.

I have the right to be heard when decisions are made about me.

I have the right to be considered when
decisions are made about my parent.

I have the right to be well cared for in my parent's absence.

I have the right to speak with, see, and touch my parent.

I have the right to support as I face my parent's incarceration.

I have the right not to be judged, blamed, or
labeled because my parent is incarcerated.

I have the right to a lifelong relationship with my parent.

(San Francisco Children of Incarcerated Parents Partnership, 2012)

Developing vocabulary to use to create an open dialogue about imprisonment is essential in dialoguing. One teacher was told by her student Tanya, "They took my dad to jail and I don't know what to do."

The teacher just looked at Tanya. She didn't know what to say or how to say it. She didn't respond. Here are some suggestions from *Friends Outside* that might help open communication and enhance safe dialogue.

"Two of every 100 children have had a parent in jail or prison."

"You didn't do anything wrong. People should not try to make you feel guilty or ashamed."

"Sometimes, it is easier not to talk about a parent who is incarcerated, but you may learn that there are plenty of other kids in the same situation."

"It's OK to love your Mom or Dad who is in jail or prison, even if some people don't think you should." (Friends Outside and California Department of Corrections and Rehabilitation, 2013, p.12)

Lastly, allowing children to ask questions and answer them honestly is an invaluable process for releasing feelings and sharing concerns. Common questions kids might ask themselves, if not aloud, are: "Is it my fault my daddy went to prison? Will I go too? Can I see my dad? Can I talk about what happened?" The following information might be reassuring:

- Relay that their parent's incarceration is not their fault.

- Give the facts about why their parent went to prison.

- Tell children what is happening to their parent.

- Share how to contact their parent if they can.

- Let children know what will happen to them.

- Describe what will stay the same and what will change.

- Acknowledge they can express feelings about a parent's incarceration in a safe way.

- Provide information on how they can visit and maintain contact with their parent.

- Give information on when a parent will be released.

- Explain that people make choices that lead to different consequences. (Adapted from Friends Outside and California Department of Corrections and Rehabilitation, 2013, p.12)

Dialoguing for children and parents involved with incarceration can be equally important and meaningful. When all family members can be honest, open, and sincere about their challenging situation, a sense of unity is created. One family was living apart for 18 months in an "immigration jail" where the brother, sister, and parents were separated from each other. After they were reunited as a family, Amanda, age 18, wrote the following: "Our parents made it clear to us that they did not leave us on purpose and that things happen for a reason. They acknowledged the devastation that it brought to us individually and as a family, but also urged us to find a positive to it. They asked us not to dwell on the past and move forward as a stronger person and family unit. Our parents made themselves available to us, and urged us to talk about and not bottle anything up."

Educators can help kids with incarcerated family members

Key findings presented from research presented by Hairston (2007) may help guide further best practice for children's well-being in schools. Findings indicate that the "majority of children of incarcerated parents do not exhibit delinquency or antisocial behavior, but they do need extra help to succeed in school" (p.33). The following suggestions by Hairston may be extremely helpful for educators.

Extra help in school

Research indicates that despite dealing with many adverse situations, the majority of school-aged children whose parents are incarcerated are not engaged in antisocial behavior or delinquency. Their self-esteem and their behaviors fall within the norm for their age groups. However, school performance problems were identified among substantial numbers of these children. The reasons that school experiences are negative for so many children whose parents are in prison have not been systematically investigated. However, school is a significant part of the lives of children and youth, and success in school is critical to their overall success and well-being. The goal of enhancing…overall school performance needs to be given high priority in initiatives designed to help them. (Hairston, 2007, p.33)

Parent–child visiting programs

Visiting programs allow incarcerated parents, usually mothers, to spend extended time with their children within the institution. The programs include day-long visits, overnight visits and child-in-residence programs. The purpose of these programs is to maintain parent–child relationships during incarceration and to decrease the negative impact of incarceration and parental separation on children. (Hairston, 2007, p.29)

Mentoring programs

The Amachi Program, based in Philadelphia, is the most visible mentoring program for children whose parents are in prison. The program is aimed at preventing intergenerational incarceration. Children are matched with mentors who commit to spending at least one hour a week for a period of at least one year with the children they mentor. The Amachi model is based on the premise that a caring adult can make a difference in a child's life and that effective mentoring can prevent children from participating in antisocial behavior. (Hairston, 2007, p.31)

Counseling and support groups

A few organizations provide counseling services and/or support groups for children with incarcerated parents. Examples include Project Seek, which operated for several years in Michigan, the Aid to Incarcerated Mothers Counseling Project in Atlanta, Georgia, Reconciliations Support Groups and Summer Camps in Nashville, Tennessee and the Center for Community Alternatives Youth Support Group in Syracuse, NY. These programs offer a setting where children of prisoners, including adolescents, can meet with peers who are also experiencing parental incarceration, talk freely about the experience, and sometimes participate in social activities together. The Amachi mentoring model has spurred interest in kids with incarcerated parents across the country. (Hairston, 2007, p.31)

Identifying challenges

It is important to identify challenges for these students.

Identifying challenges includes recruiting and retaining participants, managing the stigma that may be associated with participating in a program for prisoners' children, gaining the trust of caregivers, gaining the trust of caregivers and children, handling logistical problems related to transportation, service areas and funding requirements and the need for different programming for different age groups. (Hairston, 2007, p.31)

Telling children the truth

Studies indicate telling children the truth helps to reduce the stigma so often associated with a family member in prison. All too often adults are reluctant to speak to girls and boys about a mom or dad in prison, driving the unspoken shame of incarceration into secrecy. Although the specific consequences of such deceit are not known, researchers generally agree that children need to receive honest, factual information and to have their experiences validated (Parke and Clarke-Stewart, 2001); by trying to "protect" the child from the truth, family members may actually cause worry, uncertainty, fear, and distrust. Educating parents to overcome embarrassment about incarceration can only enhance the ease of the journey of a girl or boy without their parent. Too often kids are burdened with a secondary loss of trust in their environment, and added confusion about their life conditions as well, which inhibit children to speak about their person in prison or express feelings.

Educators can implement a *school-based loss and grief inventory* (see Chapter 1) for children that includes imprisonment and which opens doors to dialogue with parents about it. Research sampling children aged 2–7 indicates:

> that children who were told about their mothers' incarceration in an open, honest and age-appropriate manner and children who reacted with loneliness, rather than anger, to the separation from their mothers were slightly more likely than other children in the study to have secure, positive perceptions of their caregivers. (Poehlmann, 2005, in Hairston, 2007, p.17)

Conclusion

In the conclusion of Linda Goldman's (2006) book *Children Also Grieve*, she states, "What we can mention, we can manage." Linda continues:

If we, as caring and educated adults, are incapable of discussing important, and to some degree universal, life issues, how then are children to learn how to discuss them? Who will model such thoughts for them? If professionals and parents provide grief vocabulary, resources, and educational interventions, they can create a safe haven for expressing these profound and difficult life issues. (p.77)

Get on the Bus and other similar programs help children to make and keep contact with a parent while enduring the challenge of separation. These programs give young people hope that better times are coming, and allow them to see and befriend others like themselves, reducing feelings of isolation and disenfranchisement, and enhancing safety and self-esteem.

If educators can join these programs by incorporating interventions for these students into the school environment, they can become instrumental in reducing the shame and stigma so often associated with incarceration. By offering models and mentors, recognizing that imprisoned family members present complex grief and loss issues, providing opportunities for counseling and peer support groups, creating outlets for feelings, and opening communication, school personnel can begin to lift the weight girls and boys carry when living without an incarcerated family member. A student's increased capacity to learn and grow with enhanced self-esteem will surely be the by-product.

References

Bender, J. (2003) *My Daddy Is in Jail*. Chapin, SC: Youthlight, Inc.

Center for Restorative Justice Works (2015) *Annual Report*. Available at http://crjw.webaloo. com/wp-content/uploads/2017/01/CRJWannRpt2015r8sm1.pdf, accessed on 05/02/17.

Dallaire, D.H. (2007) 'Incarcerated mothers and fathers: A comparison of risks for children and families.' *Family Relations 56*, 5, 440–453.

Friends Outside and California Department of Corrections and Rehabilitation (2013) *How to Explain Jails and Prisons to Children: A Caregiver's Guide*. Available at http://friendsoutside. org/assets/pdf/How-to-Tell-Children.pdf, accessed on 05/02/17.

Goldman, L. (2006) *Children Also Grieve: Talking about Death and Healing*. London: Jessica Kingsley Publishers.

Goldman, L. (2014) *Life and Loss: A Guide to Help Grieving Children, 3rd Edition*. New York: Taylor and Francis Publishers.

Hairston, C. (2007) *Focus on Children with Incarcerated Parents*. Report for the Annie E. Casey Foundation. Available at www.f2f.ca.gov/res/pdf/FocusOnChildrenWith.pdf, accessed on 02/18/16.

Messina, N., Calhoun, S., and Braithwaite, J. (2015) *Examining the Impact of Re-Uniting Incarcerated Women with Their Children*. Prepared for the California Endowment @20111994 by The Lloyd Society.

Parke, R. and Clarke-Stewart, K.A. (2001) *Effects of Parental Incarceration on Young Children*. U.S. Department of Health and Human Services. Available at https://aspe.hhs.gov/basic-report/effects-parental-incarceration-young-children, accessed on 03/28/16.

Penn, A. (2006) *The Kissing Hand*. Terre Haute, IN: Tanglewood Press.

Poehlmann, J. (2005) 'Representations of attachment relationships in children of incarcerated mothers.' *Child Development 76*, 3, 679–696.

San Francisco Children of Incarcerated Parents Partnership (2012) *Children of Incarcerated Parents: Bill of Rights*. Available at http://friendsoutside.org/resources.htm#Bill-of-Rights, accessed on 03/28/17.

San Francisco Children of Incarcerated Parents Partnership (2016) Available at www.sfcipp.org, accessed on 05/02/17.

Sentencing Project, The (2009) *Annual Report*. Available at http://www.sentencingproject.org/wp-content/uploads/2015/10/Annual-Report-TSP-2009.pdf, accessed on 07/17/07.

Simmons, C. (2000) *Children of Incarcerated Parents*. California Research Bureau. CRB Note 7, 2, 1–11.

Spanne, A., McCarthy, N., and Longshine, L. (2010) *Wish You Were Here*. New York: Youth Communication Strategies.

U.S. Census Bureau (2009) *Custodial Mothers and Fathers and Their Child Support: 2007*. Available at www.census.gov/prod/2009pubs/p60-237.pdf, accessed on 09/11/16.

Walker, J. (2010) *An Inmate's Daughter*. Norris, MT: Raven Publishing.

Woodson, J. (2002) *Visiting Day*. New York: Puffin Books.

Resources
Contacts for visiting California prisons

California Department of Corrections website

www.cdcr.ca.gov

Chowchilla Express

Provides free transportation for the families and loved ones incarcerated at the women's prison in Chowchilla, California, to come visit.

866-918-4748 (866-91-VISIT)

Families of the Incarcerated (Archdiocese of Los Angeles Office of Restorative Justice)

Supports and empowers children and families divided by crime and the criminal justice system in Southern California and its neighboring communities.

http://communityresiliencecookbook.org/tastes-of-success/the-walla-walla-washington-story 213-438-4820 (24 hours) or 877-712-1597 (toll free)

Families_of_Prisoners@yahoogroups.com

A forum for families of the incarcerated.

Friends Care (Sacramento)

Provides services to the children and families of inmates.

sacramento.networkofcare.org/veterans/services (search by program/agency name: Children in At Risk Environments), friendsouts@aol.com, 916-446-3838

Friends Outside

Provides services to incarcerated and reentering people, their families, and communities.

www.friendsoutside.org, 209-955-0701

Get on the Bus

An annual event that offers free transportation for children and their caregivers throughout California to visit their mothers and fathers in prison.

www.getonthebus.us, info@getonthebus.us, 818-980-7714

National and state resources/services

Bureau of Prisons website

www.bop.gov

Children of Prisoners Library (CPL)

Provides free information sheets designed for people serving children of prisoners and their caregivers.

Family and Corrections Network

A network for those concerned with families of the incarcerated and a forum for disseminating information.

Prison Fellowship

Provides services and support for inmates and families.

www.prisonfellowship.org

Sesame Street's Little Children, Big Challenges: Incarceration

Provides resources for young (aged 3–8) children of the incarcerated and helps families deal with the challenges they face.

www.sesamestreet.org/parents/topicsandactivities/toolkits/incarceration

Chapter 9

LGBT Youth

WHAT IS THEIR SCHOOL EXPERIENCE?

Juan Martinez, Kari Hudnell, and Eliza Byard

"These kids have overcome so many obstacles. They shouldn't be called 'gay' teens, they should be called 'gifted' teens."

Kevin Jennings, Past Ex. Director, GLSEN

In 1990, when a group of independent school teachers came together to help improve the school experience of lesbian, gay, bisexual, and transgender (LGBT) youth, the battles they faced were unique to the time. The early days of what eventually became GLSEN (originally the Gay, Lesbian, and Straight Education Network), the leading national education organization focused on creating safe and affirming schools for all students, were focused on a very different conversation than we have today. Over 25 years ago, those teachers had to convince school administrators that LGBT youth indeed existed within the walls of their schools. The prevailing thought at the time was that being LGBT was not only a choice, but one that was made in college, not during one's middle and high school years.

Soon, the work shifted to one of safety. A crisis of bullying, harassment, and suicides involving LGBT youth swept through the country and into the nation's consciousness. To directly address these issues with students, educators, and policymakers, GLSEN developed targeted resources and a research department to help document school climate and measure effective interventions.

Launched in 1999, GLSEN's biennial National School Climate Survey (NSCS) remains the only survey of school climate for LGBT middle and high school students in the country. The survey documents the prevalence of anti-LGBT language and victimization, such as experiences of harassment and assault in school. It examines school policies and practices that may contribute to negative experiences for LGBT students and make them feel as if their school communities do not value them. The NSCS also explores the effects that a hostile school climate may have on LGBT students' educational outcomes and well-being and reports on the availability and utility of LGBT-related school resources and supports that may offset the negative effects of a hostile school climate and promote a positive learning experience.

Research findings

The NSCS serves as a valuable resource for policymakers and educators, school boards and superintendents, students and activists. The most recent edition of the NSCS (GLSEN, 2014) reported:

> *Schools nationwide are hostile environments for a distressing number of LGBT students.*

Seventy-four percent had been verbally harassed in the past year because of their sexual orientation and 55 percent because of their gender expression. As a result of feeling unsafe or uncomfortable, 30 percent had missed at least one day of school in the past month.

Thirty-six percent of LGBT students had been physically harassed (e.g., pushed or shoved) in the past year because of their sexual orientation and 23 percent because of their gender expression, while 17 percent had been physically assaulted (e.g., punched, kicked, injured with a weapon) in the past year because of their sexual orientation and 11 percent because of their gender expression.

Sixty-five percent of LGBT students heard homophobic remarks (e.g., "dyke" or "faggot") frequently or often. Thirty-three percent heard negative remarks specifically about transgender people, like "tranny" or "he/she," frequently or often.

A hostile school climate affects students' academic success and mental health.

LGBT students who experience victimization and discrimination at school have worse educational outcomes and poorer psychological well-being, including lower self-esteem.

LGBT students who experienced higher levels of victimization based on their sexual orientation had lower grade point averages (GPAs) than students who were less often harassed (2.8 vs. 3.3).

LGBT students who experienced higher levels of victimization based on their gender expression were less likely to report that they planned to pursue any post-secondary education (e.g., college or trade school) than those who experienced lower levels (92% vs. 96%).

School climate for LGBT students has improved somewhat over the years, yet remains quite hostile for many.

Increases in the availability of many LGBT-related school resources, due in part to efforts by GLSEN and other safe school advocates, may be having a positive effect on the school environment. LGBT students reported a lower incidence of homophobic remarks than ever before— from over 80 percent hearing these remarks regularly in 2001 to about 60 percent now (2014).

Verbal and physical harassment based on sexual orientation and gender expression were lower than in all prior years of the NSCS, and physical assault has been decreasing since 2007.

While the consistent reduction in anti-LGBT harassment is encouraging, the majority of LGBT students still encounter verbal and physical harassment because of their sexual orientation and gender expression. This harassment can have a significant negative impact on the academic achievement and success of LGBT students, who remain disproportionately the victims of bullying and harassment. Furthermore, the majority of LGBT students attend schools where anti-LGBT slurs are the norm and school policies and practices discriminate against LGBT students.

A case study: Coming out creates loss

It is difficult to be a teenager. It is even more difficult to be a gay teenager. LGBT youth may face more complex issues than their heterosexual peers. Significant losses occur due to difficulty in achieving the developmental tasks of adolescence. Goldman (2008) presents these tasks, which include: (1) accepting one's body as it is; (2) becoming responsible members of society; and (3) preparing for a future of economic success, marriage, and family life. Goldman (2013) writes:

> While these teens experience the challenges commonly associated with adolescent development, additional complexities arise from exposure

to stereotyping and rejection. Hidden agendas, sexual orientation, and gender identity conflicts often create larger problematic concerns in parenting, counseling, and teaching that must be recognized, overcome, and integrated into a healthy life outlook. (p.48)

WYATT: A CASE STUDY

Coming out for many students is a brave act, and sometimes LGBT students are not prepared for the consequences or tremendous difficulties they might face afterwards, as exemplified in this case study about Wyatt. His story illustrates what many adolescents might face coming out and being out, and the impact that prejudice of family, friends, teachers, and society itself has on young people, often resulting in the internalization of homophobia through hurtful projections and judgments. Self-esteem and healthy identity can plummet if a young person is forced outside the borders of what is acceptable in mainstream society. Once "out," LGBT teens may feel alienated and marginalized.

Wyatt was 16 when he came out to his parents and disclosed to them that he was gay. His father's reaction was to shove him against the wall, flee the room, and refuse to speak to him again. Dialogue between father and son stopped. Estrangement from his dad created a life of isolation he had never imagined.

Wyatt was not only alienated at home; he was taunted at school. He had come out at school a year earlier, and was bullied and ridiculed by peers in class and on social media. "You are a faggot! Stay home! We don't want you in our school!" were a few of the many messages he received. On frequent occasions walking home from school, a group of boys followed him, targeting him as gay, and threatening him almost daily. Wyatt told the school counselor, who advised him to expect these kinds of situations. Her advice was to "toughen up."

The consistency of his torment drove him to become a loner, with no one to talk to and nowhere to go. By age 16, peers, teachers, and family seemed to distance themselves, and the prejudicial slurs such as *fag* and *queer* heightened an already escalating level of self-hatred. Wyatt wrote in his diary to release the mounting feelings of despair and rage. "I hate myself and everyone around me hates me too. What's the use of living? This will never get better. I give up. It's hopeless."

Wyatt stayed home from school a lot, barely speaking to his parents. No friends called. He began taking drugs and becoming promiscuous, with nowhere to turn and no one to turn to. The stress of sexual stigma, sexual prejudice, and internalized homophobia had created a desperate situation to live with. He felt very alone.

Core stressors for LGBT youth surface as they experience the stereotyping of being a sexual minority. Herek, Chopp, and Strohl (2007) researched three major stressors that include sexual stigma, stigma awareness and felt stigma, and internalized homophobia.

Interventions for educators

> Healthy identity development and self-worth can substantially diminish for young people living in a culture where they are rejected, judged, and hated because of behaviors, sexual orientation, or gender identity. (Goldman, 2008, p.49)

Ueno's (2005) research presents LGBT youth as having higher levels of psychological distress than their heterosexual peers, mainly attributable to the interpersonal problems experienced at home and school. His findings indicate LGBT young people experience more problems with peers at school and subsequent increase in stress levels when not connected closely with other students. He found friendships "reduced psychological distress and protected them from the psychological harm associated with interpersonal problems" (p.258). Ueno concludes that the presence or lack of social support by peers at school greatly impacts interpersonal stressors for LGBT youth.

GLSEN and the students, educators, and policymakers it works with are moving the needle and doing so through four key interventions that have been tracked and measured for their effectiveness over the years in the NSCS. Muñoz-Plaza, Quinn, and Rounds (2002) researched four categories for supporting LGBT students that include increased awareness, professional training, services, and curriculum development.

Wyatt would have benefited greatly from these supports and having a safe space in school with a group of like-minded peers. Fourteen-year-old Tyler decided to join the Gay–Straight Alliance (GSA) at his school. He relayed his experience of coming out in this way: "I joined because I knew it was filled with the most accepting people this school had to offer. I felt so comfortable around them that I was able to tell everyone in the club at my first meeting that I was gay. After that

I looked forward to our weekly meetings. It was the only place in the school I could be honest about who I am."

Intervention 1: Student leadership opportunities

"I created GSAs to end the misery and isolation of being gay in high school." (Kelli Peterson, Founder of Gay–Straight Alliances in High School)

One of the key opportunities for LGBT students that make a profound impact is the existence of student leadership clubs. Over the years, these have taken the form of what is commonly known as Gay–Straight Alliances (GSAs).

According to the NSCS (GLSEN, 2014), half of students reported that their school had a GSA or similar club. Compared to LGBT students who did not have a GSA in their school, those that did were:

- less likely to hear "gay" used in a negative way often or frequently (67.2% vs. 81.1%)

- less likely to hear homophobic remarks such as "fag" or "dyke" often or frequently (57.4% vs. 71.6%)

- less likely to hear negative remarks about gender expression often or frequently (53.0% vs. 59.6%)

- less likely to feel unsafe because of their sexual orientation (46.0% vs. 64.4%)

- less likely to experience victimization related to their sexual orientation and gender expression, and felt more connected to their school community.

Research by Toomey *et al.* (2011) substantiates the positive impact GSAs have on LGBT students; the authors suggest that

school administrators and personnel should be supportive in helping students to form and facilitate GSAs in schools as a potential source of promoting positive development for this underserved population... Findings have implications for school-based personnel in that they provide one avenue through which professionals may offer and support a positive school environment for LGBT young people. Schools should support these school-based clubs given that they offer the potential for positive development and greater educational attainment. (pp. 183–184)

The importance of GSAs and similar clubs is clear, and GLSEN has produced numerous resources to help students form and grow GSAs. The GLSEN Jump-Start Guide[1] is used by new and already established GSAs across the country to help identify the club's mission and goals, as well as assess the school's climate.

This guide consists of the following eight sections designed to help student leaders bring new ideas and energy into the club and across the student body:

- Part 1: Building and Growing Your GSA

- Part 2: Tips and Tools for Organizers

- Part 3: Strategies for Training Teachers

- Part 4: Understanding Direct Action Organizing

- Part 5: Examining Power, Privilege, and Oppression

- Part 6: Creating Youth Adult Partnerships

- Part 7: Making Your Student Club Trans-Inclusive

- Part 8: Evaluation and Celebration.

The resource also offers a template for creating a journal for the GSA. A *Huffington Post* article (Huffpost Education, 2015) features student voices and the powerful difference a GSA made for them.

Intervention 2: Supportive educators

Given the immense impact that educators—teachers, school staff, and administrators—have on the climate of a school in both positive and negative ways, the existence of supportive educators might be the most critical of these interventions. It is certainly a must for the establishment of LGBT-affirming school climates.

That support can come in a number of ways, from serving as a GSA advisor and creating safe spaces, to establishing LGBT-inclusive school policies and helping to educate colleagues about the challenges LGBT students face each day. The importance of supportive educators

---

1   www.glsen.org/jumpstart

across the school day is simply invaluable. Susan Craig, at the beginning of Chapter 4, explains that "traumatic experiences alter the architecture of children's brains in ways that threaten their ability to achieve academic and social mastery. Left unattended, this affects... health, well-being, and capacity to learn."

According to GLSEN's most recent National School Climate Survey (2014), LGBT students with 11 or more supportive staff at their school were less likely to feel unsafe than students with no supportive staff (36% vs. 74%) and less likely to miss school because they felt unsafe or uncomfortable (14.7% vs. 50%). Unfortunately, only 39 percent of students could identify 11 or more supportive staff, so there is much more work to be done. To that end, for years GLSEN has made available two fundamentally important resources for educators: GLSEN's Safe Space Kit and GLSEN's Ready, Set, Respect! Toolkit.

GLSEN's Safe Space Kit[2] (Figure 9.1) provides concrete strategies that help educators support LGBT students, educate about anti-LGBT bias, and advocate for changes in their school. The Kit guides educators through assessing their school's climate, policies, and practices, while also outlining strategies that they may use to advocate for change, including posting a Safe Space sticker or Safe Space poster in classrooms or offices.

According to the NSCS, students who had seen a Safe Space sticker or poster in their school were more likely to identify school staff members who were supportive of LGBT students and more likely to feel comfortable talking with school staff about LGBT issues.

---

2   www.glsen.org/safespace

Figure 9.1 Safe Space Kit

The Kit also helps educators understand how best to be an ally to LGBT youth, including important questions to ask one self in understanding bias. Anti-LGBT bias is all around us, yet we tend to overlook the subtle biases—the anti-LGBT jokes, the exclusion of LGBT-related themes in curricula, even anti-LGBT name-calling. Subtle or not, bias has the power to hurt and isolate people. An ally's work includes recognizing and challenging your own anti-LGBT bias.

A Safe Space is a welcoming, supportive, and safe environment for LGBT students, and we must all play an important role in supporting all students. Sometimes that work is internal before we focus on external forces. Other times, the work is about policies and structures currently in place in our schools. What is important to remember is that, for many students, simply knowing that allies exist can be a source of support. One student's response appears in an interview on the Safe Space Kit (Berkowitz, 2015):

> Walking down the halls of her high school, Val rarely felt safe or secure. At age 14 and in her first year of high school, Val was bullied by her peers for being quiet and often withdrawn. "It was hard, and I was so unhappy," she says, having shed countless tears that year. "I was figuring out who I was—figuring out that I'm gay—and I was in denial. I hated myself."

The next year, Val spotted a GLSEN Safe Space sticker on the school social worker's door and decided to knock. Inside the office, Val finally said the words she had kept secret for so long. High school senior Val at GLSEN's 25th anniversary celebration explains, "I just blurted out, 'I'm gay!' and immediately burst into tears." By the end of the meeting, Val felt like she was starting over, with the social worker's support. In addition to the vote of confidence, she learned about her school's Gay–Straight Alliance club and was connected with a support group at GLSEN's local chapter.

GLSEN's Ready, Set, Respect! Toolkit[3] is focused on elementary school educators, with the goal of having students feel safe and respected, while also developing respectful attitudes and behaviors towards others. This Toolkit provides educators with help to teach about respect, and includes lesson plans that include seizing teachable moments. The lessons focus on name-calling, bullying and bias, LGBT-inclusive family diversity, gender roles, and diversity, and are designed to be used as either standalone lessons or as part of a school-wide anti-bias or bullying prevention program. The Toolkit was developed in partnership with the National Association of Elementary School Principals and the National Association for the Education of Young Children.

Elementary school is a time of rapid development for children. In addition to gaining knowledge and developing skills, these are the years during which children typically begin to develop an understanding of themselves and the world and people around them.

As such, the social environment of classrooms and schools provides the opportunity for children to initiate and develop relationships, and navigate increasingly complex peer relationships. That complexity can often lead to incidents of name-calling and the use of hurtful and biased words. If left uninterrupted by educators and other adult role models, these behaviors can take root in children's hearts and minds.

Educators are faced with an increasingly complicated world in which professional expectations are varied and intense. Many educators are under a great deal of pressure resulting from an increased emphasis on standardized test results and other accountability measures. And yet educators still strive to create culturally responsive classrooms by

---

3   www.glsen.org/readysetrespect

recognizing and encouraging the diversity of all students and their families and fostering acceptance of all people in and outside of the classroom community.

This Toolkit is designed to help educators prepare themselves for teaching about and modeling respect. It provides three sets of thematically developed and grade-span specific (K-2 or 3–5) lessons aligned with both Common Core and McRel standards as well as resources with which educators can extend learning or design other lessons. The Toolkit also supports schools endeavoring to embrace ASCD's Whole Child Initiative.

The No Name-Calling Week (2016)

In 2016, GLSEN collected images and videos of school displays and individual student work submitted as part of the Creative Expression Exhibit. Educators were invited to work with students in classes or after-school clubs to create school-wide displays that featured the message of No Name-Calling Week and the theme "Celebrate Kindness." The following are examples from students in schools throughout the United States honoring diversity.

Second grade students wrote poems and created posters on their "Recipe for Respect" wall in the school cafeteria (Figure 9.2). Students completed a hand activity where each wrote an act of kindness or a kind idea on their paper hand. It was displayed in the hall and heightened awareness of being kind every day.

Figure 9.2 "Recipe for Respect" wall

Kindergarten students celebrated differences by designing graphics related to the book *Elmer the Patchwork Elephant* that focused on diversity.

Students discussed how words hurt and shared experiences, and brainstormed on how to use words for kindness and empowerment. Once students decided on their work, they created a snowflake with that word in the center to decorate their "No Two Are Alike!" bulletin board in the main hall (Figure 9.3).

Figure 9.3 Snowflake

Students each received a T-shirt and wrote a name that they had heard used toward themselves or peers. They walked around campus with the label in an effort to create understanding and empathy. At the end of the day, students came together in a circle and reflected on what they had learned.

Intervention 3: LGBT-inclusive policies

Laws and policies that set the guidelines for what happens in our schools exist at the federal, state, district, and in-school levels. They cover a wide gamut of issues and topics, including discrimination and harassment protections for students. Unfortunately, many of these policies do not include specific protections for LGBT youth. They cover race, gender, religion, and some of the more long-settled protections, but they rarely enumerate—that is, specifically list—protections for sexual orientation and gender identity/expression.

GLSEN has been hard at work both administratively and legislatively to increase the number of enumerated protections that exist for LGBT youth. Success has been achieved at the federal, state, and local levels, but there is far more work to be done. And much like supportive educators, these policies are vital for improving school climate.

In GLSEN's most recent NSCS (2014), 56 percent of LGBT students reported personally experiencing LGBT-related discriminatory policies or practices at school and 65 percent said other students at their school had experienced these policies and practices. This included 28 percent reporting being disciplined for public displays of affection that were not disciplined among non-LGBT students.

From the same research, we know that students in schools with a comprehensive policy were less likely to hear "gay" used in a negative way often or frequently (59.2% vs. 77.1% with a generic policy vs. 80.2% for students with no policy). Additionally, those students were less likely to hear negative remarks about gender expression often or frequently (41.7% vs. 57.6% vs. 62.3%) and more likely to report that school staff intervene when hearing homophobic remarks.

Unfortunately, the education landscape is increasingly seeing a more targeted attack against the rights of students, especially transgender and gender non-conforming youth. At the same time, schools are struggling with how to establish policies not just supportive of these students, but affirming as well for all children. Rather than merely eradicate negative behavior, educators are working towards establishing positive policies inclusive of every student.

Transgender Policy

GLSEN offers a wide variety of policy resources, including model policies that educators find valuable. The most recently updated version of GLSEN's Model District Policy on Transgender and Gender Non-Conforming Students (2011) is especially timely. The resource, created in partnership with the National Center for Transgender Equality, outlines best practices for schools to ensure that all students are safe, included, and respected in school, regardless of their gender identity or expression—including transgender and gender non-conforming students. The model policy presents some objectives, key points, and alternatives to consider. It is meant to be adaptable to the specific needs of individual school districts, while keeping the original intent of the policy intact.

The following is a student voice, Katie Regittko, from GLSEN's National Student Council, underscoring the importance of more visibility in schools (2016).

> In the past year alone, there has been an exponential increase in transgender visibility... Visibility for transgender people is so important. It inspires people and gives them the hope and strength to

be who they really are. In fact, the increase in transgender visibility gave me the courage to come out as gender nonbinary and start using my preferred pronouns last October. It's amazing how recognition of transgender identities can affect a larger group of people on such a personal level.

Visibility also changes the attitudes of society. It can help to destigmatize transgender identities and open people's minds. However, what the transgender community needs in this moment is more than visibility; what we need are rights, protection, justice, and acceptance. We have our visibility; now we need action...

Intervention 4: LGBT-inclusive curriculum

School curricula are among the most local decisions you will find in the education system. Districts and schools follow a set curricula, but teachers often have the flexibility to customize and individualize lesson plans to fit the needs and priorities of their classes, students, and school environment. A curriculum and its associated lesson plans play a powerful role in a student's experience, in many cases offering a mirror for students to see themselves reflected in the subject matter, and windows to see what's possible for them in their future careers.

GLSEN's NSCS (2014) highlights just how important an LGBT-inclusive curriculum and associated lesson plans can be—both when it exists and when it is absent. The research shows that LGBT students in schools with an LGBT-inclusive curriculum were less likely to feel unsafe because of their sexual orientation (35% vs. 60%). They were also less likely to have missed school in the past month because they felt unsafe or uncomfortable (16.7% vs. 32.9%) and were more likely to report that their classmates were somewhat or very accepting of LGBT people (75.2% vs. 39.6%).

And in an area with a high need for future employees, the areas of science, technology, engineering, and mathematics (STEM) particularly stand out as fields in which an inclusive curriculum can have a significant impact. According to the NSCS, LGBT high school seniors were more likely to be interested in studying STEM or Social Science in college if their relevant high school classes included positive LGBT content (35.8% vs. 18.5% for STEM majors; 29% vs. 19.7% for Social Science majors).

Unfortunately, only 19 percent of LGBT students were taught positive representations about LGBT people, history, or events in school, which again leaves all of us with much work to do. In response to this lack of representation of LGBT people in school curricula, and disproportionate incidents of bullying and violence against LGBT youth, GLSEN, the Anti-Defamation League, and StoryCorps collaborated to create *Unheard Voices: Stories and Lessons for Grades 6–12* (2011), an oral history and curriculum project that helps educators integrate LGBT history, people, and issues into their instructional programs.

At the core of the program are brief audio interviews with individuals who bore witness to or helped to shape LGBT history in some way. Each interview is accompanied by discussion questions, activities for educators, a student reading containing biographical information about the interview subject, and historical background on the era.

Understood within this context, the resources in *Unheard Voices* can serve as a lifeline for LGBT youth and a potent bullying prevention tool. More generally, LGBT-inclusive curricula can help educators to create more honest and accurate instructional programs, as well as safer and more affirming environments for all youth. The resource includes interviews, transcripts, classroom materials, and thematic lesson plans.

Recommendations for educators

Schools can no longer ignore the presence of adolescents who identify themselves as gay, lesbian, bisexual, or transgender, or discount their deep need to question their sexuality without judgment. Educators can foster an environment that promotes this questioning, as well as refuse to partake in an ideology of compulsory heterosexuality by assuring that LGBT students have the same opportunities as their heterosexual peers. The following is the GLSEN LGBT-Inclusive School Checklist for educators.

GLSEN LGBT-Inclusive School Checklist
Policies and procedures

- Fairly enforced non-discrimination and anti-bullying/harassment policies that explicitly protect LGBT students.

- School forms and applications that are inclusive of all identities and family structures.

- A gender-neutral dress code, including for yearbook photos.

- Gender-neutral and/or private bathrooms and changing areas.

School events and celebrations

- School dances and proms that are safe for and inclusive of LGBT students.

- Proms, homecoming, and athletic events that allow for gender-neutral alternatives to "King" and "Queen."

- Valentine's Day celebrations inclusive of LGBT and non-coupled students.

- Observations of Mother's Day and Father's Day that affirm all family structures.

Course content

- Health and sexuality education that is inclusive of all sexual orientations and gender identities.

- Curriculum that regularly includes information about LGBT people, history, and events.

- Library resources and displays that are inclusive of LGBT people, history, and issues.

- Co-curricular activities.

- Athletic teams and events that are safe for and inclusive of LGBT students.

- GSAs and other student clubs that combat name-calling, bullying, and harassment.

- School publications that cover LGBT people and issues. (GLSEN Safe Space, 2016, p.28)

Educators can establish a "safe zone," with a familiar sticker or poster on the door of a guidance counselor, school nurse, coach, or administrator. A bulletin board can be displayed with information detailing support groups, school policy, implications on sexual harassment, legislation, and community activities for the LGBT community.

Teachers can recognize the importance of role models in lessons and discussions highlighting famous LGBT people, and invite LGBT guest speakers to serve as respected role models. Teachers can recognize and value the role of heterosexual allies to change the school climate by extinguishing LGBT harassment, teaching methods to stop homophobic harassment, and collaborating with staff to address prejudice in all forms of diversity (adapted from GLSEN Safe Space, 2016; Goldman, 2006).

Conclusion

School personnel have long understood that a fair and inclusive education is threatened when students' physical and emotional security is endangered. The hostile environment that exists for LGBT students in many of our schools is all too apparent. They need to be guaranteed that their school environment is a safe space with an educational climate that respects and protects all of its students, inclusive of sexual orientation, gender identity, expression, or any other difference. Every young person is entitled to learn and grow in a supportive and friendly environment with adult and peer allies.

GLSEN has presented a comprehensive approach to assure LGBT youth thrive in school by offering GSAs, projects creating kindness and respect for diversity, curricula that highlight LGBT issues and history, and policies that assure accountability for harassment and homophobia.

Our goal is far-reaching and far more comprehensive than safety alone. We strive to create an educational team founded on full opportunity and real equality for LGBT students. Teachers, principals, and counselors can effectively become a huge social support, by enhancing the natural attributes of resilience that these students assuredly possess with full acceptance and value of their sexual orientation and gender identity.

References

Berkowitz, E. (2015) 'Anti bullying program eases path for LGBT students and allies.' *Wells Fargo Stories.* Available at https://stories.wellsfargobank.com/anti-bullying-program-eases-path-for-lgbt-students-and-allies, accessed on 03/28/17.

GLSEN (2011) *Model District Policy on Transgender and Gender Nonconforming Students.* Available at www.glsen.org/sites/default/files/Trans_ModelPolicy_2014.pdf, accessed on 03/28/17.

GLSEN (2014) *National School Climate Survey.* Available at www.glsen.org/article/glsen-releases-new-national-school-climate-survey, accessed on 03/28/17.

GLSEN (2016) *Creative Expression and No-Name Calling.* Available at www.glsen.org/creative-expression-2016-highlights, accessed on 05/03/17.

GLSEN, Anti-Defamation League, and StoryCorps (2011) *Unheard Voices: Stories and Lessons for Grades 6–12.* Available at www.glsen.org/unheardvoices.html, accessed on 03/29/17.

Goldman, L. (2006) 'Creating safe havens for gay youth in schools.' *Healing Magazine*, Fall/Winter, 23–26.

Goldman, L. (2008) *Coming Out, Coming In: Nurturing the Well-being and Inclusion of Gay Youth in Mainstream Society.* New York: Taylor and Francis.

Goldman, L. (2013) 'Young People and Gender Issues: Living with Loss.' In B. Deford and R. Gilbert (eds) *Living, Loving and Loss: The Interplay of Intimacy, Sexuality and Grief.* New York: Baywood.

Herek, G., Chopp, R., and Strohl, D. (2007) 'Sexual Stigma: Putting Sexual Minority Health Issues in Context.' In I. Meyer and M. Northridge (eds) *The Health of Sexual Minorities: Public Health Perspectives on Lesbian, Gay, Bisexual, and Transgender Populations.* New York: Springer.

Huffpost Education (2015) *Gay–Straight Alliance of the Year Calls for Action.* Available at www.huffingtonpost.com/jeremy-charnecosullivan/gaystraight-alliance-of-t_b_7649956.html, accessed on 03/28/17.

Mufioz-Plaza, C., Quinn, S., and Rounds, K. (2002) 'Lesbian, gay, bisexual and transgender students: Perceived social support in the high school environment.' *The High School Journal* 85, 4, Education Module, 52–63.

Regittko, K. (2016) *We Need More than Visibility.* Available at www.glsen.org/blog/we-need-more-visibility, accessed on 05/01/17.

Toomey, R., Ryan, C., Diaz, R., and Russell, S. (2011) 'High school Gay–Straight Alliances (GSAs) and young adults' well-being: An examination of GSA presence, participation, and perceived effectiveness.' *Applied Developmental Science 15*, 4, 175–185.

Ueno, K. (2005) 'Sexual orientation and psychological distress in adolescence: Examining interpersonal stressors and social support process.' *Social Psychology Quarterly 68*, 3, 258-277.

Chapter 10

Supporting Military Students with Separation, Loss, Trauma, and Death

EQUIPPING SCHOOL PERSONNEL TO SERVE THE KIDS OF THOSE WHO SERVED

Lynda Davis

Introduction

"These kids are both inspiring and heartbreaking in their ability to continually adjust." (Surviving Marine Corps spouse)

Every school district in the country has military-connected students—children, youth, and teens—with a parent or guardian serving on active duty, in the National Guard, or the Reserves, whether state-side or overseas. In total, more than 1.2 million military dependents are students in grades K through 12, with at least an additional 100,900 enrolled in post-secondary education (Huisman, 2015). These students bring diverse experiences, great enthusiasm, and enrichment to the schools they attend, but they can also bring challenges that distinguish them from their civilian peers.

Despite their numbers, limited data on military-connected students means that districts, schools, and K-12 personnel may not even be aware of who their military-connected students are; higher education institutions are often even less aware. Since only 1 percent of the U.S. population serves in the Armed Forces, most school personnel—teachers, principals, school nurses, coaches, and counselors—are unfamiliar with the military culture in which these students live. This culture features community, resilience, and pride, but can also feature social, emotional, and learning difficulties due to challenging situations including separation, loss, trauma, and/or death. More than 10,000 children, youth, and teens have experienced at least one military-related death since September 11, 2001 (Davis, 2015).

The lack of data on, and familiarity with, military-connected students and their lifestyle often means that school personnel are unprepared to address difficulties these students may face adjusting to new curriculum requirements, instructional methods, or school climates. Despite their best intentions to ensure equal opportunities for academic and developmental success, school staff are frequently unfamiliar with these students' circumstances, or the resources available to help support them.

This chapter provides school personnel with the following information to help military-connected students: (1) a profile of military-connected students and the unique culture of military lifestyle; (2) challenges and the cumulative effect on academic and developmental success: a case study of three school-aged students; (3) risk behaviors: reactions and warning signs; (4) recommendations for educators: guidelines, tools, and resources for school and non-school personnel; and (5) peer support benefits and impact of military peer and mentor support, with a focus on the Tragedy Assistance Program for Survivors (TAPS).

A profile of military-connected students: Unique culture of military lifestyle

"Military children continually amaze us as they rise to the challenges of military life. It's a life of frequent moves, changing schools, leaving friends and making new friends." (Robert Gordon, Deputy Assistant Secretary of Defense (Military Community and Family Policy), 2011)

Characteristics of military-connected students

In the fall of 2015, over two million children, youth, and teens (from birth to age 23) were dependent on a military-affiliated (Active Duty, National Guard, or Reserve) parent or guardian. An estimated 1.381 million of these dependents were aged 4–18 years old, comprising nearly 4 percent of the nation's entire school-aged population. Less than 8 percent of military-connected students now attend Department of Defense (DoD)-run schools. Over 80 percent of pre-K-12 military-connected students attend public schools, with two-thirds living in a civilian community. Whether they attend DoD- or civilian-run schools, approximately 10–12 percent of military-connected students are served by special education programs (AACTE, 2016).

Military-connected students who live and attend school in a civilian community may find themselves with fewer military-connected peers, in addition to school personnel who are unfamiliar with the lifestyle that so strongly and pervasively influences these children's lives. This is not surprising, given the lack of information on exactly where military-connected students attend school, how they perform academically, their high school graduation, and post-college attendance percentages or workforce tracks. This lack of data makes it difficult for school personnel to identify, let alone reach out to, military-connected students (Military Child Education Coalition and American Association of Colleges for Teacher Education, 2011). Further, since most school personnel only interact with a small number of such students, given their unfamiliarity with the military lifestyle, they may feel less equipped to support them effectively in challenging situations.

> *"It used to be a big thing when a student had a parent deployed…now… sometimes we don't even know…" (Public school educator)*

Common challenges in military culture help to shape the character of military-connected children, youth, and teens. Research has shown, for example, that separation and loss can be partially offset by the often-beneficial characteristic of resilience.

Military-connected youth may function better than their civilian peers precisely because the challenges of parental deployment require them to assume more mature roles and responsibilities. Requiring students to engage in family duties can actually strengthen their ability to self-regulate; to perform intellectual tasks; and even to emotionally cope with associated challenges (Chandra *et al.*, 2010).

The roles and responsibilities that military children and young people take on during parental absence (e.g., providing emotional and financial support for their families) can serve as a source of strength for their family. According to a study reported by Bradshaw *et al.* (2010), because of their helping nature, military-connected youth may actually "possess more adaptability, accelerated maturity, and strong social skills in comparison to their civilian peers" (pp.95–96). While helpful and admirable, these additional activities sometimes interfere with the academic performance of military-connected students (Card *et al.*, 2011).

Unique nature of the military culture and lifestyle

The willingness of military-connected students to help family and to engage with others in their military community may not be expressed in the school setting where they often feel less understood and isolated. If school personnel and other students are unfamiliar with the military culture and lifestyle of these students and the challenges of separation, loss, trauma, and/or even death that they may be dealing with, they may not understand their separateness or their shy or even disruptive behavior.

School personnel will not be able to help them, or to refer them to relevant support services, when these students face situations that understandably disrupt their academic performance or behavioral stability (Easterbrooks, Ginsburg, and Lerner, 2013).

Maintaining an inter-school Grief and Loss Inventory (provided by Linda Goldman in Chapter 1) can help provide pertinent information and background.

Even if their parents are not exposed to the life-threatening dangers associated with service in a combat zone, all military-connected students regularly experience separation and loss because military families move, on average, every two years due to new duty station assignments. This is three times more frequently than their civilian counterparts, meaning that military-connected students often change schools six to nine times from the start of kindergarten to high school graduation (again three times more often than their civilian peers). This dislocation can contribute to feelings of social isolation and can have a "profound and long-lasting" impact on surviving military children (Campagna, Saari, and Harrington-LaMorie, 2014). The following students give voice to this impact:

"After moving again, I didn't even want to try to make new friends. I knew I would only have to say good-bye to them again. It's just easier to be alone." (A Navy son, a junior high school student)

"You learn to handle it. I had more than one school each year until I was in third grade." (An Army son in high school)

School personnel familiar with the military culture and lifestyle, including its high mobility, will be better equipped to understand the challenges associated with reoccurring loss that military-connected students face as they regularly leave friends and familiar school settings. Problems with school attendance, social adjustment, and academic performance are more understandable in the context of frequent education system transitions.

Challenges for military-connected students: Separation, loss, trauma, and death

> *"Military children are resilient, there's no doubt about it, but they're not invulnerable." (Dr. Keith M. Lemmon, Chief of the Division of Adolescent Medicine, Department of Pediatrics, Madigan Army Med. Center, quoted in Bock, 2012)*

Special challenges of military-connected students

> *"Our children didn't volunteer to serve, we did." (Navy spouse)*

The stress associated with parental absences, frequent moves, changing schools, and leaving friends is common among military-connected students. While they are very proud of their parents' service and their affiliation with it, life in the military can bring special challenges for these students, including:

- *separation* due to the deployment and extended absence of a parent, sibling, or other family member or friend

- *loss* of friends due to regular school transfers that follow the relocation of a parent's duty assignment every two to three years

- *trauma* due to role and family changes following the wounding, illness, or injury of a parent, sibling, or other family member or friend

- *death* of a parent, sibling, or other family member or friend.

The challenges military-connected students face—separation, loss, trauma, and death—are not completely predictable and they do not happen in isolation. They are all too often a regular part of the military lifestyle. When they occur, they impact the entire family. Yet each person reacts differently based on their age and developmental phase, their support system, their prior experience, and their resilience. They can create reactions and behaviors which are sometimes very dramatic and sometimes all too silent. To be of greatest assistance to these children in the short and longer term, adults needed to be both attentive and informed, especially in the busy and distractible school setting.

"My dad died in April and by November we had to move off base and away from everyone who we knew." (Surviving Army daughter)

These challenges mean that the culture of military children and youth is very different from their civilian peers. Because they change schools frequently, they need to adjust to differences in achievement standards, school protocols, course offerings, extracurricular activities, and academic requirements. This can be overwhelming at times, contributing to stress, isolation, and reduced self-esteem, which can, in turn, contribute to poorer school performance and lower educational attainment. Military-connected students can also face difficulties qualifying for, receiving, or continuing special needs services due to differences in district or state policies regarding regulation interpretation, required testing, and resource availability, and conflicting and confusing regulations and policies among schools. One surviving Army daughter explained, "Even before Dad died we had the challenges of my little brother's autism. Thank goodness we were very close to our neighbors on base. This made leaving them after Dad's death even harder." Some kids experience heightened stress when trying to make new friends, find a new peer group, and adjust to both a new school and new community.

"You learn to make new friends quickly but you know not to get too close because you'll move again soon." (Coast Guard son, high school student)

There appears to be a greater risk for depression and anxiety due to relocation or deployment of a parent(s), etc. Military-connected students can be separated from parents or other loved ones physically, psychologically, and/or both (see Chapter 14, Sesame Street Outreach to Military Families). This can occur before, during, or after deployment, when a parent's long-term unaccompanied assignment separates the family, or when a training assignment necessitates months apart, often with loved ones in dangerous situations. While students' reactions to parental absence vary by age, developmental stage, and other individual and family factors, a 2010 Department of Defense Report to Congress found specific deployment-related behavior patterns among military children and youth, noting that infants and preschool children are most impacted by parental deployment. Young children more often exhibit externalizing behavior (i.e., anger, lack of attention), while school-age children exhibit more internalizing behaviors (i.e., increased anxiety and fear) and lowered academic performance. Adolescents often gain greater responsibility and become more independent but lose their ability to perform well academically due to increases in depressive symptoms, behavioral problems, and emotional stress. Overall, children of all ages cope more successfully with deployment-related stress if the non-deployed parent or caregiver has positive psychological health.

In addition to the challenges of separations and loss, the military lifestyle can expose children and youth to the trauma of wounds, injuries, and/or deaths. Since September 11, 2001, over 10,000 children and youth have had a military loved one die in military service. These deaths do not stop just because there are fewer service members deployed to combat zones (Davis, 2015). Service members continue to be wounded, injured, even killed daily in more routine activities like training, and deaths from suicide.

Military-connected students who grieve the death of a loved one face specific challenges due to their unique lifestyle, the circumstances which often surround the death, and the subsequent visible traditions of military honors and burial that differ so greatly from the civilian experience (Figure 10.1).

Figure 10.1 Military honors

The more awareness that school personnel have of these and other situations, the more they can help military-connected students cope with the grief that follows a death. TAPS' *Children's Grief Guide* (2015) describes how military children and youth experience these challenges:

1. Long absences may precede the death, due to extended deployments. Young children may have trouble remembering the parent well or even at all. Likewise, they may find it difficult to acknowledge that the parent who died is gone forever this time. One army daughter shared, "Because Dad was away for six months at a time to train and then only home for three months, we were used to him being gone. My little brother didn't understand that when Dad died he was not going to come home again."

2. Children of any age may already be compromised and stressed because of the challenges of deployment. As one surviving army daughter explained, "My littlest brother was very silly at the funeral. He didn't understand that it was for Dad because Dad was dead. Dad died when he was gone, so he just thought he was still gone for work."

3. Death notification may be highly traumatic. Children living on a military installation may become fearful of strangers. Children may avoid chaplains and casualty officers because they are associated with bad news.

4. Speculation about the cause and nature of death can be very public. The condition of the loved one's remains may delay

recovery and transportation. Children may be prevented from saying goodbye by sight.

5. Shipment of personal effects may be delayed. Investigations can prolong the determination of death, thus delaying the return of belongings to the family.

6. Military funerals are public and highly traditional. They bring comfort but also attention as they involve children of all ages in considerable ceremony. One student shared, "My little brother was not able to come to the funeral because of his handicap."

7. Media attention can be significant and highly sensational. All family members can be exposed to extensive media coverage. Even young children may be asked intrusive questions or see negative reports.

8. Children of all ages become isolated from the customs and comfort of the familiar military lifestyle, its supportive community, and affiliated sense of pride because they must move a year following the death.

9. Youth may experience conflicting emotions as they have pride in a parent's bravery and service but also sadness, anger, fear, and guilt related to their death.

10. Civilian peers may lack understanding of military-connected loss and instead be judgmental or even cruel, based on their families' views of the military and/or war. New classmates and school personnel may not understand or appreciate the student's past military lifestyle and some students may even make unhelpful or hurtful comments about their loss.

TAPS, *Children's Grief Guide*

"The bullies at my school would pick on me all the time and say, 'Your dad died for no reason.'" (Surviving Marine Corps son, elementary school)

"They didn't even believe that I even had a dad. They thought I was making it all up. That I was lying about his going to war." (Surviving Army son, junior high student)

Cumulative effect of challenges on academic and developmental success

Research by the Army Research Institute for Behavioral and Social Sciences found that children exhibit emotional distress when a parent is absent for long periods of time, such as deployment to a war zone. As expected, military children, youth, and teens experience sadness and lack of concentration, and often exhibit aggressive behaviors related to their fear about a parent's safety when s/he is away (Army Research Institute, 2005). What is surprising is the finding that these behaviors tended to worsen—rather than improve—after a parent returned from a deployment. In fact, ongoing research that is focused on military children, youth, and teens indicates that families can be impacted by a service member's deployment-related separation for a generation following the conclusion of a family's military service.

Military-connected students live with the awareness that their parent or other uniformed loved one is at risk not only during deployment in times of war but every day. Regular training exercises, service-related illnesses (including post-traumatic stress), and even the reality of suicide are ever present in the life experience of military-connected students. This daily exposure to the stressors of deployments, injury, and even death has an impact (Cohen, Mannarino, and Deblinger, 2006).

The cumulative impact of the presence of danger is one significant difference between military-connected students and most of their civilian peers. Military-connected students may have a greater need for support and understanding from school personnel, especially in times of separation, loss, trauma, death, or the anniversary of a death. They should not assume that bereavement and mourning have discrete and sequential stages or timelines or that even all military-connected students grieve alike.

"It's hard because I didn't get to give him a goodnight kiss at all last year, and now I don't get to give him a goodbye kiss either." (Army elementary school student)

A CASE STUDY OF THREE SCHOOL-AGED STUDENTS

For one Army family with three school-aged children (Figure 10.2), the challenges of separation, loss, trauma, and death came all at once and more than once, creating a tsunami that still impacts their lives, each differently, years later.

Ashlynne was only ten years old when her father, an Army Sgt. 1st Class, died in a training accident in California. At the time, her next younger brother, who has autism, was eight, and her youngest brother was five. She struggled in various, but different, ways than her brothers as they all transitioned from the known culture of the home, friends, and school on their familiar military installation to new civilian communities and schools.

Figure 10.2 Ashlynne and brothers

A solid A+ student before her father's sudden death, Ashlynne tried very hard to maintain that record in school to reduce stress in the home and to let her mother concentrate on the challenges that her two younger brothers were experiencing. To most adults, and to her teachers, Ashlynne looked "perfect."

Her next younger brother of eight was enrolled in a special needs classroom in the school on the military installation where they lived. Because of his autism, every attempt was made to maintain his life as it was before his father's deployment and death. As long as his surrounding circumstances remained stable, so did he. For most adults, especially his teachers, the focus was on his need for structure and support. The school supported him by continuing his enrollment through elementary school, even when the family moved off-base and the other children were required to change schools. Another surviving army daughter with a similar experience explained, "Because of this handicap, my little brother just needed the school to keep his routine—to keep him on a normal schedule. He could not understand Dad's death as a loss but he responded to a change in schedule as a loss."

Ashlynne's youngest brother, age five, expressed his grief behaviorally. In the school setting he acted out in class and did not pay attention. Despite his ability, his grades slipped to C– because he refused to do his work. To most adults, including his teachers, he seemed difficult and even annoying; this meant his mother often shouldered the requirement to devote additional attention to help him with his schoolwork.

As a young woman of 20, still coping in many ways with the death of her father, Ashlynne and her brothers, then 18 and 15, were struck with yet another heartbreak when they lost their Air Force Veteran mother to suicide. This loss, in the final week of her sophomore year of college, occurred outside of the supportive military culture she and her brothers had known after their father's death.

To many others, including faculty and administrators, she became someone to avoid because of the stigma of suicide and their uncertainty and discomfort over what to say. Despite their accommodation of the temporary delay of exams, she felt alone and isolated on campus. This put her at considerable risk.

Ashlynne and her youngest brother began attending the TAPS Good Grief Camps the first year after their father's death. As college students grieving the loss of their mother too, they became mentors to other children and youth who were just beginning their own grief journey. The special benefits of the TAPS peer support for military-connected school-aged children and youth can best be described by their comments: *"Good Grief Camp was the only place we could go and not feel like outsiders. It's where we went to be with other kids like us who had lost a parent in the military. It was the only place we ever went where kids didn't ask us about why we only had one parent. It was the only place we truly felt safe emotionally and where we acted like, and were treated like, normal kids."*

Now a college graduate, Ashlynne has built on her experience of separation, loss, trauma, and grief, and the strength gained from peer support to incorporate her father's love for education, and her mother's spirit of service, into her mission to support other military-connected students in their pursuit of higher education as the Director of the Education Support and Scholarship Program at TAPS.

Risk behaviors for military-connected students
Reactions to separation, loss, trauma, and/or death

"Any child old enough to love is old enough to mourn." (Dr. Alan Wolfelt, 2006)

A student's response to the death of a parent or loved one is influenced by their relationship to the deceased, loss history, cultural customs about bereavement, and network of support. Students of a similar developmental age and with a common background, like military-connected children and youth, are more likely to respond with similar expressions and behaviors. For example, preschoolers may regress and have emotional outbursts (temper tantrums, sudden fears), while children may have physical ailments (stomach upsets, headaches, vomiting). Youth may become almost adult-like as they take on the responsibilities of the deceased or remaining parent. Teenagers may have strong emotional responses like depression and even turn to drugs, alcohol, and/or sex to express their grief. Many of the physical, emotional, cognitive, and behavioral signs of grief in military-connected students are commonly missed or misinterpreted by school personnel, and even by parents (see the common signs of grieving children, Chapter 1). School personnel should be alert to these and other behaviors in the school setting. School-based resources and/or referral to specialized services and organizations should be considered quickly, especially if the behaviors become debilitating or are prolonged.

Warning signs that military-connected students are challenged

"Be aware of 'red flag' grief related behaviors…that signal a possible need for referral, assessment, and intervention." (Kaplow, Layne, and Pynoos, 2014)

Military-connected students who are at risk for experiencing traumatic grief include those who have experienced the following:

- pre-existing health and mental health problems

- parents who have had multiple deployments

- single-parent families with that parent deployed

- dual-military parent families with one or both parents deployed

- living in homes away from military communities

- limited access to local, community-based resources. (Adapted from the National Child Traumatic Stress Network, Military and Veteran Families and Children, 2014, p.1)

Military-connected students may show signs of serious stress in response to: *separation* from a military-affiliated parent; *loss* of a familiar military home, community, and school; *traumatic* exposure to bad news and exposure to wounds, illness, and/or injury; or the *death* of a parent, other family member, or friend. The Educational Opportunities Directorate of the Department of Defense, in their *Educators Guide to the Military Child during Deployment* (2011, p.5), identified that the following signs may indicate that a military student is in acute distress and needs to be referred for immediate evaluation:

- unfocused agitation or hysteria (intentionally hurts or cuts themselves, seems at risk for hurting others)

- disconnection from peers and adults (disregard for personal appearance and hygiene, or exhibits a possible drug or alcohol abuse problem)

- serious depression or withdrawal (continued crying, intense sadness, withdrawn, non-communicative)

- auditory or visual hallucinations (expresses violent or depressed feelings in "dark" drawings or writings)

- prolonged major change that continues for more than six weeks (difficulty concentrating in school, inability to resume normal classroom assignments and activities).

In the article "Helping military kids cope with traumatic death" Goldman (2008) identified other behaviors (i.e., threat of suicide or preoccupation with suicide, harmful acts to other children or animals) as potential indicators that a child may benefit from professional help (see Chapter 2 on complex grief issues). School personnel who know to look for these and more subtle behaviors can help grieving military-connected students who may be at risk or who are expressing these or other "red flag" signs of complicated or complex grief. Once familiar with these behaviors, they also need to know about the resources available to assist them and the students so that they can act quickly to normalize the student's experiences and to engage assistance.

Recommendations for educators supporting military-connected students

Whether they are considered at risk or are showing the "red flag" signs of complex grief, military-connected students will often need support as they regularly face the challenges of separation, relocation, loss, trauma, and/or death in the context of their military lifestyle. In order to better assist them, school professionals should employ age- and child-specific guidelines in the school setting such as those below, adapted from the Educational Opportunities Directorate of the Department of Defense (2011, pp.6–7).

Guidelines for military-connected students in school settings

- *Focus on the classroom environment and students*: maintain routines; emphasize learning; and attend to students' emerging needs.

- *Provide structure*: maintain a predictable, structured schedule with specific rules; apply standard consequences; and provide support and consistency for students.

- *Maintain objectivity*: respond in a calm and caring manner; answer questions in simple, direct terms; and transition students back to normal studies and activities.

- *Reinforce safety and security*: end discussions with a focus on the child's safety and that of all loved ones and the military.

- *Be patient*: reduce student workload; anticipate temporary slowdown in work; and accommodate disruption in learning.

- *Listen*: be approachable, attentive, and sensitive; and recognize the unique needs of children coping with separation, loss, trauma, and/or death.

- *Be sensitive to language and cultural needs*: respect the challenges students have trying to express their feelings; and recognize the difficulty of trying to interpret these feelings accurately.

- *Acknowledge*: validate students' feelings; and help them to develop a realistic understanding of the circumstances.

- *Reinforce anger management*: expect some angry outbursts; reinforce age-appropriate anger management; and ensure a climate of nonviolence and acceptance.

Resources for the academic setting

To assist school personnel in the academic setting, particularly when a military-connected student is experiencing loss or death and is in mourning, schools can utilize customized resources, or refer to specialized organizations that have proven their value across the ages, stages, and types of grief that are often faced by these students. Sesame Street, in Chapter 14, presents a comprehensive program for young children on deployment, loss associated with the military, and death. Through Muppet-engaged vignettes and storylines, military-connected students can join a cyber peer group of other military-connected peers and families, and feel understood and connected. These programs and downloadable materials also provide educators with a forum for discussion and inclusion.

Resources for the non-academic setting

School personnel can play an invaluable role in the support of military-connected students by not only using tailored resources in their classroom but by helping surviving parents and other caregiving adults identify resources for the home. They can also refer the family to organizations that offer comprehensive support (i.e., TAPS) and resources (Carroll and Wolfelt, 2015). The DoD Educational Opportunities Directorate Guide (2006) offers suggestions that teachers can share with caregiving adults to help them reinforce the interventions that are being used in the academic setting, including the following:

- Identify where comfort can be found (e.g., quiet time alone, physical action, reading).

- Clarify the situation together and brainstorm solutions.

- Help process the expression of grief through activities:

- Create a ritual, like lighting a candle, visiting the grave, or cooking a meal.

- Stick to a routine to maintain a sense of safety.

- Acknowledge that it takes time (even decades) to heal.

- Draw how you feel.

- Tell the story of loss over and over.

- Write a letter to the deceased.

- Make a memory book. Figure 10.3 is from a Navy memory book for a dad that had died in military service from his son.

- Spend time with other bereaved children.

- Look at photos together in order to open a dialogue (Figure 10.4), or play together and share precious memories.

Figure 10.3 Navy memory book page

Figure 10.4 Memory photo collage

Peer support for military-connected students

"Shared joy is a double joy; shared sorrow is half a sorrow." (Swedish proverb)

Grieving children feel less alone when they are with other children who have also experienced the death of a loved one. Because grieving together can promote healing together, one of the most effective interventions for students facing loss and grief is to provide a safe, secure, and confidential setting to socialize with peers who share similar challenges. This socialization helps normalize their feelings and behaviors as natural, and offers them companionship and understanding.

Civilian schools and therapeutic settings may offer grief groups for students, but often there are not enough military-connected children or youth to enable the full sharing of experiences unique to their military culture. Without this chance to share common circumstances (e.g., death of a parent in combat), military-connected children may remain isolated.

Being with others who share similar experiences allows children and youth to express their grief without fear or shame, especially when the death has been associated with circumstances that are unusual or different from the majority of other students. Grief support programs for military-connected children and youth not only make accommodations for differences in developmental phases but they incorporate special resources that recognize the unique military lifestyle that is the reference for the loss.

One specialized peer support program for grieving military children and youth is TAPS,[1] which has provided access to Good Grief Camps and Military Mentors to over 9,000 school-aged kids (and 50,000 adult family members) since 1994. TAPS provides resources (i.e., peer support, military mentors, seminars, camps, free counseling, books, and scholarships for school-aged survivors) to ensure that the experience of grieving military-connected children is acknowledged, respected, supported, and normalized both in, and beyond, the school setting. Good Grief Camp participants:

- meet others their own age with similar loss experiences

---

1   www.taps.org

- learn that they are not alone in their thoughts or feelings
- participate in special, developmentally appropriate grief work activities
- discover how to cope with the pain and confusion they are experiencing
- receive a trained military mentor who acts as big brother or sister
- engage in ceremonies and rituals to honor the sacrifice of their loved one
- create a network of friends to lean on as they move forward.

TAPS programs for children include pairing with screened and trained Military Mentors at Good Grief Camps for Young Survivors and Good Grief Camp Outs. These Mentors and events provide a safe and supportive atmosphere in which children and youth learn coping skills, establish and identify support systems, and discover that they can have fun again without forgetting their loved ones.

Conclusion

The death of a military parent has a lasting impact on the children they leave behind. Whether that impact follows a natural course of mourning and transition or involves a traumatic response that is debilitating and permanent will depend in part on the child's own loss history and resilience and the assistance he or she receives from family, friends, caregivers, teachers, counselors, and clinicians.

Military students are wonderfully resilient and rich in the range of experiences they bring to their academic life. These experiences do however include the many challenges of separation, loss, trauma, and even death that are part of the military lifestyle. Their cumulative effect on a military student's academic and developmental success is often hard to see, hard to assess, and even harder to support, especially by teachers and administrators with little knowledge of, or exposure to, the military culture.

Knowing the range of possible reactions to separation and loss—whatever the cause—and the warning signs of risk behaviors, will enable adults to demonstrate an informed respect for the military student's circumstances. School personnel with ready access to tools and resources, such as those provided in this chapter, will better equip them to engage with these students in a supportive, academic setting. It will also help them make the best suggestions for therapeutic-type services, including peer support, outside of school.

Those educators who can acknowledge and address the needs of a military student grieving—whether it's the loss of old friends, the separation from a deployment parent, the trauma of an unexpected family medical emergency, or the death of a beloved parent—will provide options for healing and learning that help promote wellness and success in every area of their life.

References

AACTE (American Association of Colleges and Teacher Education) (2016) *Operation Educate the Educators.* Available at www.aacte.org/programs-and-services/operation-educate-the-educators, accessed on 03/29/17.

Army Research Institute, U.S. Army Community and Family Support Center, Department of Defense (2005) *Highlights, Survey of Army Families.* Available at www.armymwr.biz/docs/saf5childreportoct05.pdf, accessed on 05/04/17.

Bock, F. (2012) *Building Resilience in Military Children.* Available at www.army.mil/article/87489/Building_Resiliency_in_Military_Children, accessed on 03/29/17.

Bradshaw, C.P., Sundhinaraset, M., Mmari, K., and Blum, R.W. (2010) 'School transitions among military adolescents: A qualitative study of stress and coping.' *School Psychology Review 39,* 1, 84–105.

Campagna, H.R., Saati, T., and Harrington-LaMorie, J. (2014) 'Adolescent grief: The death of a U.S. service member.' *Coping with Loss in Adolescents.* Washington, DC: Hospice Foundation of America.

Card, N.A., Bosch, L., Casper, D.M., Wiggs, C. *et al.* (2011) 'A meta-analytic review of internalizing, externalizing, and academic adjustment among children of deployed military service members.' *Journal of Family Psychology 25,* 4, 508–520.

Carroll, B. and Wolfelt, A. (2015) *Healing Your Grieving Heart after a Military Death: 100 Practical Ideas for Families and Friends.* Ft. Collins, CO: Companion Press.

Chandra, A., Lara-Cinisomo, L., Jaycox, L.H., Tanielian, T. *et al.* (2010) 'Children on the homefront: The experience of children from military families.' *Pediatrics 125,* 16–25. Available at http://pediatrics.aappublications.org/content/125/1/16, accessed on 03/30/16.

Cohen, J., Mannarino, A.P., and Deblinger, E. (2006) *Treating Trauma and Traumatic Grief in Children and Adolescents.* New York: The Guilford Press.

Davis, L. (2015) *Grief Support for Military Children: A Guide for School Personnel.* Arlington, VA: TAPS.

Department of Defense (2006) *Report on the Impact of Deployment of Members of the Armed Forces on Their Dependent Children.* Available at http://download.militaryonesource.mil/12038/MOS/Reports/Report_to_Congress_on_Impact_of_Deployment_on_Military_Children.pdf, accessed on 03/30/16.

Easterbrooks, M.A., Ginsburg, K., and Lerner, R.M. (2013) 'Resilience among military youth.' *Military Children and Families 23,* 2, 99–120.

Educational Opportunities Directorate, Department of Defense (2011) *Educators Guide to the Military Child During Deployment.* Available at https://www2.ed.gov/about/offices/list/os/homefront/homefront.pdf, accessed on 03/30/16.

Goldman, L. (2008) 'Helping military kids cope with traumatic death.' *TAPS Magazine 14*, 3, 22.

Gordon III, R. (2011) *April, Month of the Military Child (Kids Serve Too!).* Available at www.dodlive.mil/index.php/2011/04/april-month-of-the-military-child-kids-serve-too, accessed on 03/29/17.

Huisman, S. (2015) 'What you need to know: The military student data identifier.' *Families on the Homefront.* Available at www.familiesonthehomefront.com/what-you-need-to-know-the-military-student-data-identifier, accessed on 03/30/16.

Kaplow, J.B., Layne, C.M., and Pynoos, R. (2014) 'Parental grief facilitation: How parents can help their bereaved children during the holidays.' *International Society for Traumatic Stress Studies.* Available at www.istss.org/education-research/traumatic-stresspoints/2014-december/parental-grief-facilitation-how-parents-can-help-t.aspx, accessed on 03/29/17.

Military Child Education Coalition and the American Association of Colleges for Teacher Education (2011) *Operation Educate the Educators.* Available at https://aacte.org/programs-and-services/operation-educate-the-educators, accessed on 03/30/16.

National Child Traumatic Stress Network (2014) *Military and Veterans Families and Children.* Available at www.nctsn.org/resources/topics/military-children-and-families, accessed on 03/29/17.

Tragedy Assistance Program for Survivors (TAPS) (2015) *Children's Grief Guide.* Available at http://quickseries.com/index.php?prodcode=01-0687-100-01, accessed on 05/04/17.

Wolfelt, A. (2006) *Companioning the Bereaved.* Ft. Collins, CO: Companion Press.

Military resources for educators

Air Force: www.afcrossroads.com (click on family separation)

Army: www.goacs.org (click on family readiness)

Center for Loss and Life Transition: www.centerforloss.com

Department of Defense Education Activity: www.defense.gov

Department of Defense Educational Opportunities: www.militarystudent.org

Marine Corps: www.usmc-mccs.org (click on deployment information)

Military Child Education Coalition: www.militarychild.org/pdf_files/deploymentr2.pdf

National Association of School Psychologists: www.nasponline.org

National Child Traumatic Stress Network and National Center for PTSD—Psychological First Aid for Schools Field Operations Guide: www.nctsn.org/sites/default/files/pfa/school/1-PFA_for_Schools_final.pdf

National Children, Youth and Families at Risk Initiative: www.cyfernet.org

National Guard: https://www.nationalguard.com

National Guard Youth Site: www.guardfamilyyouth.org

National Military Families Association: www.nmfa.org

Navy: www.lifelines2000.org (click on deployment readiness)

Reserves: www.defenselink.mil/ra (click on family readiness)

Tragedy Assistance Program for Survivors (TAPS): www.taps.org

Chapter 11

Trafficking and Commercial Sexual Exploitation in Schools

Eve Birge

Introduction

This chapter is written with the hope that it will shine a little light in a dark corner and that we—as a community of educators, parents, and caring adults—will continue to build on progress taking place the world over. Child trafficking is a difficult issue to think about, let alone talk about. But if we want to see a world that is free of it, we need to face it, recognize what we are seeing, and know what to do to stop it. We need to understand the impact of trafficking on our students as it relates to teaching, learning, and self-esteem.

Throughout the chapter, a story will unfold that illustrates the problem; it is a fictional story based on hundreds of thousands of true stories, some relayed to me through my work in this area over the last decade. The issue of human trafficking and its manifestation in our nation's schools has become an increasing focus for me in my work. As you'll learn, students in every school across America are vulnerable to recruitment by traffickers. Some groups are particularly susceptible: young people experiencing homelessness and young people with a history of child welfare involvement.

In this story we will meet children and adults; victims and perpetrators; bystanders and interveners. These labels seldom reflect the reality—victims become perpetrators; perpetrators were victims; someone is compelled to act; someone else is silenced. The goal is to see past the labels and focus instead on the unique role we can play to keep children safe in our schools, homes, and communities.

Definition, prevalence, and misconceptions

Human trafficking is the world's second most profitable criminal enterprise, sharing this position with the illegal arms trade, second only to the illegal drug trade (U.S. Department of Justice, 2016). Human trafficking is modern-day slavery. Sex and labor trafficking don't just happen in other countries. Modern-day slavery is a reality in communities across America and, increasingly, we're seeing that schools are targets for recruitment. And it's the children in our schools who are already under duress, often through no fault of their own, who are the targets. For example, the National Center for Missing and Exploited Children reports that, in 2014, one in six runaways were likely victims of child sex trafficking.

Each one of us has a role to play if we want to prevent the trafficking of our nation's children and youth. It is important to define the following terms:

- *Sex trafficking*: The recruitment, harboring, transportation, provision, or obtaining of a person for the purpose of a commercial sex act.

- *Commercial sex act*: Any sex act on account of which anything of value is given to or received by any person.

- *Severe forms of trafficking*: Sex trafficking in which a commercial sex act is induced by force, fraud, or coercion, or in which the person induced to perform such act has not attained 18 years of age; or the recruitment, harboring, transportation, provision, or obtaining of a person for labor or services, through the use of force, fraud, or coercion, for the purpose of subjection to involuntary servitude, peonage, debt bondage, or slavery. (Trafficking Victims Protection Act, 2000)

CASE STUDY, PART 1

In this story, you will read about children, the traffickers who prey on them, and adults that take notice and intervene. The characters are based on real people I've come across in my work. On any given day, if you search national press outlets for stories about child trafficking and the commercial sexual exploitation of children, you will read dozens of stories that sound similar to—and are even more alarming than—what you're about to read. The material is difficult, but as caretakers and advocates for these children, it's important for us to understand that this is happening, and our most vulnerable children are most susceptible.

> "I believe no one is talking to young people because it's a heavy topic, and in some cases, like mine, it was bound to happen because of how I grew up." (Student, survivor)

The victims: Chelsea and Jacob

Twelve-year-old Chelsea had never heard of human trafficking or commercial sexual exploitation. She learned about slavery in her middle school history class, but not about **modern-day** slavery. She didn't know that sex trafficking is a form of modern slavery that exists throughout the United States and all over the world, or that 26 percent of the world's trafficking victims are children (International Labour Organization, 2012). Even if she had known that girls typically enter into the commercial sex market between 12 and 14 years of age, she didn't know what the "commercial sex market" was.

She didn't realize that the inappropriate intimate advances of her uncle when she was in elementary school significantly increased her vulnerability to sexual exploitation and trafficking; she barely remembered what had happened. What she knew about sex was what she had seen in movies or on-line and heard from her friends. The idea that girls her age make up the majority of victims in the commercial sex market, which includes prostitution, pornography, stripping, and escort services, had never crossed her mind. *Why would it?*

> "There are so many young victims because pimps know that the younger you are the easier you are to manipulate." (Student, survivor)

If she had been aware of this crime, she might not have agreed to go with her friend Jacob to the house of an older man he'd only recently met.

Jacob is an 11-year-old runaway. His mother left the family when he was four. His father's violent outbursts terrified him and finally drove Jacob on to the streets around his 11th birthday. He'd grown up with little money, in a family and a neighborhood that was disempowered and under-resourced. Jacob was a target for victimization.

Two days after leaving home, an older man, named Steve, approached Jacob. He was waiting outside Jacob's school. Steve asked if he was OK, treated him with kindness and respect, bought him dinner, and invited him to "crash" at his house. After a few days, he offered Jacob his own room and gave him a brand new PlayStation. Initially, the only thing he asked was for Jacob to introduce him to his friends at school.

Jacob didn't know that pimps and drug dealers approach many runaway, homeless, abused and at-risk children within days of them landing on the streets. He certainly didn't know that runaway and homeless youth are the most vulnerable to being recruited into the sex industry (Estes and Weiner, cited in IOM (Institute of Medicine) and NRC (National Research Council), 2013). He'd never even had sex. Jacob's history—inadequate supervision and care by his parents, exposure to domestic violence, and now homelessness—are risk factors, and no one was there to protect Jacob or cultivate his resilience.

Possible risk factors associated with child trafficking:

- lack of personal safety

- isolation

- emotional distress

- homelessness

- poverty

- family dysfunction

- substance abuse

- mental illness

- learning disabilities

- developmental delay

- childhood sexual abuse

- promotion of sexual exploitation by family members or peers

- lack of social support. (Office of Safe and Healthy Students, 2015)

The trafficker: Steve

Steve profits from the control and exploitation of Jacob, Chelsea, and dozens of other children. He's part of a highly profitable global criminal enterprise, generating billions of dollars in annual profits. He operates according to the dynamics of supply and demand, and the demand in his community, and communities nationwide, is great.

He considers himself a matchmaker, a businessman; but Steve is a child sex trafficker, an exploiter. He coerces children from his local middle school to participate in sex acts, pornography, and Internet-based exploitation, including stripping. He lures children by providing them with food, shelter, money, and gifts. He targets and takes advantage of the imbalance of power between an adult and a child. This is child abuse.

Steve recruited Jacob outside of his school after his classmate told Steve that Jacob had talked about running away from his father. He could often be seen in front of the middle school, but he had also recruited children at little league games, the mall, on the street, and close to a local community shelter.

Technology

Steve also uses technology and the Internet in nuanced ways to reach young victims and to find clients. He "friends" children on social media sites, claims he's a talent or modeling scout, and poses as a good-looking peer. In this way, he coerces children into sending personal information and pictures.

> "The media plays a role because young girls are attracted to music that is...about the trap life...and [then] they're cool because they're doing it until they're getting beat and think death is the only way out." (Student, survivor)

The way Steve uses technology is always evolving. He's provided with opportunities to share images and advertise. He has threatened to "out" children via social media and expose what they have done to their friends or families. This is one way he maintains control over them.

Tactics

One of his friends, also a trafficker, uses tracking software to monitor his young victims. But Steve prefers to use a "caregiver" relationship with the children to coerce or manipulate them into sexually exploitative acts. He grooms them gradually, and eventually persuades them to recruit their friends or fellow students. He exploited Jacob and Chelsea's vulnerability and their life circumstances: their existing trauma, low self-esteem, isolation from family or friends, lack of basic resources, and, in Jacob's case, homelessness. He met their emotional and physical needs; he provided food, shelter, and care. Many traffickers use physical force, violence, and threats, but Steve relies on manipulation to keep his victims reliant on him. He is also skilled at making his victims feel responsible for their victimization.

The numbers

Steve feels invincible. He knows that sexual violence is the most underreported crime in America (National Association of Social Workers, 2001). The statistics on sexual exploitation and trafficking appear low or are unavailable. He knows why: most of the children are too afraid or ashamed to tell anyone. Or they are too attached to their trafficker.

Trafficking is difficult to detect and identify—these are some of the reasons why:

- shame and fear

- stigma associated with forced prostitution

- power and control of the trafficker

- student's inability to recognize or admit that he or she is a victim.

Steve is savvy. It's not lost on him that human trafficking is the world's second most profitable criminal enterprise (U.S. Department of Justice, 2016). He can use and sell his victims again and again; he wouldn't have a renewable resource if he sold guns or drugs. And most people assume he's a parent or uncle when they seem him with a child rather than a child abuser.

The venue

Chelsea, Jacob, and Steve live in a suburban neighborhood, but its close proximity to a city, a major port, and a busy highway corridor have made their community, and communities throughout the state and nation, attractive places for exploiters and traffickers. Steve has exploited children in urban and rural areas; he's moved around a lot. He finds victims—and clients—wherever he goes. And with the rise of the Internet he can be virtually anywhere as long as he has a cell phone or a computer with a web cam.

In Steve's current location, the local middle school students have been his primary target. Although schools are beginning to see signs of trafficking among students, school communities often are not trained to know what they are seeing; and when they are, they don't know what steps to take. If school staff understood the risk factors and dynamics of sexual exploitation and trafficking, they would have taken steps to protect children like Chelsea and Jacob. In this case, and countless others like it, the school was not prepared.

Educators can create a safe, supportive school

"We can better educate young people by educating them on signs and talking to survivors." (Student, survivor)

While it's important to talk to children about risk-reduction strategies, adults are responsible for protecting them. And schools have a unique role to play in the fight to end trafficking. Not only are they uniquely positioned to see signs of vulnerability, risk, and need, but the fact is that building a safe, supportive environment enables a focus on learning. Children can't learn if they don't feel safe.

Behavioral indicators of a victim

In Jacob's case, he stopped attending school on a regular basis and seemed to have a coached response when answering questions about his whereabouts. He started carrying a cell phone, flaunted cash and gifts, acted out in class, and talked to students he'd never associated with.

Chelsea distanced herself from her friends, and became isolated, withdrawn, and uncharacteristically shy. She was forgetful and didn't pay attention in class, barely ate, and did not appear to be taking care of herself. In both cases, the signs were there, but for too many months no one noticed or identified these potential signs of abuse, neglect, and exploitation.

"Most teachers don't see it because girls [and boys] know that if anyone finds out you will be beaten, burned, or something of that nature, so it's hidden very well."

"Teachers should look for a change in behavior...more sexual, loud, violent, missing more school, revealing clothes, bruises." (Students, survivors)

Possible behavioral indicators of a child sex trafficking victim include, but are not limited to, the following:

- an inability to attend school on a regular basis and/or unexplained absences

- frequently running away from home

- references made to frequent travel to other cities

- bruises or other signs of physical trauma, withdrawn behavior, depression, anxiety, or fear

- lack of control over a personal schedule and/or identification or travel documents

- hunger, malnourishment, or inappropriate dress (based on weather conditions or surroundings)

- signs of drug addiction

- coached or rehearsed responses to questions

- a sudden change in attire, behavior, relationships, or material possessions (e.g., expensive items)

- uncharacteristic promiscuity and/or references to sexual situations or terminology beyond age-specific norms

- a "boyfriend" or "girlfriend" who is noticeably older and/or controlling

- an attempt to conceal scars, tattoos, or bruises

- a sudden change in attention to personal hygiene

- tattoos (a form of branding) displaying the name or moniker of a trafficker, such as "daddy"

- hyperarousal or symptoms of anger, panic, phobia, irritability, hyperactivity, frequent crying, temper tantrums, regressive behavior, and/or clinging behavior

- hypoarousal or symptoms of daydreaming, inability to bond with others, inattention, forgetfulness, and/or shyness. (Office of Safe and Healthy Students, 2015)

Trafficking not only put these children squarely in harm's way, it also put the school in jeopardy. Human trafficking is child abuse, and teachers are mandatory reporters.

CASE STUDY, PART 2: A PROTOCOL
FOR SERVICE PROVISION

Eventually, Ms. Johnson, a school resource officer (SRO), noticed that Jacob's dress and behavior had changed and tried to get in touch with his parents. When his father told her that Jacob had left home, she contacted the school counselor who had developed a rapport with Jacob during a time when his grades were slipping.

Together, they met with Jacob and listened to him in a non-judgmental, caring way. He pieced together a story that was incomplete and he seemed guarded. They shared their concern with Jacob and their commitment to helping him and ensuring his needs were met.

> *"I've had numerous students report that they don't feel safe or comfortable around certain students because they know those students are trying to recruit/pressure girls to be involved." (School counselor)*

Ms. Johnson began a school-wide investigation. The school's concerns were quickly validated and corroborated by a number of students who knew Jacob. Jacob eventually admitted he was scared for his safety and the safety of a number of his friends. He disclosed Steve's whereabouts and, with Ms. Johnson's aid, law enforcement opened a formal investigation.

When the counselor became aware that Jacob and Chelsea were being victimized, she acknowledged their bravery in sharing and let them know that what had happened was not their fault. She was trained to remain calm and focused and did not press them for information. She reassured them that she would be their advocate and a consistent support. After learning more details about their experiences, the counselor put together a detailed report for child welfare and they were able to provide Jacob with home and social services, including ongoing counseling, and Chelsea with wraparound services, including long-term individual and family counseling.

This event was devastating to Jacob, Chelsea, and the lives of the other students who were victimized. It scarred families and the community and had a considerable impact on the school district. School leaders realized that in order to rebuild a trusting, healthy learning environment, they had to know what to do to prevent trafficking and protect their vulnerable students. Through training and professional development, their school community became familiar with the risk factors and indicators. The district developed a clear protocol that addressed trafficking and provided step-by-step instructions for staff.[1] This protocol did not feel like a burden on school staff—it relieved them and placed responsibility for action with school counselors and psychologists, local mental health and child welfare partners, and law enforcement.

"I see all types of students with very different backgrounds involved. It's the Special Education students that I am most concerned about." (School resource officer)

Engaging partners: Service providers, and local law enforcement

Leaders in this school district recognized that the first partners they needed to reach out to would be the service providers and local law enforcement. These partners could help them identify the scope and prevalence of trafficking in their community. Moreover, they realized that before they put this issue in front of their school staff, they needed resources and supports in place to field questions, calls, and incident reports. School leaders knew that Jacob and Chelsea were not the only victims, nor were they the first. The school community just didn't know what they were seeing or how to address it. Once they realized the signs and behavioral indicators, reports might go up, and if they did there needed to be a support network and accountability plan in place for school staff, students, victims, and perpetrators.

"The students that have abuse and neglect in their backgrounds are most vulnerable. It's the girls that are eager to be loved and have positive male attention that I see get lured into the game." (High school principal)

Educating staff and parents: Creating a safe environment

The school then required professional development training for staff with student safety as a primary function: school counselors and psychologists, social workers, resource officers and police, nurses, and principals. Awareness training was offered to the rest of the school community: teachers, cafeteria workers, bus drivers, janitorial staff, etc. They were familiarized with the protocol and what should be done when there is a suspected trafficking incident.

Concurrently, school leaders shared information with the Parent–Teacher Association (PTA), starting with a few parents who they felt could carry the message in a clear way that focused on prevention and student

---

1   Sample protocol: https://safesupportivelearning.ed.gov/human-trafficking-americas-schools/sample-protocol-school-districts.

well-being. Several school leaders—representatives from the school and the PTA—then reached out to the school board to be sure they understood the issue, its impact in the surrounding community, county, and state, and what the school community could do to address and prevent trafficking and the commercial sexual exploitation of children.

> *"A safe school is a place where all students feel safe and know that there are adults who will protect them." (High school principal)*

Conclusion

This is a story about sex trafficking, but labor trafficking is also taking place in neighborhoods nationwide. This is just one story among millions. Children and their traffickers come from every walk of life and can be found in every environment.

I hope you remember this story and take the information to heart in your work with constituents, communities, neighbors, and friends. It's up to each of us to raise awareness about trafficking, find out about existing resources, and learn what to do when we come across a potential victim.[2]

Even more important than intervention is that we work together to build a more resilient generation of young people by focusing on trauma-informed and holistic care, prevention, and early education.

References

International Labour Organization (2012) *New ILO Global Estimate of Forced Labour: 20.9 Million Victims.* Available at www.ilo.org/global/about-the-ilo/newsroom/news/WCMS_182109/lang--en/index.htm, accessed on 03/29/17.

IOM (Institute of Medicine) and NRC (National Research Council) (2013) *Confronting Commercial Sexual Exploitation and Sex Trafficking of Minors in the United States.* Washington, DC: The National Academies Press. Available at www.ojjdp.gov/pubs/243838.pdf, accessed on 05/04/17.

Modern Slavery Research Project (MSRP) (2017) *Labor and Sex Trafficking Among Homeless Youth* (executive summary, 8 pages, PDF). Available at www.loyno.edu/news/story/2017/4/19/3918, accessed on 05/30/2017.

National Association of Social Workers (2001) 'Commercial child sexual exploitation: "The most hidden form of child abuse," says NASW member Richard Estes.' Press conference.

---

2   If you don't know who to call or need additional resources, you can contact the National Human Trafficking Resource Center toll-free hotline, 24 hours a day, 7 days a week, at 1-888-373-7888. Support is provided in more than 200 languages. You can also email them at nhtrc@polarisproject.org.

Available at https://www.socialworkers.org/pressroom/2001/091001.asp, accessed on 03/29/17.

National Center for Missing and Exploited Children (2014) *Child Sex Trafficking.* Available at www.missingkids.org/1in6, accessed on 05/04/17.

Office of Safe and Healthy Students (2015) *Human Trafficking in America's Schools.* Washington, DC: U.S. Department of Education, Office of Elementary and Secondary Education, Office of Safe and Healthy Students. Available at https://safesupportivelearning.ed.gov/human-trafficking-americas-schools/risk-factors-and-indicators, accessed on 03/29/17.

Trafficking Victims Protection Act (2000) Public Law 106-386, October 28. Victims of Trafficking and Violence Protection Act of 2000. Available at www.state.gov/documents/organization/10492.pdf, accessed on 03/29/17.

U.S. Department of Justice (2016) 'Sex trafficking law enforcement task force highlighted during national slavery and human trafficking prevention month.' Press release. The U.S. Attorney's Office, District of R.I. Available at www.justice.gov/usao-ri/pr/sex-trafficking-law-enforcement-task-force-highlighted-during-national-slavery-and-human, accessed on 03/29/17.

Part III

THE SOLUTION

Achieving Student Well-being

"Start by doing what's necessary; then do what's possible; and suddenly you are doing the impossible."

St. Francis

Chapter 12

Leading Students Who Are Hurting Using a Strengths-Based Approach

Jonathan J. Doll

Introduction

There are many reasons to help students across our land who are hurting, often emotionally, during their progression through the teen years—and one of them is the prevention of self-harm and school violence. These tragic events stem from students who are feeling hurt or misguided in life, and also include other motivations/precursors. However, an approach that is counterintuitive yet could hold great promise to all students is to teach them about their strengths. Then educators can let these uplifting life-components help provide encouragement for our hurting young people and the educational and family/community systems around them.

The strengths-based methodology is drawn from the important work of the late psychologist and researcher, Dr. Donald O. Clifton, of Gallup, Incorporated (Parker, 2015). His work led to the creation of the Strengths-Finder Tool and the bestseller *Strengths Based Leadership* (2007) by Tom Rath and Barry Conchie. Also, Gallup (n.d.) has created a similar tool called *Strengths-Explorer* for young adults aged 10 through 14 years old. These important tools comprise a revolutionary method to provide support to students and schools as explained by one of my *Huffington Post* articles (Doll, 2015a).

It's important from the onset of this discussion to keep the focus on *providing support*—rather than only thinking that we must insulate ourselves from threats and yet not help in preventing these behaviors. In other words, an approach that can take a student's *inner* pain and turn that pain into *something promising* is a method to consider.

Goldman suggests, in Chapter 2, that "many of the behaviors and difficulties in learning are pain-based rather than merely 'oppositional,'" as exemplified in her case study of a traumatized child named Tyler. Goldman also elaborates on Bath's (2008) suggestion to address three crucial elements of healing: "the development of safety, the promotion of healing relationships, and the teaching of self-management and coping skills" (p.18). The strengths-based methodology provides just that level of success and hope.

When we think about providing support, it must be strategic, relational, and with the ability to influence how students will act *tomorrow*, not just today. Moreover, this entire context should be thought of within the leadership of a school or a district (or set of districts) because, like an orchestra, amazing sounds do not just manifest on their own, but require superb conducting and well-trained participants.

Also, as we think about the students who could potentially engage in acts of self-harm or school violence, they are a largely heterogeneous group. Of school shootings, the youngest shooter was only six years old, in Flint, Michigan (Rosenblatt, 2000). And most certainly, the range of students who commit or threaten to commit violent acts spans age groups, cultures, and even, occasionally, gender. The victims can be as young as kindergarteners, such as in the Sandy Hook Elementary shooting, with so many young students experiencing the death of a friend, the violence of the attack, and the long road to healing.

To make this clear, an analysis of school shooters from Columbine to the present showed that 96 percent of them were males (Doll, 2015b). One of the defining characteristics of this analysis of troubled individuals was that they took at least one life through the use of a gun in schools or on school property. But as stated, these people also all share one thing: they were not using their strengths for any common good and, worse yet, many of them never even knew what their strengths were.

This chapter will broadly call for the increased use of student strengths in education, and even in the correction of students. But one thing needs to be made clear. Strengths are not just for students who are hurting, they are for everyone. And like the adage that says "Hurt people hurt people," so also "Strengths-empowered people find and help others excel using strengths."

A strengths-based approach: Howard County Schools

With that said, it is possible for entire schools and districts to adopt the use of strengths for students, teachers, leaders, and even parents and community. For instance, the Howard County Public School System in Ellicott City, Maryland, is a shining example of this practice in action. Ebony Langford-Brown, who heads the School Improvement and Curricular Design work in Howard County, is an ardent supporter of strengths. She explained their use of strengths district-wide with students from grades 4 on up through high school, as well as with all the teachers and leaders in the district.

As a *strategic*[1] leader, Langford-Brown reminds us that having a deep understanding of one's strengths is essential when helping students to become the best they can be. When an entire district is strengths-focused, students will develop a firm understanding of the creative gifts and abilities they possess. Moreover, knowledge of these *strengths* can really be helpful for educators so that student behavior is not seen from a deficit paradigm, but rather as a catalyst in fulfilling the potential in each student through the exercise of personal strengths.

But to get to the place of full implementation of a strengths-based approach, as in the example of Howard County Schools, requires a much more comprehensive understanding of strengths, their benefits, and their application in areas of most need.

Understanding the strengths-based approach: A technique for students and educators

In gaining an understanding of the meaning of a strengths-based approach, students and faculty members can both engage in the following activity. Students are first asked to write out their own top three strengths (in their own opinion). Even without a deep understanding of strengths yet, it should not be too difficult to make an initial guess at one's top strengths. A complete list of strengths can be found in Table 12.1, as derived from the book *Strengths Based Leadership* (Rath and Conchie, 2007) and the Gallup website (Rath and Conchie, 2009). Also, if better wording for a strength comes to mind (than in the table), the student should use that instead.

---

1 Ms. Langford-Brown's strengths are (1) *Restorative,* (2) *Relator,* (3) *Responsibility,* (4) *Strategic,* and (5) *Learner.*

Table 12.1 The four strengths-based leadership themes (Rath and Conchie, 2009)

Executing	Influencing	Relationship building	Strategic thinking
• Achiever	• Activator	• Adaptability	• Analytical
• Arranger	• Command	• Developer	• Context
• Belief	• Communication	• Connectedness	• Futuristic
• Consistency	• Competition	• Empathy	• Ideation
• Deliberative	• Maximizer	• Harmony	• Input
• Discipline	• Self-Assurance	• Includer	• Intellection
• Focus	• Significance	• Individualization	• Learner
• Responsibility	• Woo	• Positivity	• Strategic
• Restorative		• Relator	

The Strengths-Finder Tool gives a person aged 18 or over a list of their top five strengths and a number of resources to learn how to fully utilize their strengths in life. Also, the adolescent Strengths-Explorer Tool gives a young person their top three strengths.

This methodology has been amazing. My top five strengths are: (1) *Strategic*, (2) *Ideation*, (3) *Individualization*, (4) *Learner*, and (5) *Woo (Win Others Over)*. Since having learned these strengths, I have been able to unlock my own untapped talents in writing and advocacy, things I long had been thinking about and suggesting but never had the confidence to pursue. In similar ways, teenagers can see many benefits in their lives through a solid understanding of personal strengths. To begin with, strengths replace timidity or even boldness in areas that are unhealthy. In other words, strengths help a person focus on what really matters, and ways they can contribute in life. Second, strengths can elevate a person in areas they never expected, giving them a newfound sense of self-esteem and understanding about their own talents. For teens, this can be especially helpful in areas where peer pressure and feelings of inadequacy are being experienced or even are at lifetime highs. As a small example of a strength that provides focus to this chapter, consider the strength *Woo*, which means to Win Others Over. That process of developing a greater sense of team in serving students who are experiencing distress is one of my primary aims for this chapter.

The great news is that you do not just have to guess in order to find out your strengths or those of your students. There are a number of ways to determine students' strengths or your own using either free or fee-based tools. Thus, a wise reader can take the freeway of strengths to ascertain their top three multiple intelligences from Howard Gardner's groundbreaking work in 1983 (*Frames of Mind: The Theory of Multiple Intelligences*) and 1999 (*Intelligences Reframed: Multiple Intelligences for the 21st Century*). To ascertain one's multiple intelligences, an example of a free online tool includes the one provided by LiteracyNet (n.d.).

Alternatively, adults can deeply investigate the comprehensive educational products of Gallup, Incorporated, which includes both the Strengths-Finder for adults, Naviance career and college readiness materials for older students,[2] and the Strengths-Explorer website for adolescent students aged 10 to 14.[3]

What is strengths-based leadership?

To create the Strengths-Based Leadership tools, Gallup, Incorporated studied 20,000 leaders of major companies and organizations around the world with the goal of finding out what made them successful. They also surveyed thousands of people who were followers to find out what they valued in their leaders. The result was the creation of an online Strengths-Finder Tool that helps young people ascertain their strengths under four domains: *Executing* (getting things done), *Influencing* (creating organizational momentum), *Relationship building* (getting and keeping everyone together), and *Strategic thinking* (going beyond the here and now to make the future into a reality).

Even though the strengths-based techniques were designed with business leaders in mind, they are fully applicable to students and learning. When I train school leaders to use strengths in education, an important understanding I develop in participants is that when they are better able to teach using their strengths, their students are going to have better experiences learning as well. Even more so, the gift that a solid understanding of strengths gives to students in the learning process is that it conveys an immediate sense of importance to them of themselves as people by their inherent gifting *inside of them* instead

2   www.naviance.com/college-and-career-readiness-platform
3   www.strengths-explorer.com

of being based on what they can do. In other words, *everyone* has strengths, not just the best basketball player, best math student, or fastest runner on the track.

But what does each of these domains look like at a school level?

Executing. People with top strengths in the executing area are the ones who help their organization complete its goals. Sometimes these people lead the charge or other times they give focus to disparate coworkers to thus create a unified vision in order to reach a common goal. People with executing skills are the shoes of an organization. In terms of education, these students are classroom leaders and the ones who develop and lead organizations in their school or community.

Influencing. This area tends to be under-represented among groups of educators and academic researchers, but is essential to completing organizational tasks. In order for people to move towards a desired target, they need someone who rallies their support, enthusiasm, verve, and passion. In short, that's an influencer. Influencers are the necessary eyeglasses of insight and even correction for an organization. These people are skilled in conveying the truth with tact. Students who have strengths in influencing are diplomats. They can easily find a common goal when different ideas are presented or can create a crucial truce between different peer groups.

Relationship building. People who are relationship-oriented certainly do not hide in quiet offices. Instead they are comfortable being center stage or on the wings rallying those on the sidelines. Relationship builders want to share the stage with as many as they can bring on board. Like influencers, relationship builders also rally the troops. The key distinction is that relationship builders understand how to keep the group together even amidst competing aims, intentions, strengths, and even limitations. Relationship builders are the glue of an organization. In schools, relationship building is often visible on the outside, but a gift in this area means that a student is really good at creating, deepening, and maintaining connections with diverse sets of students and even adults.

Strategic thinking. Lastly, strategy thinkers are the ones who may sometimes seem to have a far-off look in their eyes when discussions are in the here and now. Strategic thinkers are always listening and taking in new information and assimilating it to a broader scheme.

Their value comes in that they are always looking at next steps, including far-off benefits, as well as potential complications and how to mitigate them. Strategic thinkers are the shoelaces of an organization. In schools, strategic thinking is often a goal of the learning process. It is unfortunate, at times, when educators try to make every student into a strategic thinker. Keep in mind that everyone can exercise this skill, but some students can show this even more by independently coming up with strategic ideas on a frequent basis.

Educators will want to encourage strengths-based behaviors in students because it helps students develop confidence and focus. Especially when educators begin to recognize and build upon strengths in students who struggle with various types of distress, it will be like throwing them a life preserver. Strengths in students can very well be the boost that they need to climb out of most types of distress or trouble.

Nevertheless, the metaphors that were used previously of shoes, eyeglasses, glue, and shoelaces may seem a bit too abstract until you have had the chance to try out these things for yourselves—and to help your students do the same. The strengths-based leadership approach is not intended for use in taking over your organization or the lives of your students, but rather to give an appropriate focus and emphasis on what *is good* in each person—coworkers, collaborators, and co-learners (our students). After all, the use of a strengths-based leadership approach intends to keep everyone in an organization learning and trying to assimilate new information in a way that strengthens the organization and all of its members.

A demonstration of strengths with hurting students

This brings us back to students who are emotionally hurting, especially those who might engage in school violence unless put on a better pathway. We should also remember that those who have been threatened or exposed to a traumatic event are an equally hurting group. The reason we first investigated our own strengths and wrote them out before helping others is so that we can better understand the strengths of students. This important capacity for empathy is both a strength and a skill.

In December 2015, I did strengths-based leadership training at a K-12 alternative school that had actually had a school shooting threat months earlier. It was clear to me that students were still on edge and apprehensive about anything that they were unfamiliar with. However, as I delved into the idea that *every student* had strengths and gifts, students began to perk up, and develop an internal sense of enthusiasm. In fact, when everyone was sharing their strengths reports with one another, there were smiles and signs of confidence that quickly replaced fear, worry, and intimidation. These strengths are also helpful for students who make mistakes in helping them get back on their feet and contributing to their family and community again. The strengths-based leadership method enabled students in this school to bounce back and to see and experience hope again.

Moreover, one of the teachers from that training reported on how valuable and even life changing the strengths-based leadership process was for her as a teacher. She said, "My greatest strength is my ability to contribute to a situation. I can give my impact and advice when needed." Interestingly enough, that statement stemmed from her top five strengths. Using the Strengths-Finder, her strengths were: (1) *Input*, (2) *Achiever*, (3) *Connectedness*, (4) *Learner*, and (5) *Woo*. In other words, she knew how to connect new information, relationships with students, learning, and achievement to help her troubled students succeed. Similar insights took place with all of the students at the school as well.

Strengths-based leadership: Working with students challenged by life issues

If you want to use strengths-based leadership in your school or institution, you need to be intentional about it. One way is to start by training the faculty within the school. As a result, they will gradually become more sensitized to teaching students and encouraging the strengths in all of their students.

It is actually quite common in American society to think in terms of strengths and weaknesses. Unfortunately, we sometimes focus too much on weaknesses and lose the potential for positive change. As we do this, it is routine in education that we continually try to get students to stop engaging in things that we estimate to be weaknesses for them. However, this estimation on our part can be faulty if we do not accurately see a student's strengths or, worse, that we misinterpret strengths as being weaknesses. In contrast, the strengths-based leadership approach aims to reform education by motivating students and adults through a continued emphasis on strengths.

Through strengths, educators are more positively focused on valuable traits rather than hurtful ones. And the argument I would posit is that the power of strengths can outweigh deficits and lead to lasting changes across the educational context. Thus, a process of becoming empowered by strengths means to understand and apply one's strongest characteristics to each and every situation encountered and think of solutions that use these strengths.

Up until now, this investigation has been at an elementary stage of understanding. By providing an example of strengths being used in a school setting, we will go deeper into what strengths look like in action. As such, a clearer method for introducing strengths can be gained. The following is a three-step process for training the adults in a building on strengths. It is a process that should be led by a school leader or whomever in the school/district that has a deep understanding of their own strengths and how to train in them. To become that strengths-empowered educator, all you need to do is read the *Strengths Based Leadership* book (Rath and Conchie, 2007) and begin utilizing the power that is in your own strengths.

A strengths-based module

There are five steps to implementing a strengths-based work module for educators and caring adults, and each aims at a deeper understanding of strengths in the context of the individual staff member's work experience. The goals are personal excellence and also organizational excellence.

1. *Strengths Based Leadership* (Rath and Conchie, 2007) will be used as a guide for each staff member. An introductory meeting (Step 2, below) will be created to give this book to staff and explain its purpose. Teachers will be expected to review the first part of the book (pages 1–99) and then use the Strengths-Finder Tool.

2. *Meeting 1 (30 minutes)*: The school leader will explain the strengths-based leadership process and what this can lend

to their institution. The book will be given out to each staff member at the meeting.

3. *Homework to do before Meeting 2 (due in two weeks)*:

a) Staff will review pages 1–99. From these pages, they will consider what four amazing leaders did in the course of leading powerful organizations including Teach for America. Teachers will ask themselves if there are any overlaps between skills they can apply in school from the four domains: *executing, influencing, relationship building,* and *strategic thinking.*

b) Staff will each take the strengths survey, which is located in an envelope at the end of the book. This should be done in a quiet place and takes about 30 minutes. The code from the book will take them to a website where they each take the "test."

4. *Meeting 2 (45 minutes to 1 hour)*: In a workshop format, the school leader will briefly review the four strength domains, where the strengths of the whole school/institution are, and what benefits this can have to all who work there. After that, teachers will engage in a collective discussion regarding individual strengths, along with questions and answers.

5. By teaching your school faculty and staff about their own strengths, the dialogue amongst educators should naturally shift towards positives and assets in both students and educational situations. This can be a much-needed transformation in some schools, especially those that might have a history of backbiting, distrust, or isolation.

Comparing the case of two schools

Now that we have an introductory understanding in the use of strengths in a building, let's compare two schools. One of them is using strengths-based leadership and the other is not. It should be noted that, in the subsequent examples, the idea of emotional pain in students would be termed more simply as *distress*.

School 1: A strengths-based approach

So, imagine two completely different educational contexts. In the first school, strengths-based ideas were boldly put in place with adults and all the hurting, or *distressed*, students. This meant that the school works out its positive value for students by actually helping them realize their true strengths in life and learn how to better apply them in difficult situations.

Specifically, boys who struggle behaviorally and/or emotionally in this type of school were proactively given tactile or kinesthetic types of service to help reconnect themselves to both the social fabric of the school and also to help them continually have opportunities to make amends and restitution for past mistakes. When students made mistakes, they were directed towards their strengths using a form similar to the *Middle Grades Strengths-Based Referral Form* (see below) to enable students to quickly realize they are valuable even during the process of correction. This form can easily be adapted for working with younger or even older students.

Also, the adults in that school work with *Strengths-Explorer* and *Naviance* materials to help these students find their strengths. Because this sense of reconnection is *hands-on*, it was perceived as being much more *accessible* and *real* for both students and adults. In addition, students no longer felt as much fear of getting in trouble because they understood that their school was using student mistakes to help build character and maturity.

Furthermore, as parents, guardians, and community members become more involved in strengths-based solutions, they find that distressed young people really appreciate being involved in relationships that reach out to them to help them find their value in society. For example, one student who was coached in learning her strengths was able to talk about larger challenges faced at school and think of positive strategies for the next year when she would be at college. Another was replacing behaviors rooted in weaknesses with ones using strengths. As a result of such interactions, the school developed a deeper connection with parents and community members and was more focused on building strengths rather than just preventing weaknesses. It was not a perfect world at this school by any means—but it was much better than the alternative.

✓

MIDDLE GRADES STRENGTHS-BASED REFERRAL FORM (ADAPTED FROM DOLL, 2015C, PP.160–161)

Student name _____ Grade _____

Date _____

Teacher name _____

Staff name _____

1) What are three strengths that I have in general? (To be filled out by the student.)

a) _____

_____

b) _____

_____

c) _____

_____

2) Today, what actions did I engage in? Be specific. Start with "I."

_____

_____

3) How did my actions affect others in the classroom or elsewhere?

_____

_____

4) To get back into class, I will:

Stop: _____

Start: _____

5) My improvement plan. List three things you can do to solve this problem. Start with "I will..."

a) _____

_____

b) _____

_____

c) _____

_____

6) How do I plan on making up the work I missed during this incident?

_____

7) Do you have any additional thoughts?

_____

Additional teacher/counselor comments: (need to include family/follow-up):

_____

School 2: A traditional approach

Now consider the second school, where it is *business as usual* with regard to student discipline. In this school, when student thefts, fights, and other incorrigible behaviors occurred, the school made regular use of exclusionary (out of school) discipline practices. It was clear to students that there was no place for them with their peers when they made large mistakes. So, in a given school year, there were a half a dozen or more out-of-school suspensions and even an expulsion or two. These numbers could have been much higher, but escalating punishments by the administrators had the desired effect of silencing the students.

There is a delicate balance in schools that use traditional discipline where the common thought is that, if punishments can be used to "make an example" to other students, then discipline problems will decrease. The only problem is that schools like this one are often using fear to create change instead of strengths, training, and a practice of encouraging *all students*.

Both schools' end-of-year party: Punishments vs. rewards

Fast forward to the end of the school year in both of these schools. Each of the schools planned an end-of-year party for students. Here is what these parties looked like.

In the first school, where the strengths-based leadership approach was used with students who made significant mistakes, the end-of-year party was *for all* of the students who realized their strengths that year. Thus, these students—*every last one of them*—are honored for their strengths publicly, before the rest of the school. This even meant that students who made mistakes but then learned their strengths were celebrated for their strengths. In addition, something public and positive was done for these students to take the place of the stigma and negative sting of making mistakes.

And though it is a relatively unheard-of practice to honor students who formerly get into trouble at school, it was found to be quite useful in deepening positive changes these students made over the course of a year. More importantly, the whole group of students who learned and were empowered by their strengths were asked *in front of their peers* if learning about those strengths helped them engage in safer, more productive school behaviors, and if they thought that they had a better chance of a successful future and life outcome as a result. The answer was a resounding "Yes."

After each young person had a chance to share—*somewhat vulnerably*—with the rest of the student body in a safe, trust-infused atmosphere, then the school leadership came forward and congratulated these students and also all of the other students in the school who made the changes possible. Thus, the school honored the students that *already knew their strengths well enough so they did not need to get in trouble during the school year.* Then everybody celebrated the comprehensive work of change—it was a true end-of-year party for all!

We should remember what President Barack Obama wisely said at the Sandy Hook Prayer Vigil in 2012: that *we all need to change* in order to find solutions to lethal school violence. So, in this first school, President Obama's wise words were fulfilled. Wow! Amazing!

Next, let's talk about the end-of-year party in the second school. This was where traditional discipline practices—*including semi-frequent suspensions and expulsions*—were used as often as school leaders deemed necessary. At the party for this school, there were games, clowns, and even a dunk tank with chagrinned teachers in crazy-looking clothes. Sounds like it was a fun recipe for celebration, right?

Oddly, however, the students quickly formed two groups, as any astute observer could see. There were the students who were distressed and most likely were punished during the year. For these students, the end-of-year party was simply not all that joyous. Some distressed students skipped the party; a couple smoked coffin nails behind the bleachers outside the school. Still others milled around aimlessly among all of the happy students—*the ones who were not causing mischief and who have better grades.*

Lastly, there were a couple of distressed students who were not at the party—and not through their own choices. One was expelled and was now in juvenile hall. The other was expelled in October for half of the school year, and that student never returned to any school, ever. For these two expelled students, the trip down the road leading to a lifetime of hardship has already begun. Sadly, one could accurately say that the school leaders in that school had simply kicked the can down the road for these students.

The funny thing was that a number of the distressed students at the school already knew about these two expelled students. Their punishment served as a constant reminder to all distressed students that certain punishments were coming to anyone who would not change.

Sadly, the only promises they felt would ever come true involved punishments of one kind or another.

But I would ask the reader: *How are students in America going to change if we don't sacrifice ourselves, and our egos, and give them the skills, the strengths, the forgiveness, and the support that they need in schools in order to be a part of that change?* In other words, how can students change if we don't intentionally help them? The process of change is hard, and that is why we need to help each other and help our distressed students so often underserved in our school systems.

So, I have shared about two schools in the previous illustration: one that fostered a *strengths-based approach* and the other which relied on the tired old method of *exclusionary discipline* along with *zero-tolerance policies* to continually send a message to deviant students without actually helping them change. It's amazing how easy it is for educators to transition from working in one of the schools to the other. All they have to do is to learn their own strengths and then pass that knowledge on to the other teachers and students.

Comparing the schools at the end of a year reveals a tension that is often overlooked in our society. While both school parties were joyous in different ways, students' experiences were quite different. In the first school, the distressed students who changed their behavior were *consistently excited* about their future. Also, the students who were already successful have a better understanding of how they can support the distressed young people they encounter in life—*a method that works* has been modeled for them.

However, in that second institution where the distressed students were being pushed out of school slowly and steadily, there was very little joy to be found among these distressed students. Perhaps even those working in a school like this would lack the right level of passion as well. And for distressed students, their schooling experiences were only the beginning of a life that was well acquainted with pain. Over time, school had taught them nothing that they did not already know from their own experiences and hardships outside of school. Change could come, but these students really felt that they had not learned it in time.

This is a modern-day tragedy with regard to what should be expected from our educational system. Yet it is completely within our power as educators to change it. I want to go to the first school, manage the school leaders, and meet the students. Don't you?

Where to go from here

We have over 97,000 schools in America, and we are just one nation amid a world of growing children (U.S. Department of Education, 2014). How many do you think would benefit by a strengths-based approach? One, two, 100, 10,000, 50,000, or even all of them? I leave it to the reader to put their highest expectation around the correct number. My persuasive argument is that a strengths-based approach can help all students in every school.

In closing, here are some apropos words from the 26th U.S. President, Theodore Roosevelt, where he quoted a Virginian's steadfast motto on the topic of perseverance and dedication. These words carry well the thoughts of inspiration (Hardies, 2013) and have received their share of elaboration over time (Brewton, n.d.). In his memoir, President Roosevelt remarked:

> Do what you can, with what you've got, where you are. (Roosevelt, 1926, p.327)

With those words, it is important to note that President Roosevelt suffered from severe asthma complications as a child. From the Oval Office, however, he was known as the *conservationist president* and was responsible for an amazing solution, authoring the American Antiquities Act in 1906 and declaring many of our national monuments including Muir Woods, the Petrified Forest, and the Grand Canyon (National Park Service, n.d.).

That said, we should all be making solutions in our lifetime for the troubles that we've seen, right? After all, it is essential for all of us to focus our work on supporting students towards our capabilities and all that we can do to have the greatest impact. In this way, rather than chasing after things we are not and circumstances we do not find in our daily experience, we can simply accept the things, experiences, and strengths that we do have. It's definitely a word of wisdom to close this discussion on finding strengths in students who are hurting and those impacted by them.

By utilizing strengths across an entire school community, the process of correcting students can be transformed in an exciting journey of self-discovery. It is hoped that the reader and also a very large group of adults and students can be helped along the way.

References

Bath, H. (2008) 'The three pillars of trauma-informed care.' *Reclaiming Children and Youth 17*, 3, 17–21.

Brewton, S. (n.d.) *Squire Widener vs. Theodore Roosevelt.* Available at https://suebrewton.com/tag/do-what-you-can-with-what-you-have-where-you-are, accessed on 03/29/17.

Doll, J. (2015a) 'How to use a strengths-based approach with youth at risk of violence.' *Huffington Post*, 25 November. Available at www.huffingtonpost.com/jonathan-j-doll-phd/how-to-use-a-strengthsbas_b_8642044.html, accessed on 03/29/17.

Doll, J. (2015b) *Ending School Shootings: School and District Tools for Prevention and Action.* Charleston, SC: CreateSpace Independent Publishing Platform.

Doll, J. (2015c) *Completed PBIS Report.* Available at www.endingschoolshootings.org/Resources/Form 3 Completed - PBIS Incident Report.pdf, accessed on 03/29/17.

Gallup (n.d.) *The Strengths-Explorer Tool.* Available at www.strengths-explorer.com, accessed on 03/29/17.

Gardner, H. (1983) *Frames of Mind: The Theory of Multiple Intelligences.* New York: Basic Books.

Gardner, H. (1999) *Intelligences Reframed: Multiple Intelligences for the 21st Century.* New York: Basic Books.

Hardies, R. (2013) *The Spirit of All Souls: Letter from Rob.* Available at www.all-souls.org/sites/default/files/documents/Spirit-2013-01.pdf, accessed on 03/29/17.

LiteracyNet. (n.d.). *Assessment: Find Your Strengths Multiple Intelligences Tool.* Available at www.literacynet.org/mi/assessment/findyourstrengths.html, accessed on 03/29/17.

National Park Service (n.d.) *Theodore Roosevelt and Conservation.* Available at https://www.nps.gov/thro/learn/historyculture/theodore-roosevelt-and-conservation.htm, accessed on 03/29/17.

Obama, B. (2012) *Remarks by the President at Sandy Hook Interfaith Prayer Vigil.* Available at https://www.whitehouse.gov/the-press-office/2012/12/16/remarks-president-sandy-hook-interfaith-prayer-vigil, accessed on 03/29/17.

Parker, E. (2015) 'Advice to R.I.: Focus on strengths, not weaknesses.' *Providence Journal*, October 24. Available at www.providencejournal.com/article/20151024/NEWS/151029540, accessed on 03/29/17.

Rath, T. and Conchie, B. (2007) *Strengths Based Leadership: Great Leaders, Great Teams, and Why People Follow.* New York: Gallup Press.

Rath, T. and Conchie, B. (2009) *What Makes a Great Leadership Team?* Available at www.gallup.com/businessjournal/113338/what-makes-great-leadership-team.aspx, accessed on 03/29/17.

Roosevelt, T. (1926) *An Autobiography*, in the *National Works, Volume XX.* New York: Charles Scribner's Sons.

Rosenblatt, R. (2000) 'The killing of Kayla.' *Time Magazine*, March 5. Available at http://content.time.com/time/magazine/article/0,9171,40342,00.html, accessed on 03/29/17.

U.S. Department of Education (2014) *Expansive Survey of America's Public Schools Reveals Troubling Racial Disparities.* Available at www.ed.gov/news/press-releases/expansive-survey-americas-public-schools-reveals-troubling-racial-disparities, accessed on 03/29/17.

Chapter 13

The Expressive Arts

A VEHICLE FOR CHANGE

Eric Green, Jennifer Baggerly,
Ronnie Nowicki, and Michael Lotz

Introduction

Professional school counselors, educators, and mental health professionals have a responsibility to ensure the success of every student,
especially underserved students who have experienced loss and trauma.
Young people who are affected by death and other traumas need
developmentally appropriate support structures and mental health
strategies to promote their academic and social success. Traditional
talk therapy adapted to children is not necessarily developmentally
appropriate (Landreth, Baggerly, and Tyndall-Lind, 1999). In
addition, psychotherapy outcome literature indicates that talk therapy
does not consistently produce moderate or large effect sizes for some
populations of children (Green and Drewes, 2013; Weisz, McCarty,
and Valeri, 2006). However, expressive arts approaches such as play
therapy have been found to produce a moderate effect size for children
(Lin and Bratton, 2015).

Two developmentally appropriate paradigms of educational
support/mental health care in P–12 (pre-school through 12th grade)
are expressive arts and play therapy with children in small group and
individual settings. These approaches have demonstrated improvements
in children's feelings of interpersonal security, externalization
of affect in a psychologically healthy manner, and stress levels related
to school-based anxiety (Green and Drewes, 2013). Therefore, this
chapter covers the use of expressive arts, including play therapy, with
school-aged children affected by loss, grief, and trauma, in an effort to
support their social, career, and academic success.

First, a comprehensive literature review of current research-supported practices related to integrating expressive arts and play therapy with school-aged children experiencing challenging life events is provided. Second, a case study illustrating expressive arts is included from the first author's recent work with bereaved children in schools. Finally, the chapter concludes with practical suggestions for school counselors and educators when incorporating expressive arts with underserved youth and the challenging issues they face that have been presented in many chapters.

Childhood loss and grief: A brief overview

Children's comprehension of death and non-death-related loss is formulated by their developmental capacities, viability of support systems, and the ability (or not) to accept the finality of loss (Hunter and Smith, 2008; Nguyen and Gelman, 2002) and change. Grief is an ongoing life process, not just a specific emotion or unique event, which impacts an individual's physical and emotional health as well as behaviors. It can be particularly challenging for children to make sense of loss because they often do not possess a point of reference for difficult life events. Nor do they necessarily have the cognitive capacity to understand the dynamic process of matriculating through the grief process. Compared to adults, children typically have less experience coping with aberrant emotions, thoughts, and feelings. Therefore, they often find it challenging to verbally express complex issues such as interpersonal loss (Green and Connolly, 2009). Since children often find comfort in communicating through play and more creative mechanisms, such as expressive arts, they may benefit from non-verbal/creative means of communication during the adjustment period following difficult life events.

As young children develop, their understanding and cognitive awareness of loss and grief typically increases. Their sources of information about death and other tragedies may come from watching television, hearing others talk about it, asking caretakers, or having direct experiences of losing a pet, family member, or peer. The developmental stages for children's understanding are presented in Chapter 1.

Girls and boys attending school in the 21st century face many losses. For example, one out of every 20 children who are 15 years or younger will experience the death of one or both parents (Owens, 2008). In addition, societal and global issues of poverty, abuse, immigration, and military deployment create an overlay of trauma for children already facing challenges in the classroom. Students may have hidden emotions of grief that are too difficult to speak of or even formulate through words. "By opening communication through the expressive arts, educators can create a bridge between a student's *inability* to share and release thoughts and feelings and their *ability* to access these inner states safely as part of a healing process" (Goldman, 2011, p.21).

School-aged children depend upon surviving caregivers and family members as they work through appropriate sadness and anger over their interpersonal loss (Christ, 2000). Other factors that affect the grieving process include: family cohesiveness, how often the family is willing to discuss the matter together, how each member copes with the loss, and any other major life stressors (Green and Connolly, 2009). The permanent absence of an important person in an individual's life can inflict persistent emotional distress by impairing normal functioning of schedules and relationships (LaFreniere and Cain, 2015). Therefore, a lack of early psychosocial support for students during challenging life events can lead to an onset of mental health concerns and inhibit learning and growth. Symptomatology of depression such as hopelessness, self-doubt, isolation, and apathy may surface, as well as various levels of anxiety (Christ, 2000). Educators can become that significant adult who forms a connecting bond of caring through the expressive arts.

Creating loss and grief awareness in schools

School counselors, teachers, administrators, and other educators benefit when they are cognizant of the common signs of grief in school-aged children (Goldman, 2012, and Chapter 1). When children affected by death and other grief-related issues go unnoticed, their risk for various psychosocial and physiological responses increases. Common signs of childhood grief manifesting outwardly in schools include outbursts and aggressiveness in the classroom, poor grades, inability to concentrate, and a sudden proclivity expressed by children to be alone. Other signs include nightmares, crying unexpectedly, frequent stomachaches and headaches, increased conflicting relationships, and impulsive choices.

Typical children do not like to act or appear different from their peers; therefore, children who display grief-related symptomatology at school may have serious psychosocial adjustment difficulties. Some youngsters may try to normalize their grief responses by not talking about their loss at school or they may continue to talk about the deceased loved one in the present tense during classroom conversations (Goldman, 2015). Young people may experience difficulty when they attempt to externalize their feelings and thoughts to people they do not trust. Children's reluctance to verbalize their distress following a death or loss is a major rationale for using expressive arts with a bereaved child. Play and art allow students to appropriately communicate their hidden emotions and develop a more personal acceptance of the loss (Green and Connolly, 2009).

Expressive arts with school-aged children: An overview

Expressive arts therapy provides children an opportunity to access their creativity to gain an understanding of difficult life events and emotions (Near, 2013). Play constitutes children's therapeutic work. Toys allow them to communicate; while play may be seen as a metaphorical language (Landreth, 2012). Expressive arts integrate play, art, music, writing, and other creative avenues to facilitate personal change and an alteration of behaviors in children with a variety of psychosocial needs. Unconscious projections may be externalized through the child's therapeutic, educational, and creative work, which may bring about symptom relief. Expressive arts facilitated by a trained teacher, guidance counselor, or other mental health professional are generally viewed as a socially acceptable mode of therapeutic engagement that may help alleviate emotional distress in children (Green and Drewes, 2013).

The specific types of expressive arts therapy that will be discussed in this chapter include play therapy, art therapy, sandplay therapy, and music therapy. Each modality has its own unique way of engaging school-aged children's imaginations, which may facilitate healing during difficult and challenging periods of grief and loss. Expressive arts therapy has been successfully applied to a variety of girls and boys from diverse backgrounds, and the next sections will demonstrate how each type can benefit underserved students in a school setting.

Play therapy

Play is considered a fundamental aspect of early life, and it has been shown to improve the social, emotional, cognitive, and physical domains of children (Green and Drewes, 2013). The therapeutic powers of play assist children in making sense of their world and can help resolve various distressing and traumatic life events (Association for Play Therapy, 2013). It serves as a route for children to express emotions and feelings through imagination, symbolism, and fantasy (Russ, 2007). Play therapy allows the counselor to enter the child's experience, which can facilitate growth and healing in a way that is congruent with the developmental age of the child.

Although there are several theoretical models of play therapy, Child-Centered Play Therapy (CCPT) is most relevant in working with children and grief and loss. CCPT involves children leading and directing their own play, with an educator or therapist as a participant-observer who provides beneficial responses such as tracking play behavior, reflecting feelings, building self-esteem, setting therapeutic limits, facilitating understanding, and enlarging the meaning (Landreth, 2012). Children are able to examine their experiences in a psychologically and physically safe environment—one in which the teacher, counselor, or therapist unconditionally accepts the child's play and is permissive.

Landreth (2012) suggested that children should have access to a fully equipped playroom that contains real-life toys, aggressive toys, and toys that facilitate expression, such as a counselor's office or early childhood classroom. The use of sand trays is recommended from this theoretical perspective because of the unstructured properties of sand and water. Children have access to scooping, shifting, piling, and burying in the sand with various types of items and toys. The teacher, counselor, or school psychologist does not need to direct the student in any way, and the experience during play can be relaxing and soothing for the child. To begin the session, the child-centered play educator or mental health professional may simply say, "Welcome to the playroom. In here, you can play with all of the toys in most of the ways you'd like." This open invitation sets the stage for the child to be in control of the healing process. Afterwards, children typically play out different themes (e.g., power, seeking safety, good vs. bad, nurturing, etc.) occurring in their lives and work out solutions to old problems through the symbols afforded by the various toys and the beneficial relationship within the playroom.

Toy telephones can create a private role-play conversation with a loved one. For example, Juan was five years old when his dad was deported. "I really miss my dad," he explained to his kindergarten teacher. He picked up the play toy telephone in the classroom and began an ongoing, ever-present dialogue with Dad. "Hi Daddy. How are you? I love you. I really miss you. I don't understand why they had to take you away. Are you OK? Let me tell you about my day." This projective prop created a safe path for Juan to work through challenging spaces without the need to directly verbalize them. "This play allows and provides an outlet for thoughts and feelings and helps participants adapt to their life situation" (Goldman, 2002, p.123).

Students can use props to recreate a disaster setting with doctors, nurses, firemen, and policemen through projective play. Ellie pretended to be a nurse helping those hurt at the Pentagon crash, and Tyler put on the fire hat and gloves and said, "Don't worry, I'll save you. Run for your lives." These children "felt empowered through play to take action and control over the difficult experience they had witnessed" (Goldman, 2005, p.122). Adam survived Hurricane Katrina. He used the sand table in the guidance counselor's office to place figures of himself, Mom and Dad, and his dog Cooper. "I couldn't find my dog, my house was gone, and all of my stuff was missing. Me and my mom and dad were scared. We didn't know if help would ever come." The effectiveness of CCPT after disasters was demonstrated by Shen (2002), whose findings suggested a significant reduction in anxiety and suicidal ideation in children who received CCPT after a Taiwanese earthquake.

Art therapy

The process of creating art can be a tool to assess the feelings and perceptions of children's internal worlds and permits communication between their inner and outer affective spheres (French and Klein, 2012). The modality of expressive art has foundations within three predominant theoretical paradigms: psychoanalytic, developmental, and cognitive-behavioral therapy. The psychoanalytic theories of both Sigmund Freud and Carl Jung have influenced the art therapy field. Margaret Naumburg (1987) integrated aspects of both Freudian and Jungian theory in practice. Naumburg's approach focused on unearthing unconscious material through the use of free association about non-directed or spontaneously produced artwork. Donald Winnicott's contribution to object relations theory has influenced art therapy by describing how children place greater value on particular objects than the item itself, which becomes a transitional object. The artwork created by a child in a safe environment in school can serve as a transitional object by functioning as a reminder of what was experienced during the process of using expressive arts (Malchiodi, 2003).

Developmental art activity emphasizes the comprehensive understanding of the normative process of cognitive, emotional, physical, and artistic development of children and the precept that creative artistic activities offer normative experiences and promote increased social, emotional, and cognitive functioning for all individuals (Green and Drewes, 2013; Malchiodi, Kim, and Choi, 2003). In contrast to the psychoanalytic approach to art activities, the cognitive-behavioral therapy approach implements techniques such as self-instruction training and stress inoculation training. Self-instruction training teaches behavioral techniques to students such as coaching impulsive students towards completion of drawing and coloring projects (Meichenbaum and Goodman, 1971).

When infusing art interventions, teachers, counselors, school psychologists, and therapists should carefully consider the child's treatment goals and objectives (Silverstone, 2009). Professionals must also carefully consider to what degree they will interact with the child and facilitate the use of art media throughout the time with the student (Rubin, 2005). Some children need the educator or mental health professional to be intermittently verbal (e.g., guiding, tracking, encouraging) throughout the process, while other girls and boys may need the adult to witness their process in silence. Either way, one should remain attuned to verbal, non-verbal, visual, and metaphorical methods of communication as indicators of clinical significance (Kaplan, 2003). The teacher or mental health professional may observe the completed art product and ask the child to describe the artwork through the use of open-ended questions. Through the discussion of the student's artwork, the adult gains an understanding of the child's symbolic language depicted within their art. It is essential for them not to assign meaning to the content of the image based on personal associations and projections.

The following examples illustrate the broad canvas of emotions and imagery that can be created by drawing and clay. In Chapter 1, Goldman shared 11-year-old Michelle's drawing after her mother's fatal car crash (Figure 1.2). Research suggests that many children locate their deceased person in a place called heaven. Michelle drew a picture of her mom in heaven surrounded by friends and family, her dog, and a castle where only the great live, like her mom. Her mom loved Elvis. She drew his house with lots of disco dancing and a buffet of her favorite foods. Drawing pictures about heaven "helps children feel comforted and safe if they can hold a positive image of where their person is" (Goldman, 2009, p.42).

Michelle also drew a picture of her *Magical Place* after Mom died (Figure 13.1). She explained it was a place with rainbows and flowers and everyone got to meet God. Michelle said she liked to look at the picture: "It makes me feel good."

Figure 13.1 Magical Place (Goldman, 2002, p.118)

Dr. Laila Gupta conveyed another poignant example during her keynote speech at the Montreal Association for Death Education and Counseling Conference. She spoke of her work with children living with war, disaster, and trauma and relayed the experience of a young boy and his accompanying drawings about his story. This boy from Rwanda had witnessed his father being murdered before his eyes. Dr. Gupta encouraged him to create four drawings as follows: (1) life before the tragic event, (2) the boy's experience of the event, (3) how life is now, and (4) what would he like life to be in the future. Dr. Gupta incorporated the concept of creating a keepsake book; ending with a future hopeful outlook. Through art expression, the boy was encouraged to share his experience, ending with a future hopeful outlook. He drew himself as an automobile mechanic. Art as a grief technique allowed a safe vehicle for expression in many ways (Goldman, 2011, p.20).

Sculpting is another expressive vehicle that can open a path to easier communication and sharing. "Clay has a very calming effect for children and they can gain a feeling of mastery by…pounding, squeezing, pinching, ripping, smoothing, and poking it" (Goldman, 2014, p.83). Alexa, age 10, was enraged at police for arresting her dad, resulting in her father's imprisonment. She recreated the scene of police invading her home and taking her dad away while she, Mom, and her little brother Marcus were left crying and screaming at the door. She sculpted the police, her dad, and her family when this traumatic incident took place. Then Alexa took the policeman's image and smashed it, crying, "I hate you! I hate you! You took my father away." Clay represented a safe avenue to express rage through a projective play scenario.

Sandplay therapy

Sandplay allows children to use symbols in the form of various sand miniatures, sand, and a sand tray to communicate their inner thoughts, feelings, fantasies, and experiences in the presence of a supportive therapist. It is mostly non-verbal and non-directive. Sandplay is based upon and influenced by the psychological principles of Carl Jung and was officially developed by Swiss therapist Dora Kalff. The modality of sandplay allows children a *free and protected space* (Kalff, 2003) where their imagination is stimulated and the natural healing powers of the psyche are enlivened. They feel safe and encouraged to play and express themselves through difficult issues, such as grief and bereavement, without the fear of being interrupted, analyzed, or judged by anyone.

The sandplay work begins by introducing the girls and boys in a calm tone that allows them to explore the playroom and choose for themselves what might be fun to do. Creating a free and protected space in which students can access their internal state is an essential role of the empathic sandplay caring adult. Children are introduced to both wet and dry sand, sand trays, and the sand miniatures that will be used to generate a sand picture. The sand miniatures are used to stimulate the child's imagination and represent the many dynamics in their personal world. The child symbolically communicates their personal issues through the display of their sand picture and their choice of sand miniatures, which may allow a teacher or mental health professional to comprehend or conceptualize these issues during the sandplay process. As sandplay is purely non-directive, there are no interventions or directive techniques in Kalffian sandplay.

The adult plays the role of a supportive witness to the creation of sand pictures during the process of sandplay. While occupying the role of witness, they sit closely near the child, allowing the space to be a window into the child's inner world. The teacher, counselor, or mental health professional typically will take notes on the order of miniatures chosen and how they are placed in the picture, the child's comments during the process, as well as their own thoughts. Then they may verbalize, "Is there anything you'd like to share about your sand picture? You don't have to if you don't want to. Completely up to you." There is little to no verbal processing after a child completes the sand picture. The sand picture created may be added to the child's file/personal records.

The creation of the sand picture emerges in the context of a nonjudgmental relationship. The sand picture and the caring relationship enable the child to search for their conceptualization of life, death, grieving, and living. The therapeutic dyad allows the young people the free and sheltered space to reflect on the loss, say goodbye, and/or share their emotions at their own pace and choosing (Green and Drewes, 2013).

Music therapy

According to the American Music Therapy Association (2013), music therapy is the clinical and evidence-based treatment that uses music interventions to address the needs of young people. Music has been found to inspire imagination and exploration. It stimulates language and can be used to develop listening and social skills that build confidence for social interaction (Green and Drewes, 2013). Music plays an integral part in the cognitive, physical, social, and emotional health of children, and can be healing for students in a school setting. Other studies have found a correlation in which children are less anxious and have decreased levels of arousal when presented with music relaxation techniques and their own choice of music (McFerran, 2010; Pelletier, 2004).

Music therapists utilize live music or recorded music based on what best suits the child and situation. However, some research supports the use of live music in therapeutic outcomes because of its enhanced quality and potential to be inventive and flexible (Green and Drewes, 2013). There are several ways to engage the child with music such as through listening, performing, and improvising. These can be used in a classroom, guidance setting, or music program. Listening to music can be a source of relaxation, entertainment, and exploration of emotions for the student based on the song. Young people often enjoy performing music by singing a song or playing an instrument, which can help them connect with their emotions. This connection may improve upon their sensorimotor and cognitive skills. Improvising musical selections in a safe, healing space may help facilitate growth in spontaneity and teach the child how to properly react to the unexpected. A common music technique to use with students for self-exploration would be to have them bring in a favorite song or one that summarizes how they see themselves. This can give caring adults an opportunity to gain a better understanding of the student by having them explore why they chose this song and explain how it is relatable to them.

Another effective music technique with children and teens is to ask them to bring in a song about their person that died or left, or a challenge they are facing. Andrew was a 14-year-old boy who loved music. After 9/11, Andrew's school counselor asked his class to bring in music to describe their emotions about this traumatic event. One student played "God Bless America" and explained how much America meant to him, especially since his mother had just received citizenship. Another classmate shared the song "From a Distance" and explained her vision of world peace. Her father had died in combat in Iraq. Andrew loved the song "My Hero" and explained that was just how he felt about the firemen and policemen that were injured or killed helping others during the traumatic event. He said, "I wish I could be like that" (Goldman, 2011, p.20). "Qualitative investigations have indicated that music peer groups may be beneficial for struggling adolescents. The existing relationship between young people and music serves as a platform for connectedness and emotional expression that is utilized within a therapeutic, support group format" (McFerran, Roberts, and O'Grady, 2010, p.541).

Using expressive arts with underserved children in schools

According to the ASCA National Model's (2012) outline of a comprehensive and developmentally appropriate school counseling program, the use of expressive arts and play therapy in elementary, middle, and secondary schools can be effectively included in response services such as preventative and direct interventions (Trice-Black, Bailey, and Riechel, 2013). Professional educators and school counselors can use play, art, sandplay, and music during individual and small group counseling sessions as well as classroom guidance lessons to give students separate outlets of communication. Furthermore, expressive arts and play therapy can be used with grieving students from all backgrounds as they attempt to communicate the many difficulties they are experiencing during any traumatic life process. Research has found this modality to be sensitive to diverse cultures, socio-economic status, and the varying levels of academic and language abilities (Trice-Black *et al.*, 2013). Expressive arts and play therapy can be used successfully with school-aged children to support personal self-discovery and fulfillment as they grieve and reconcile their loss. The following case study illustrates the implementation of expressive arts with a grieving child in a school system, and how the therapeutic relationship became a vehicle of change and hope.

CORDELL: A CASE STUDY

Cordell was an 11-year-old African-American male who relocated from the southern tip of Florida to the northern Florida panhandle with his mother following his grandfather's death (all identifying information in this case has been altered to protect client confidentiality). Cordell was referred to his new middle-school counselor because his teacher expressed concern over his self-isolation and unwillingness to participate in group activities with his peers. His math teacher also reported that Cordell appeared despondent at times, especially when other children spoke about their family members in the classroom setting. Cordell had no history of behavioral problems and was a "B" student at his former school in southern Florida. He also was a member of the tennis team and drama club. He enjoyed drawing, and he indicated his preference of engaging in artistic and creative activities. Cordell was especially close to his grandfather who had died suddenly and unexpectedly of a heart attack at age 74. Cordell reported that his grandfather became his primary father figure after his biological father remarried and discontinued contact with Cordell at a young age.

Cordell was emotionally distraught about his grandfather's death, and he expressed feeling alone and saddened. His mother indicated that he lost interest in playing tennis following his grandfather's passing, and he had been eating nearly twice as many snacks and portions at dinner than before his grandfather's death. The school counselor agreed to meet with Cordell for an initial six weeks (two 20-minute sessions per week) to help him express difficult emotions related to his grandfather's death, acclimate to his new school environment, and build new peer relationships. The school counselor provided him a free and sheltered space to process any grief issues that were interfering with his academic success.

In the school counselor's office, there were two sand trays (a wet tray and a dry tray), hundreds of diverse sand miniatures (Figure 13.2), crayons, markers, construction paper, psycho-educational books, an Ipad to play music and videos, and puppets. Over the first three sessions, Cordell spoke very little about what was bothering him. Instead, he self-soothed by manipulating the sand with his fingers. He would scoop it, cup the sand, and try to build a sand structure, but he did not choose to place miniatures in the sand trays, nor was he expected to do so.

Figure 13.2 Sand miniatures

During the second and third sessions, he did verbalize to the school counselor that playing with the sand felt cool to the touch, and he smiled for a couple of seconds at a time. The school counselor remained quietly supportive of Cordell during these relationship-building sessions, which usually occur during the first few weeks of engagement.

During the second week, Cordell, still relatively quiet, asked if he could draw. The school counselor indicated that he could make the decisions of what to do during their time together.

He looked at the counselor's "Color Your Mandala" workbook. The counselor explained, "These images are mandalas. They are often circular shapes that represent wholeness. You're welcome to use any of the art materials that you'd like to create your mandala. And after you're done, I might ask you to write the story of your mandala on the back of the page, and sign and date it. But you don't have to if you don't want to. How does that sound to you?" He responded affirmatively.

Over the next several weeks, Cordell created many mandala images and wrote the story of the mandalas as well. He started each session by playing in the sand, as it appeared to kinesthetically calm him. The school counselor, with Cordell's permission, played soft, relaxing music in the background and did not track Cordell's movements but remained relatively quiet while Cordell created. After about a month, he created a mandala filled with multi-colored flowers (Figure 13.3).

Figure 13.3 Flowers

This image, and the resolution of the image between the child and the counselor, represented a breakthrough moment in the grief work. Cordell called the mandala "Flowers." He also wrote a poem with it:

A patchwork of colors. A sudden release. A relief.
A thing in the making. A soul forever changing.
Death is blooming. Life is assuming.
Be calm. Be reborn. Be magical. Breathe.

He seemed affectively moved as he shed a couple of tears after sharing the poem he wrote on the back of his mandala. He then, after over a month into the counseling relationship, shared that his grandfather had died and that he missed him. His eyes welled with tears, and the counselor reassured him that he was there with him and deeply felt the pain of his loss. Cordell gave the counselor a hug, then returned to class.

During these first several weeks of counseling, Cordell's teacher reported that he seemed to be more engaged in class and was exhibiting less dissociation. Also, his math teacher reported that she observed him helping another child with his homework and socializing a bit more at recess with peers. After about two months of individual counseling, Cordell was referred to a "children in transition" group so he could continue his adjustment to the new school and processing any residual grief issues.

He continued coloring mandalas, including a traditional circular mandala (Figure 13.4) that he titled "Blue." Cordell reported to his counselor that while he missed his grandfather terribly, he was also comforted by the fact that his grandfather's favorite color was blue, and he mentioned that his favorite color was blue.

Figure 13.4 Blue mandala

He was able to find strands of memories and draw strength upon them during his bereavement. He also became a "big brother" to a younger child who lost his grandmother, and this socially responsible behavior seems to have helped Cordell heal as well.

At the end of the semester, Cordell was still sad at times as he missed his grandfather very much. But he was less isolated, slightly more engaged in school, and participated regularly in artistic and creative outlets toward coping and healing.

Recommendations for school counselors and educators

As illustrated in the case study above, expressive arts served as a vehicle for change during a student's adjustment period to loss. Cordell went from feeling somber and disconnected to re-engaging in peer relationships and altruistically helping younger schoolmates in his new environment. Educators and school counselors can create a systematic approach to help grieving children in their schools by incorporating the expressive arts into their daily program through the following suggestions:

- The guidance counselor can prepare their office with projective miniature objects, stuffed animals, and a sand table for projective play.

- Teachers can have an art center in each classroom to allow for spontaneous drawings.

- Music can be incorporated into daily activities to promote an expression of feeling.

- Creative experiential learning (CEL) approaches can be provided to students.

CEL is an educational method that teachers and educators can include in their classroom curricula to improve students' retention and knowledge. CEL allows students to participate in creative activities, reflect, make connections, and apply learning by contemplating the things they are doing (Green and Drewes, 2013). Through CEL, students are encouraged to be active learners, leading to higher orders of thinking, such as the application, evaluation, and synthesis of concepts. CEL requires that teachers and educators reconfigure traditional teaching methods such as lecturing or doing worksheets to more creative activities that engage students. CEL can facilitate self-expression and openness, increase self-awareness and problem solving, as well as support self-care (Green and Drewes, 2013).

To prepare for CEL, teachers and educators need to be intentional in creating a positive and trusting classroom environment. This preparation includes addressing any concerns students voice and permitting group discussions. Dyads and small groups can be formed to further engage students in creative activities. Teachers and educators need to maintain ethical boundaries throughout the process by respecting students' autonomy and ensuring their well-being. The physical learning environment needs to contain enough space for students to move around for the various expressive arts activities and contain the necessary materials. In order to be invested in this nontraditional social constructionist approach, students need to be encouraged to take ownership of their learning.

The process of CEL involves obtaining informed consent, using various expressive arts to teach concepts, processing and debriefing, as well as ongoing assessment (Green and Drewes, 2013). Sandplay, mandalas, psychodrama, poetry, and music can symbolically communicate concepts being learned. For example, teachers can ask students to:

- place sand miniatures in a sand tray to represent juxtaposition of characters in a book

- color sections of mandalas in different colors to learn about percentages

- write poems or make art projects about prominent scientific events or findings

- create dramatic role plays about historical people.

Furthermore, teachers and educators can use video media to help students learn material and illustrate important concepts. CEL can enrich the lives of students and increase learning when used correctly.

Implications

There are three implications regarding the use of expressive arts with bereaved youth in school settings. First, counselors and educators can help youth in crisis when they recognize that expressive arts, especially those using play, drawings, sand, and music, are a child's developmentally appropriate mechanism of communicating. Thereby, children must be afforded the free and sheltered space to matriculate through the grief experience at their own pace and volition so that they can succeed in the academic setting. Second, the inherent vulnerability entwined with this type of depth work necessitates that counselors obtain advanced professional development, certification, and supervision in the specific modality practiced. Resources such as CEL and *Integrating Expressive Arts and Play Therapy with Children and Adolescents, 3rd Edition* (Green and Drewes, 2013) can be accessed to ascertain processes and procedures for ethical practice. Finally, counselors and educators are encouraged to regularly engage in their own creative outlets as part of renewal and self-care. In doing so, they will be fully present to serve as a vehicle of change for our underserved youth.

References

American Music Therapy Association (2013) *What is Music Therapy?* Available at www.musictherapy.org/about/musictherapy, accessed on 03/29/17.

American School Counselor Association (ASCA) (2012) *The ASCA National Model: A Framework for School Counseling Programs, 3rd Edition.* Alexandria, VA: ASCA.

Association for Play Therapy (2013) *About APT.* Available at www.a4pt.org/?page=AboutAPT, accessed on 03/29/17.

Christ, G.H. (2000) 'Impact of development on children's mourning.' *Cancer Practice 8*, 72–81.

French, L. and Klein, R. (eds) (2012) *Therapeutic Practice in Schools: Working with the Child within: A Clinical Workbook for Counsellors, Psychotherapists and Arts Therapists.* London: Routledge.

Goldman, L. (2002) *Breaking the Silence: A Guide to Help Children with Complicated Grief, 2nd Edition.* New York: Taylor and Francis.

Goldman, L. (2005) *Children Also Grieve: Talking about Death and Healing.* London: Jessica Kingsley Publishers.

Goldman, L. (2009) *Great Answers to Difficult Questions About Death: What Children Need to Know.* London: Jessica Kingsley Publishers.

Goldman, L. (2011) 'Valuing expressive therapy in grief work.' *ADEC Forum 37*, 1, 20–21.

Goldman, L. (2012) 'Helping the grieving child in the schools.' *Healing Magazine*, 26–29.

Goldman, L. (2014) *Life and Loss: A Guide to Help Grieving Children, 3rd Edition.* New York: Taylor and Francis Publishers.

Goldman, L. (2015) 'What complicates grief for children: A case study.' *Healing Magazine*, 6–10.

Green, E.J. and Connolly, M.E. (2009) 'Jungian family sandplay with bereaved children: Implications for play therapists.' *International Journal of Play Therapy 18*, 2, 84–98.

Green, E.J. and Drewes, A. (eds) (2013) *Integrating Expressive Arts and Play Therapy with Children and Adolescents, 3rd Edition.* Hoboken, NJ: John Wiley.

Hunter, S.B. and Smith, D.E. (2008) 'Predictors of children's understandings of death: Age, cognitive ability, death experience, and maternal communicative competence.' *Omega 57*, 143–162.

Kalff, D. (2003) *Sandplay: A Psychotherapeutic Approach to the Psyche.* Cloverdale, CA: Temenos Press.

Kaplan, F. (2003) 'Art-Based Assessments.' In C.A. Malchiodi (ed.) *Handbook of Art Therapy.* New York: Guilford Press.

LaFreniere, L. and Cain, A. (2015) 'Parentally bereaved children and adolescents: The question of peer support.' *Omega: Journal of Death and Dying 71*, 3, 245–271.

Landreth, G. (2012) *Play Therapy, 3rd Edition.* London: Routledge.

Landreth, G., Baggerly, J.N., and Tyndall-Lind, A.M. (1999) 'Beyond adapting adult counseling skills to counsel children: The paradigm shift to child centered play therapy.' *Journal of Individual Psychology 55*, 3, 272–287.

Lin, Y. and Bratton, S.C. (2015) 'A meta-analytic review of child-centered play therapy approaches.' *Journal of Counseling and Development 93*, 1, 45–58.

Malchiodi, C.A. (2003) 'Psychoanalytic, Analytic, and Object Relations Approaches.' In C.A. Malchiodi (ed.) *Handbook of Art Therapy.* New York: Guilford Press.

Malchiodi, C.A., Kim, D.Y., and Choi, W.S. (2003) 'Developmental Art Therapy.' In C.A. Malchiodi (ed.) *Handbook of Art Therapy.* New York: Guilford Press.

McFerran, K. (2010) *Adolescents, Music and Music Therapy: Methods and Techniques for Clinicians, Educators, and Students.* London: Jessica Kingsley Publishers.

McFerran, K., Roberts, M., and O'Grady, L. (2010) 'Music therapy with bereaved teenagers: A mixed methods perspective.' *Journal of Death Studies 34*, 6, 541–565.

Meichenbaum, D.H. and Goodman, J. (1971) 'Training impulsive children to talk to themselves: A means of developing self-control.' *Journal of Abnormal Psychology 77*, 115–126.

Naumburg, M. (1987) *Dynamically Oriented Art Therapy: Its Principles and Practices.* Chicago, IL: Magnolia Street.

Near, R. (2013) 'Expressive Arts with Grieving Children.' In C.A. Malchiodi (ed.) *Art Therapy and Health Care.* New York: Guilford Press.

Nguyen, S.P. and Gelman, S.A. (2002) 'Four and 6-year-olds' biological concept of death: The case of plants.' *British Journal of Developmental Psychology 20*, 4, 495.

Owens, D. (2008) 'Recognizing the needs of bereaved children in palliative care.' *Journal of Hospice & Palliative Nursing 10*, 1, 1–10.

Pelletier, C.L. (2004) 'The effect of music on decreasing arousal due to stress: A meta-analysis.' *Journal of Music Therapy 41*, 3, 192–214.

Rubin, J.A. (2005) *Child Art Therapy, 25th Anniversary Edition.* Hoboken, NJ: Wiley.

Russ, S. (2007) 'Pretend play: A resource for children who are coping with stress and managing anxiety.' *NYS Psychologist 19*, 5, 13–17.

Shen, Y. (2002) 'Short-term group play therapy with Chinese earthquake victims: Effects on anxiety, depression, and adjustment.' *International Journal of Play Therapy 11*, 1, 43–63.

Silverstone, L. (2009) *Art Therapy Exercises: Inspirational and Practical Ideas to Stimulate the Imagination.* London: Jessica Kingsley Publishers.

Trice-Black, S., Bailey, C.L., and Riechel, M.K. (2013) 'Play therapy in school counseling.' *Professional School Counseling 16*, 5, 303–312.

Weisz, J.R., McCarty, C.A., and Valeri, S.M. (2006) 'Effects of psychotherapy for depression in children and adolescents: A meta-analysis.' *Psychological Bulletin 132*, 1, 132–149.

Chapter 14

Media and Social Impact

SESAME STREET HELPS STUDENTS

Rocio Galarza and David Cohen

Introduction

Sesame Workshop, the producer of Sesame Street and other educational programs, is a long-recognized expert in developing materials that support the cognitive and emotional well-being of young children and their families (Fisch and Truglio, 2000). Through its popular, long-running television show, its beloved Muppets, and various media resources, Sesame Workshop has demonstrated a commitment to supporting families and educators with young children in many different circumstances on an array of topics discussed in this resource. In addition to areas related to school readiness, such as literacy and numeracy, the U.S. Social Impact arm of Sesame Workshop, responsible for community outreach efforts, has covered sensitive topics such as the incarceration of a parent, death, and military deployment. There are few resources on these topics that are geared toward very young children and those who care for them; and by using the positive power of media and its Muppets, Sesame Workshop seeks to fill this gap. These materials can be used to not only help families in vulnerable situations, but also to raise awareness among educators, caregivers, and other professionals, and instruct them on how to help young children and families in need to cope with the challenges they face.

Children who are able to communicate their feelings and experiences, and have access to caregivers they feel are trustworthy and available, are more likely to cope successfully with challenging and adverse circumstances (McCubbin and McCubbin, 1996). Through storybooks, videos, and apps, Sesame Workshop is able to connect with girls and boys, and educators and parents, around topics they might be reluctant to address, and help promote conversation and resilience (Oades-Sese *et al.*, 2014). There are a number of ways that Sesame Workshop is uniquely positioned to help young people and their families in trying circumstances, as well as the providers who serve them. In general, one has an easier time learning how to approach and deal with a sensitive topic when it is coming from a familiar and trusted source (Kotler, Roberto, and Lee, 2002; Lauricella, Gola, and Calvert, 2011; McGuire, 1989).

Sesame Street and its characters are well known by both kids and adults for providing entertaining, comforting, and educational fare. The friendly faces of the Muppets (Figure 14.1) and adult cast provide a warm and welcoming space for introducing and illustrating tough topics.

Figure 14.1 Muppets

In addition, by portraying difficult and emotionally complex situations, such as when a parent dies, or is deployed or incarcerated, in age-appropriate ways, Sesame Street is able to convey what young children may be experiencing as well as model effective words and actions of caring adults. Further, by portraying these scenarios in its own unique ways, Sesame Workshop can help *normalize* situations that vulnerable families and children might otherwise feel to be stigmatizing and alienating, and at the same time raise awareness among those who are not as knowledgeable of the challenges they face. Finally, by delivering these media-based resources both online and via hands-on materials, Sesame Workshop is able to reach children, families, educators, and others who serve them wherever they may be.

Outreach initiatives

Looking at the outreach initiatives for young children and their families who are dealing with incarceration, military deployment, and death of a parent will illustrate the ways Sesame Workshop teaches educators, caregivers, and providers about these issues and how they can help. These resources raise awareness among providers and educators, and also give them tools to explain and highlight difficult themes in ways that maximize coping, understanding, and acceptance.

Sesame Workshop reaches out to a broad range of children, educators, and parents throughout the world that are facing challenging situations. It serves them in this digital age as an example of what can be done on a grand scale to provide information and resources for grieving kids on television, Internet, video, and downloadable materials.

Incarceration

Cortina and Trutt present in Chapter 8 an effective intervention, the *Get on the Bus* Project, highlighting awareness that incarceration impacts not only the person who is incarcerated but also his/her entire family. There has been a large increase in the number of children impacted by incarceration; 2.7 million children under age 18 have a parent in state or federal prison in the United States, an increase of 80 percent since 1991. Further, these numbers may be underestimated, since collecting information about these children is difficult given that they are "virtually invisible for several reasons, such as stigma, lack of communication among social service agencies, and limited definition of 'family' from the U.S. criminal justice system" (Harris and Graham, 2010, p.12). In response to the number of families affected, and the dearth of relevant resources for younger children, Sesame Workshop developed the *Little Children, Big Challenges: Incarceration* initiative.

Through videos, print materials, and digital media, *Little Children, Big Challenges: Incarceration* helps caregivers and providers with activities, tips, and strategies that promote coping and caring. Young children with incarcerated parents often experience upheaval in their family life, and are often not told the truth about their parents' incarceration due to a fear of being ostracized, or simply because their caregivers do not want or know how to discuss it. These young children may also blame themselves to make sense of their situation, and believe they must have done something wrong to cause the parent's incarceration (Fritsch and Burkhead, 1981; Hairston, 2007).

The initiative's main messages for children center on the following themes:

- You are not alone.

- There are people who will care for you.

- It is OK to feel many different ways.

- It's not your fault.

The main goals of the initiative for adult caregivers are the following:

- Talk openly and honestly with your child in an age-appropriate way.

- Keep consistent routines.

These goals are repeated throughout all the components of the resources: guides for caring adults, videos, as well as a storybook. For example, in the guide for adult caregivers there is a list of questions phrased the way a child would ask them, accompanied by age-appropriate responses:

Question: "Where is Mommy / Daddy?"

Answer: If the parent has been convicted: "Mommy / Daddy is in a place called prison for a while. Grown-ups sometimes go to prison when they break a rule called a law. She / he is not there because of anything you did. This is not your fault."

If the parent is not yet convicted: "Mommy / Daddy is in a place called jail. She / he's there because she / he may have broken an important grown-up rule called a law. Right now people are trying to figure out what happened" (Sesame Street in Communities, n.d.)

The videos included in the resources portray a Muppet child character, Alex, talking to other Muppet friends Abby and Rosita and a trusted adult character, Sofia, about his incarcerated father. As Alex, Sofia, Abby, and Rosita talk, we learn age-appropriate definitions of incarceration, we see Alex open up about his worries and feelings— being sad and angry, feeling he might be to blame for his father's incarceration, feeling alone and different from his peers—and we watch how Alex's friends comfort him, and promise that they "will always be there for him." Other videos include real children talking about having an incarcerated parent, how they cope, and what makes them feel better.

Because helping children and incarcerated parents connect and maintain contact can help the family cope with the separation and stigma of their situation (Adalist-Estrin, 2011), the resources also include an animated story of a young girl preparing to visit her father in prison. We watch as she prepares to see him, and the rules she has to follow while at the prison, as well as specific details about what her dad is wearing, and how she says goodbye. The story can help prepare a child about what he/she should expect when visiting a parent in prison or jail by showing it in a simple, straightforward way.

The videos described above and illustrated in Figure 14.2 help define incarceration, show real children experiencing a parent's incarceration, can spark conversations about feelings, or help prepare a child and educate caregivers about what to expect when visiting a parent in prison or jail. Cortina and Trutt, in Chapter 8, introduce a meaningful paradigm that allows kids to visit family members in prison by exploring the project, *Get on the Bus*.

Figure 14.2 Talking about incarceration

In summary, the Sesame Street *Little Children, Big Challenges: Incarceration* content illustrates how adults can talk to young children about incarceration in an age-appropriate yet honest way, how to answer their questions, and how to reassure children that they are not alone and will always be cared for. Appropriately, "You Are Not Alone" is the name of the song that accompanies this initiative, and reinforces its message of support and comfort:

You are not alone, I've been there too.
Many children have, many are like you.
You're not alone, I'm by your side.
My ears are here to listen, my arms are open wide.

Caring for a child who has an incarcerated parent can be challenging, particularly when one is unfamiliar or uncomfortable dealing with such a situation. Resources like *Little Children, Big Challenges: Incarceration* help familiarize the incarceration experience in a simple, compassionate, "Sesame Workshop" way by including easy-to-use tools for providers to help children and their families, such as providing concrete answers to questions a child may ask, and modeling the appropriate behaviors of children and adults in the safe, accepting setting of Sesame Street. Further, the tone and familiarity of the stories and their themes might help children identify with the characters, and aid in sparking conversations that might help young children begin to express their own feelings and stories (Amer, 1999).

Deployment

Sesame Workshop approached the difficult topic of a deployed parent in a similar fashion with its *Talk, Listen, Connect* project (Figure 14.3). Lynda Davis underscores in Chapter 10 the specific challenges military children face in schools. The experience of military families, whether active duty, National Guard, or Reserves, may be foreign to many kids, educators, and other caring adults. Through its friendly and familiar child and adult characters, as well as research-based content, *Talk, Listen, Connect* not only helps those children and families who are dealing with a parent's deployment, it can also educate those unfamiliar with military families' experiences.

Figure 14.3 Children and deployment

Parents of preschoolers may think that, because their preschool child is so young, they are immune to stress and challenges when their parent is deployed. However, while young children may not be able to fully comprehend what a deployment entails, they are often confused about why their parent is leaving, they long for the deployed parent, may worry about their safety, and they may experience difficulty transitioning with reintegration when their deployed parent returns home (MacDermid *et al.*, 2008). Being able to communicate with young children about deployment can play a key role in helping them cope (Cozza, Chun, and Polo, 2005). For these reasons, the *Talk, Listen, Connect* resources focus on the following messages aimed at helping military families with young children between the ages of two and five build a sense of stability and resiliency during times of separation by offering age-appropriate strategies for coping when a parent is deployed, specifically:

- Modeling age-appropriate conversations between preschoolers and adults using the Sesame Street characters.

- Teaching adult caregivers the importance of, and strategies to promote, communication with a young child about the experiences he/she is going through, including helping children talk about feelings.

The *Talk, Listen, Connect* initiative delivers these goals throughout its materials, and in ways that educators, parents, and other caring adults can easily use with the children they care for and love. For example, in one of the videos Elmo must cope with his father leaving "for lots and lots of days" (Figure 14.4). When Elmo's dad is deployed, he and Elmo create new routines that ease the pain of separation and help maintain a sense of stability. For example, Elmo and his mother develop a new bedtime ritual: No matter where they are, the family—Elmo with his mom at home, and his father who is away—will say goodnight to "the same moon" before going to sleep. Videos of actual military families depict their real-life experiences and the strategies they use when a mother or father is deployed, such as drawing and sending pictures, or having an adult help write a letter. And, when Elmo is confused by his nervous feelings when his father returns home, it is depicted in a manner that would be typical of a preschool child—he's excited to see his dad, but nervous too. Elmo's father explains that it is normal to have these feelings, and it might take a while to figure out how to be together again. Elmo uses a preschooler's language to describe what he is experiencing, and we see Elmo's father model appropriate listening skills, as well as age-appropriate explanations in his responses to Elmo.

Figure 14.4 Talking about deployment

Showing these videos to kids and asking follow-up questions may help them articulate verbally or in some other way what they themselves experience at these times (Tubbs, 2015). By providing *virtual peers* who appropriately express and model the feelings, behaviors, and experiences common to families facing similar challenges of having a deployed parent, the videos may prompt parents and children to articulate their own feelings and experiences. Another advantage of having a video component is that one can view it multiple times if necessary, and highlight any key moments that providers may feel would be most helpful to a particular child, teacher, or parent. These videos also provide basic information for educators and providers about the challenges children with a deployed parent may face and how to help them cope.

Death

Perhaps the most difficult experience for a young child is the death of a parent or other close family member, as explored by Linda Goldman in Chapter 1. Some estimate that 5 percent of children in the United States lose one or both parents by age 15 (The Dougy Center for Grieving Children, 2004), and suggest that the proportion is substantially higher in lower socioeconomic groups (Osterweis, Solomon, and Green, 1984). Emotional or social problems resulting from the death of a parent that are not adequately addressed can become sources for added difficulties in adulthood, including psychiatric difficulties (Busch and Kimble, 2001).

Children are especially vulnerable to psychological problems after the death of a parent. Their vulnerability may be exacerbated by survivors, who may not be able to provide sufficient comfort and support because of their own bereavement (Osterweis *et al.*, 1984). Moreover, as noted in this volume and elsewhere, special considerations should be given when working with young children: they do not yet comprehend the permanence of death, their emotions fluctuate, they worry about others in their lives and who will take care of them, and, like children dealing with incarceration, may blame themselves for what has happened to their parents (Busch and Kimble, 2001; The National Child Traumatic Stress Network, 2008).

The Sesame Workshop materials, *When Families Grieve*, is one tool those working with children can use to help ease a child's pain by supporting the expression of feelings, promoting open and age-appropriate communication about death and what it means, and providing concrete strategies and activities to help children and families cope.

The key messages for children in *When Families Grieve* are the following:

- There are things you should know about death.

- You might feel many different feelings and that is OK; what you are going through is normal.

- There are people who care about you and are there for you.

- Remember and talk about your loved one who died.

- You can be happy again.

Key messages for educators, adult caregivers, and parents include the following:

- Talk with your child.

- Help children adjust by providing structure.

- Take care of yourself.

The videos included in the Sesame Workshop resources illustrate these aspects of a young child's experience and understanding of death, and portray appropriate ways trusted adults could help them. As with other Sesame Workshop outreach initiatives, the main messages are emphasized throughout the various components of the project.

For example, in one of the *When Families Grieve* videos, Elmo is talking about his Uncle Jack with his father, and how Elmo cannot wait to see him at a picnic. Elmo's father explains that they had talked about how Uncle Jack died, and so cannot be at the picnic. When Elmo says he will just show it to Uncle Jack "next time" and that he can call him on the phone, his father explains, "When someone dies, their bodies stop working. They don't eat or breathe or talk on the phone. Uncle Jack died." (See Figure 14.5.) Elmo's father asks him if he has any questions, and a suddenly carefree Elmo asks if his father can help him put a kite together to take to the park.

Figure 14.5 When families grieve

The video can instruct caregivers by illustrating how an adult can talk openly and honestly about death, in language that a young child can understand. And by portraying how young children might act when discussing death, switching abruptly to another topic, the video also helps normalize what might seem like strange behaviors, which are actually not at all unusual. In Chapter 1, Goldman explores the common signs of grieving children, and the importance of normalizing unfamiliar grief reactions for bereaved families.

The storybook and live action videos with real families illustrate ways that children can remember their loved one, and how it is normal to feel different emotions.

Creating a memory box of special items that remind you of the person who died, celebrating their birthday, or doing things in their memory are a few suggested ways families can remember someone. Memory boxes and picture albums are important tools that enable children to share feelings and ideas. A memory table also allows kids to share meaningful objects that link them to loved ones (Goldman, 2014).

The videos and songs illustrate the different emotions one can feel, and explain that it is normal to have different feelings at the same time. Feeling angry and sad about someone dying, or relieved if someone has died after a long illness, is not unusual.

Showing these situations on Sesame Street helps normalize them, and can provide some comfort and reassurance. The videos may also serve as an avenue to explore children's feelings; after watching the videos or reading the storybook, children might be asked about how the characters were feeling or what they did, which may help spark discussion about children's own feelings (Amer, 1999).

Sesame Street's grief project (Figure 14.6) is able to meet the needs of adults who many find it difficult to tackle the challenging topic of death in ways that are comforting and developmentally appropriate for a child (Goldman, 2014).

Figure 14.6 Sesame Street's grief project

Addressing an international audience

Sesame Workshop reaches not only millions of kids within the United States, but also millions more beyond. Girls and boys all over the world feel the global reach of Sesame Workshop in over 30 international adaptations of Sesame Street.

As with vulnerable children, to reach children internationally, Sesame Workshop aims to create a place that will be familiar and safe. It is, therefore, crucial that international Sesame Street resources are culturally relevant, and include the familiar look and feel of the society in which children live. The importance of cultural context in the creation of these Sesame Street adaptations, or "co-productions," stems from the notion that a child learns best in a culturally relevant space (Rogoff, 2003). For this reason, Sesame Workshop ensures that the co-productions are indigenously produced: the production, research, and curriculum staff all hail from the country where the adaptation is being produced, and the curriculum and characters fit with the priorities and values of that country (Cole and Lee, 2016).

One example of this process is the creation of the Zari character (Figure 14.7) for the Sesame Street co-production in Afghanistan (*Baghch-e-Simsim*). Zari, an Afghan girl Muppet, serves as a model to Afghani children for girls' empowerment, physical well-being, nutrition, and diversity appreciation. By having Zari—who shares the language, culture, and appearance of an Afghani child—present these topics in age-appropriate and culturally appropriate ways, Afghani children will be more likely to attend to the messages *Baghch-e-Simsim* strives to convey.

Figure 14.7 Zari

Further, by including strong female characters like Zari who interact with their male counterparts in equal, supportive, and mutually respectful ways, Sesame Workshop productions convey positive messages of equity and kindness, and are able to do so in locations where young girls and women have limited social, educational, or professional opportunities (Cole and Lee, 2016).

Recommendations for educators

Educators play a unique role in a child's world, one that provides comfort, confidence, and encouragement. This role is especially important to young children in extraordinary circumstances, who may lack the knowledge and skills they need to cope, or even lack another consistent, caring adult in their lives. The Sesame Street resources described here enable educators to fulfill their role and help vulnerable children in concrete, age-appropriate ways. A few important recommendations for how educators can make best use of the resources might be helpful.

- *Keep in mind the main messages for children and educators in the resources.* The key messages are woven throughout the materials, and enable educators to easily reinforce and clarify them for the children in their care.

- *Encouraging children to express themselves, and empowering adults to engage children in age-appropriate conversations around even the most difficult topics, is a common goal for these Sesame Street initiatives.* It may seem daunting for even professional educators working with children to address difficult challenges when these situations are beyond the educator's own experience. When the popular characters on Sesame Street face the same challenging situation, educators are able to familiarize themselves with it, and also facilitate conversations by, for example, exploring with the child similarities between him/her and their familiar Sesame Street friends, or identifying the Sesame Street character's feelings and how to express the feelings appropriately.

- *Decide what tools best fit the child's and your program's needs.* Programs are different, as are the children being served. The Sesame Street resources are delivered in a variety of formats to allow children and educators to select what would work best for them. For programs with limited online connectivity, print resources may be a useful format. For a child who gravitates toward videos or interactive tools, educators may want to incorporate the online resources into their work with the child. Because all the components—online, print, video—all convey the same key messages, they can be used alone or together by educators to help the children in their care.

Conclusion

The Sesame Workshop initiatives described above share some key elements that help children, educators, and families, but also serve to guide and teach the dedicated provider who serves them. These elements include key messages of open, age-appropriate communication, and having an available and caring adult in the child's life. These messages are woven into the child-directed materials (videos, storybooks, and apps), and carry through to the adult-directed resources of the initiatives, specifically the caregiver guides and particular live-action videos. The simple, straightforward Muppet stories of Elmo and his furry friends as they navigate difficult situations with the help of caring adults are ideal vehicles for learning about topics such as deployment and incarceration, how young children might experience these situations, and how adults can help them cope. Listening to Elmo or his friends Alex and Jesse talk about a parent who died, or is deployed, or is incarcerated, imparts insight into what a child is feeling, while also providing basic information about these experiences. Adult-directed content provides additional information, in a simple, approachable style, about specific aspects of these experiences, such as the deployment cycle and how to cope, preparing for a visit with a parent in prison, or answering difficult questions a preschooler might ask about death.

Moreover, because these are media-based resources, they are extremely versatile, and can be used and accessed in a variety of settings at any time: home visits, school, clinics, trainings, parenting classes, community events, classrooms, or on the go. The downloadable materials were created so that they can be incorporated into existing programs and curricula, whenever providers would find it useful. The versatility of the content, combined with the friendly, familiar, and furry characters who live on Sesame Street, produce initiatives that strengthen understanding of the experiences of vulnerable children, highlight their needs and hopes, encourage and build a stronger capacity to learn, and enable educators, parents, and other caring adults to help these children cope.

References

Adalist-Estrin, A. (2011) 'Why maintain relationships?' *Children of Prisoners Library: Facts and Issues. CPL 102.* Available at www.fairshake.net/wp-content/uploads/2012/04/Children-of-Prisoners-Library.pdf, accessed on 05/04/17.

Amer, K. (1999) 'Bibliotherapy: Using fiction to help children in two populations discuss feelings.' *Pediatric Nursing 25*, 1, 91–95.

Busch, T. and Kimble, C. (2001) 'Grieving children: Are we meeting the challenge?' *Pediatric Nursing 27*, 4, 414–418.

Cole, C. and Lee, J. (2016) *The Sesame Effect: The Global Impact of the Longest Street in the World.* New York: Routledge.

Cozza, S.J., Chun, R.S., and Polo, J.A. (2005) 'Military families and children during Operation Iraqi Freedom.' *Psychiatric Quarterly 76*, 4, 371–378.

The Dougy Center for Grieving Children (2004) *Helping Children Cope with Death.* Portland, OR: The Dougy Center for Grieving Children.

Fisch, S. and Truglio, R. (2000) *G is for Growing: 30 Years of Research on Sesame Street.* New York: Lea's Communications Series.

Fritsch, T.A. and Burkhead, J.D. (1981) 'Behavioral reactions of children to parental absence due to imprisonment.' *Family Relations*, 83–88.

Goldman, L. (2014) *Life and Loss: A Guide to Help Grieving Children, 3rd Edition.* New York: Taylor and Francis.

Hairston, C.F. (2007) *Focus on Children with Incarcerated Parents: An Overview of the Research Literature.* Available at https://repositories.lib.utexas.edu/bitstream/handle/2152/15158/AECasey_Children_IncParents.pdf?sequence=2, accessed on 04/04/17.

Harris, Y.R. and Graham, J.A. (2010) *Children of Incarcerated Parents: Theoretical Developmental and Clinical Issues.* New York: Springer.

Kotler, P., Roberto, N., and Lee, N.R. (2002) *Social Marketing: Improving the Quality of Life.* Thousand Oaks, CA: Sage.

Lauricella, A.R., Gola, A.A.H., and Calvert, S.L. (2011) 'Toddlers' learning from socially meaningful video characters.' *Media Psychology 14*, 2, 216–232.

MacDermid, S.M., Samper, R., Schwarz, R., Nishida, J., and Nyaronga, D. (2008) *Understanding and Promoting Resilience in Military Families.* West Lafayette, IN: Military Family Research Institute, Purdue University.

McCubbin, H.G.A. and McCubbin, M. (1996) *Family Assessment: Resiliency, Coping and Adaptation—Inventories for Research and Practice.* Madison, WI: University of Wisconsin.

McGuire, W.J. (1989) 'Theoretical Foundations of Campaigns.' In R.E. Rice and C.A. Atkin (eds) *Public Communication Campaigns, 2nd Edition.* Newbury Park, CA: Sage.

National Child Traumatic Stress Network, The (2008) *Traumatic grief in military children: Information for families.* Available at http://www.nctsnet.org/nctsn_assets/pdfs/Military_Grief_Families_final3.pdf, accessed on 01/01/16.

Oades-Sese, G., Cohen, D., Allen, J., and Lewis, M. (2014) 'Building Resilience the Sesame Street Way.' In S. Prince-Embury and D. Saklofske (eds) *Resilience Interventions for Youth in Diverse Populations.* New York: Springer.

Osterweis, M., Solomon, F., and Green, F. (1984) *Bereavement: Reactions, Consequences, and Care.* Washington, DC: National Academy Press.

Rogoff, B. (2003) *The Cultural Nature of Human Development.* New York: Oxford University Press.

Sesame Street in Communities (n.d.) *Ask Me Anything*. Available at www.sesamestreetincommunities. org/activities/ask-me-anything, accessed on 05/04/17.

Tubbs, A. (2015) *Bibliotherapy for Children Coping with a Loved One's Military Deployment: What do Children's Books Tell Us?* Available at http://scholarsarchive.byu.edu/etd/4391, accessed on 02/26/16.

Chapter 15

Catching Kids Before They Fall

A PRINCIPAL'S PERSPECTIVE

Jim Sporleder

My goal in this chapter is to reach you through your heart so that I may introduce a "new lens" of seeing, a way to gain a greater understanding of students that come to school with challenging issues that can interfere with your day as the leader in your building, or disrupt the learning environment in your classrooms. Consider a few reflective questions. Are you spending so much time on behavior issues in the office that you feel it's interfering with your ability to be the instructional leader you have been trained to be? Are the behavior challenges that you are seeing in the classroom getting better each year, or are they becoming increasingly overwhelming? Are the behaviors you are seeing in your classroom interfering with your ability to teach? My last question: Is your own personal stress level increasing each year in managing the escalated behaviors you are seeing? As I travel the country, I hear the same stories from teachers: "We spend the majority of our time managing behavior rather than covering the content that we are responsible for to prepare our students, and get them ready for the high-stakes testing that we are being evaluated on with students' test scores."

A core problem we face today is one of emotional dysregulated adults working with emotional dysregulated students. It is not a good combination when they interact together. NoBullying.com (2015) defines emotional dysregulation as

> a condition in which the person cannot effectively modulate his or her emotions... In children [it] is marked by extreme emotional instability, above and beyond the normal ups and downs of regular

mood swings. Often, the child's response to the world around him is inappropriate… A child with Emotional Dysregulation may react more negatively than would be expected. The child may scream, cry, throw things, or challenge the teacher further.

As we begin to gain a greater understanding of our students, we are more prepared to gain a greater understanding of ourselves. Educators are people that have normal triggers that push buttons. Unless we truly understand our students, we can't incorporate the understanding that their behavior is not about us. Their behavior is about what they may be experiencing outside of school or from past traumatic events. Students do not wake up in the morning and plan how to destroy our day. Many students wake up in the morning in a toxic environment of fear, abuse, or neglect. Adults responsible as caregivers may have caused the deep-seated pain within these students.

Another pattern I have noticed in my travels is the development within a school of a list of the top ten disrupters in a school building. It takes very little time for that list to be formulated. Implementing some trauma-informed strategies, Lincoln High School staff members were able to remove a high percentage of students from their list of "Students of Concern" once the action plan was developed and put into action.

What is changing the landscape of our classrooms and schools?

Longhi and colleagues present the Adverse Childhood Experiences (ACEs) research (2015), which, together with our increased knowledge about the impact of trauma on the developing brain, tells us that the percentage of trauma-impacted students entering our classrooms is on the rise. In Washington State alone, we know that 45 percent of a class of 30 students has been impacted by the ACEs they bring with them to the classroom. What does that look like?

This provides a more accurate picture of our classrooms, and it helps understand "why" you are feeling additional stress, and "why" you are seeing the increase in disruptive behaviors. If we look at the "Zero Tolerance Policies" that have been around for just over 20 years, we see that they are failing miserably. In fact, the research shows that our schools are no safer today than when these policies were put into place (American Psychological Association Zero Tolerance Task Force, 2008). When you combine the ineffectiveness of these policies with the *Pipeline to Prison* research (Losen, 2015), the compelling fact is that excessive suspension of students for mundane infractions has nothing to do with making our schools safer. What is also disturbing about this study is that the suspension of minority students is disproportionately more than their white peers for the same infractions. The research indicates that the younger students are when suspended from school, the higher the likelihood that these students will fall on the slippery slope into our prison system.

> If the only tool you have is a hammer, you tend to see everything as a nail. (Maslow, 1966, p.15)

Take some time to reflect on Maslow's statement. If a student's behavior doesn't change after being hit by the hammer, what is our normal practice? We use progressive discipline and we hit the student with a harder consequence over and over again. The students we keep using traditional punishment with to correct their behavior are the very students that begin to disengage from the learning environment and eventually disconnect themselves from school. We have to put the hammer down and look at our students with empathy, not as a nail to be hit until we influence them in becoming a high school dropout.

As I take a step back and look at our educational system, I see too many of our students falling without a caring adult relationship(s) present to catch them. These are the students that the system labels and judges within our schools. We label them as being lazy and unmotivated, classroom disrupters, defiant, and disengaged, and we predict that they will end up dropping out of school. What is so discouraging is that our predictions are more accurate than not.

Why we need a "New Approach to School Discipline"

First, we need to look at what neuroscience tells us about brain development and how it impacts behavior before we can accept that traditional disciplinary practices are no longer effective with a high percentage of our students. It will require the reader to look deeply into current disciplinary practices and, hopefully at the end of this chapter, make the paradigm shift to look at each student with a deeper understanding: to see that the behavior is not about *you*, the behavior is about the student. It's critical to understand that the "caregiver" of the child may be responsible for some of their brain development. Kids raised in a toxic home environment can have higher levels of cortisol flooding their brains, which puts them into a Fight-Flight-Freeze mode. Their homes may be so unpredictable that they develop survival brains. These aren't bad brains, they are brains that are a result of the dysfunction, abuse, and violence they are either the witness to, or the victim of. When students are in the high-escalated state, they physiologically cannot take in new knowledge or problem solve.

As Dr. John Medina, author of *Brain Rules* (2014), shares, when our traumatized students are in the escalated state of Fight-Flight-Freeze, their behavior is out of their control. Our traditional way of addressing a student who is escalated is to confront them, which escalates the student to a higher emotional state and defiance. Traditional thinking is that the student is choosing to misbehave and needs immediate consequences. The traditional approach to discipline is to react to the behavior and then tell the student the consequence when they are already escalated. Heather T. Forbes, in her book *Help for Billy* (2012), explains that when we reprimand or give consequences to a student that is highly escalated, it is like trying to communicate with a lizard brain. The student at that moment does not have the ability to problem solve or connect with our reaction. Figure 15.1 illustrates why these students are not prepared to learn from their emotional dysregulation, unless we, the adult, teach them.

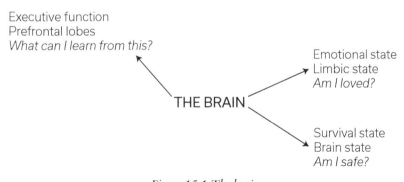

Figure 15.1 The brain

Most children that come from healthy homes and families come to school ready to learn. They function from the prefrontal lobes, where they can demonstrate their ability to learn and to problem solve. These students understand the cause and effect of their behavior and academic achievement. The trauma-impacted student influenced by toxic homes and toxic caregivers may be functioning from the lower parts of the brain and cannot understand cause and effect. They come to us lagging behind developmentally and cannot problem solve nor take in new knowledge when they are in this emotional state.

As you can see from Figure 15.1, the trauma-impacted student isn't functioning anywhere near the frontal lobes and physiologically can't learn when escalated. It is out of their control and they are dependent upon caring adults at school to teach them how to self-regulate and feel safe. Knowing that brain development is the responsibility of the "caregiver," neuroscience tells us that the brain drives behavior. Therefore the students that we see disrupting our classes do not respond to traditional consequences, which are mainly focused on punishment. The thought is that if we provide the right punishment, the student will learn a lesson and won't be eager to misbehave again. However, the reality is that the students do not connect the dots of their behavior with the consequences. We need a new approach that will teach our students how to come down from an escalated state to a calm emotional state. We then have the opportunity to teach self-regulation.

With a trauma-informed model, these kids can thrive over time. This paradigm shift in our approach is an effective method that still sets boundaries, holds students accountable, and teaches students how to use specific strategies to calm down. When a student is calm, you can help them move from the lower part of their brains to the prefrontal lobes where they can learn and problem solve. It is critical to know that the behavior you are witnessing is rooted in fear, fear of failure, and not feeling emotionally or physically safe.

I was invited to attend the Hope to Resilience Conference in the spring of 2010. It became the beginning of my transformation.

When I returned to Lincoln High School after attending the Hope to Resilience Conference, I felt like I had been hit by a lightning bolt after hearing Dr. John Medina's keynote presentation. I was so moved by his presentation that I began searching for a curriculum to help implement trauma-informed practices into Lincoln High School. I learned very quickly there was no curriculum. I realized we needed to use the trauma-informed theory to discover concepts necessary to implement into schools that were aligned with current research. This led me to eventually co-write a curriculum for schools, *The Trauma Informed School* (Sporleder and Forbes, 2016).

Before asking staff to change their approach to student discipline, I first had to change my approach. Moving away from my traditional disciplinarian practices was a big adjustment for me. One challenge when I arrived at Lincoln was the disregard of authority and reasonable requests. The common response from the students was F--- you, or F--- off, or completely ignoring a staff request. For example, students would walk into class and put their feet up on the desk with a defiant "I don't have to do what I don't want to do." When a student was asked politely to remove their feet from the desk, it was "F--- you." "Please take your head phones off while I'm teaching." "F--- you." Student walking out of class without permission: "You'll need to stay in class—please return to your seat…" "F--- you." I observed very quickly that the disregard of a reasonable request from staff had to be addressed with strong discipline, and it had to be very consistent.

In my traditional style, I gave students a three-day-out-of-school suspension for any time they directed their "F--- you" to a staff member. If the student escalated in my office, I added additional days. I had never experienced a school culture so out of control and influenced by specific gang members who kept the tension very high and unpredictable. To gain control, I used out-of-school suspensions and had students arrested for any disorderly conduct, any gang conflict, any assaults and fights, and any verbal threats to a staff member. Slowly, the tension in the building began to come down, and the kids began to understand that safety was a top priority of mine.

Implementing a trauma-informed approach for our students

I began moving away from out-of-school suspensions, and towards keeping students in school as much as possible for disciplinary consequences. I assigned In-School Suspension (ISS) for infractions that would have been out-of-school discipline before my new learning. What I quickly noticed was that students were begging me to give them out-of-school consequences rather than coming to school and being placed in the ISS room. When I asked why they preferred suspension to being assigned to ISS, many responded, "ISS is boring and I would rather be out of school." I knew I was on the right track when I finally realized that, for many students suspended out of school, it is a free day without any supervision from home. I also realized keeping kids in school was a more effective form of accountability than giving free days out of school. This accountability piece was holding them accountable to attending school, not lying around at home or roaming the streets. Students began keeping up with their school work rather than coming back after a 3–5-day suspension which put them further behind in their school work and set them up for failure.

The value of students being supervised by a caring adult was palpable. It resulted in building positive relationships with the students being assigned to ISS. It is critical to have the right supervisor in the ISS room. The person must know when a student needs some time to process, and when to be firm and have students engaged with their school work. If that person sets the ISS room up as a punitive consequence, it is set up to fail. There will always be infractions that require an out-of-school consequence or legal action, but what I learned during the years we were trauma-informed was that developing positive relationships with students teaches them alternative ways to handle specific situations, such as communicating to teachers before they are triggered to react from their brain stem. Teaching them about how to respond when they feel triggered provided options they could use to self-regulate. Even in situations when infractions required out-of-school suspensions or legal interventions, relationships could be nurtured and developed.

Teachers provide a trauma-informed approach with students

A kindergarten teacher, Mrs. Pearl, shared the following story with me: "I have a little guy, Joey, who is really struggling. His emotional outbursts can be unpredictable. He goes into a rage and can present himself as a safety threat to the classmates. The other day he took off his shoes and threw them against the wall, frightening the other children. I approached the little guy in a calm manner, wrapped my arms around him, and said, 'You're safe, let's step out in the hallway.'" He was escalated, screaming that he didn't want to go to the hallway, and he wanted to fight. Mrs. Pearl explained she took Joey outside the classroom and sat down on a chair with her arms around him. She told me his heart was beating so hard that her hand was moving with the beat of his chest. She stayed calm, held him, kept telling him he was safe, and asked him to breathe with her (she had taught her class breathing techniques, so this was not something new to Joey).

At first Joey did not want to breathe, but with reassurance that he was safe and getting help, he began to do his favorite breathing exercise, taking deep breaths and letting them out. Mrs. Pearl's hand began to settle as the boy's heart rate came down. Finally, she couldn't even feel the boy's beating heart. Joey let out a big breath and said, "I'm OK now." Then he began to cry. "I just want to be back in the blue house, I want my mommy." You see, the blue house was the last time he was with his mom before she was sent to prison on drug charges. His father took him and moved in with his grandmother. Soon after, Dad abandoned Joey. In Chapter 8, Cortina and Trutt present a resourceful project, *Get on the Bus*, that helps children and teens bond with incarcerated family members. *Get on the Bus* is an empowering tool for students and an effective resource for educators.

In our traditional practices, we would have called the office and asked that the boy be removed from the classroom. There is a very good chance that Joey would have been sent home for the day, only reinforcing the pain and abandonment he might already have felt inside. It could also send a message to Joey that he is bad, and unworthy to stay in school. *With the trauma approach, he was loved, taught a strategy to help him calm down, and was able to see his teacher as a safe adult.* Later in the day, he told the teacher, "I love you and wish I could live with you." Did the little guy stop having emotional outbursts? No, but they started to happen less frequently, and he trusted his teacher as a safe adult who was there to help him. Not all of our students come to us with the healthy brain development necessary to behave appropriately. Many struggling students need caring adults in their lives capable of teaching them the resiliency skills needed to change behavior strategies to self-regulate. As Craig explains at the end of Chapter 4, "Trauma-sensitive schools do not replace learning with discipline. Rather, they rely on positive relationships and neurologically based instruction to nurture children's inherent capacity for self-regulation, and increase their capacity for academic achievement and social mastery."

A trauma-informed model

At Lincoln we began to implement a trauma-informed model school-wide. The staff learned the following three essential concepts and they became daily practice for the majority of our school staff:

- Drop your personal mirror; the behavior is not about you, it is about what the student is going through.

- Do not confront the behavior when a student is highly escalated. Have systems in place to allow the student time to calm down. If you confront the student during the emotional upset, you will escalate their behavior. When they have calmed down, they are ready to problem solve and learn.

- Develop understanding of why we would use this approach.

Research validates that when we create positive adult relationships with students, we have the opportunity to influence their life path. We become a part of their life that teaches resiliency, and helps them discover their self-worth and value. Trauma-impacted students with no interventions cannot see beyond tomorrow. They feel hopelessness. They have been beaten down much of their lives, and the predictable outcomes with no intervention may be more accurate than for those who come from poverty. With positive adult interventions, a student can find healing that leads to hope for their future. That outcome is what should drive us to change our paradigm around school discipline. Adults have the opportunity to be that one person that can change the outcome from hopelessness to *hope*. That is a priceless gift we can offer our struggling students. We can do this by adhering to the following three concepts:

- Drop our personal mirror.

- Allow students time to de-escalate.

- Provide a caring adult relationship that influences resilience and hope.

The following is an example of a trauma-informed strategy using these concepts.

A CASE STUDY: TRAUMA-INFORMED STRATEGIES AT THE SECONDARY LEVEL

A neighbor called Lincoln High School reporting students smoking pot in the alley behind their house. When our School Resource Officer (SRO) and Intervention Specialist responded, the students saw the SRO's car coming and one of them threw the pot off to the side. Then the three students were brought back to school, obviously highly under the influence. They were separated before talking about the incident. The SRO, Intervention Specialist, and I each had one student to interview. When I looked into the eyes of Tony, the student in my office, he appeared to have been smoking pot heavily.

My conversation started out like this: "Tony, I can tell that you are smoking a lot of pot, just by looking into your eyes. I'm not judging you, but something tells me you must be under a lot of stress to be smoking this heavily." Tony slowly looked up at me and nodded his head. I continued: "Tony, you don't have to answer my question, but if I were to ask you where your stress level is from a 1–10 scale, where would you tell me it would be?" Tony's response was: "I am at a ten." I thanked him for sharing and then I told him that a stress level of ten was too much for one person to carry or be able to function. I followed up with: "Tony, are you smoking pot before you come to school?" His response was "Yes." I then asked, "Tony, are you smoking pot every day at lunch?" Tony responded yes. I then asked: "Tony, are you smoking pot in the evening as well?" Tony again responded yes. I then shared: "Tony, you don't have to answer this last question, but we need to wrap some support around you so that you don't have to smoke that much pot to handle your stress level."

Tony looked up at me and said: "Sporleder, I can't smoke enough pot to block the thoughts that are going through my head." I asked if he felt comfortable telling me what those thoughts were. Tony responded: "Sporleder, I lost my older sister in a house fire. Everyone got out of the house except my sister. It haunts me that I wasn't there to save her." Then tears started streaming down his face as he shared that he wasn't there for his youngest sister who was just four years old when beaten to death by her foster parent.

At this point he was sobbing: "I should have been there to save my little sister, I would never have allowed anyone to beat her." I just listened and validated how sorry I was that he was carrying such a heavy load. I told Tony: "I couldn't even imagine how painful your experiences have been. What I can tell you is that I *love* you and I would like to offer help from our health center so that you can get support from a person who has expertise in helping kids who have had horrible things happen in their lives. I would never try to force anyone into counseling, but I want to offer you the opportunity to have someone help you with the enormous amount of stress that you are under. You can't function with the level of stress you are carrying, and you can't function with the amount of pot you are smoking to try and block out the tormented thoughts going through your head." Tony looked up at me and said he would like to try the counseling.

In a trauma-informed approach, the accountability comes at the end of the conversation. I then said: "Tony, you are under the influence at a level in which you won't be able to function in your classes." I told him that I was going to send him home for one day, but before I let him go, I wanted to walk him to the health center, introduce him, and make an appointment for when he returned to school. At that time we still did not know which of the students threw the pot to the side before our SRO pulled up. Therefore, we had students under the influence, but no charge for possession of the pot.

Before taking Tony to the health center, he disclosed: "Sporleder, I am the one who threw out the pot when I saw [the SRO] Matt's car." I responded that it takes character to be able to come forward and take responsibility, and that I admired that quality that he was displaying. However, I shared with him that, by telling us he was in possession, Matt would have to cite him, and he would have to go to court for the citation. Tony nodded his head and said: "I understand." Then Tony asked me for a favor, and I said of course! "I live with my uncle and we are moving to a new apartment—would you mind giving me one more day out so I can help the family move?" I granted his request.

Over the weeks ahead, I saw a new person transforming. Tony shared that the counseling sessions were really helping him a lot. I could see his face clearing up and a daily smile as I checked in on him. A couple of months later, I called Tony to my office to let him know about the positive changes I was seeing in him. I said once again that he did not have to answer my question, but I felt I could tell he wasn't using pot to try and drown out his thoughts and feelings. Tony smiled and said: "Sporleder, I might smoke pot once a week. The counseling and this school have helped me more than I can say." We hugged and I sent him back to his classroom. *In a trauma-informed model, you can't always reach 100 percent of the students, but you can love them unconditionally 100 percent of the time.*

Teacher examples of using trauma-informed practices

One of the biggest mistakes I have seen in classrooms is not understanding that trauma-informed practices are for all of our students. A second grade teacher shared that one of her students, who came from a wonderful home, walked into her class one morning and was very upset and quiet. The teacher approached the student and quietly said, "Honey, you seem very upset today, is there anything that I can help you with or that you might want to share?" The little girl just broke down and sobbed. It took some time before she finally was able to explain that her parents had euthanized their dog and she was very sad. Then the little girl said her daddy went on a business trip. She missed him and that made her sad too. The teacher validated the girl's feelings and told her that if she needed anything during the day to just come and ask. Before the little girl left for home, she expressed how much she appreciated her teacher's help and thanked her.

A second student that came to school that day also looked very upset and ready to burst into tears. The teacher approached the second student in the same manner. "Honey, you really look like you are upset, is there anything that I can do for you to help you with your feelings?" The second student shared, "Daddy beat Mommy up last night and I'm scared." The same exact approach was taken with the two students, but with different interventions and procedures for the student who witnessed her daddy beating her mommy up. I hope you can see the value in how the teacher approached both students.

For a trauma-informed approach to be effective, the systems and practices must be put in place for the students to access. At Lincoln, students were taught about their emotional triggers, and allowed to request a timeout if they felt they were going to have an emotional blow up. This allowed students to identify their triggers and use the timeout opportunity to self-regulate.

Educators have asked me, "How long was your line to get into timeout so that the student didn't have to do their class work?" The answer is that there was never a line. When you are in positive relationships with your students, they appreciate the opportunity to have choices so that they remain regulated. We allowed students to stay in timeout (ISS room) until they felt they were able to handle returning back to their schedule. If a student needed to spend the rest of the day in timeout, we made sure they got their class work so that they would not fall behind. Sometimes we became aware that a student experienced a horrible night due to family issues, homeless issues, or an early morning drug raid by SWAT. We would let them know we were aware of their rough night and allow them to go to the ISS room and get some sleep on the sofa there.

Educators often ask, "How long was the line for those wanting to avoid going to classes and were making up stories to evade class?" My answer is that there was never a line. In fact, I usually saw the student sent to ISS for sleep back in the flow of their school day in just a short time. Checking in on them, students shared that they felt rested enough to go back to class. When you create positive adult relationships, kids appreciate the care and rarely take advantage of the offer.

I also allowed teachers to ask students if they needed a timeout, or ask them to go to timeout, so that they could talk about the issue later. These examples are based on building a good momentum of success in school. One student told a visitor, "I love my school. The staff here care about all the students, like a family."

Creating meaningful conversation

Whenever approaching a disruptive student or one that is starting to escalate, approach them calmly, and speak in a quiet voice so others can't hear the interaction. Conversations are as simple as the following examples:

"Why did you pull me out into the hall!" "Because I respect you and did not want to have this conversation in front of your peers."

"I'm trying to teach and you are making it difficult for me by being disruptive. What do you need from me right now so that I can teach and your needs are met?"

"I wanted to check in with you. You seem like you are really upset and it's making it hard for me to be able to teach. Are you OK? What do you think will help you so that I can teach? You know how much I care about you, but you are so disruptive right now; I want you to go to Shelly in the ISS room and take a timeout. You're welcome back this period if you feel you can come back and engage in the class work."

"It seems like you didn't get much sleep last night, so how about putting your head down on the desk and resting—that way you are OK and I can teach."

"John, you know I hate writing referrals to the office, but everything that I have tried to help you isn't working. Maybe you need some time to talk with Sporleder or Brooke; I care about you, it's just not working out today."

We had one boy at Lincoln who always wanted to just put his head down on his desk. If someone walked by the room, they might think he was disengaged and not having a good day. Actually his teacher had asked him not to blurt out answers and to give other kids a chance to respond. He decided that putting his head on the desk would help him do that. So what a passerby saw wasn't necessarily what was actually happening. The student looked disengaged, but was actually participating.

If we look at Maslow's hierarchy...

Maslow's research tells us that if we don't meet the social and emotional needs of our students, we will get very little bumps of growth in academic achievement and see a higher dropout rate. Statistics on discipline data at Lincoln from 2009 to 2013 indicate a reduction from 600 referrals to 320, 280, and 242 by 2013. The number of students out of school ranged from 768 to 96 in suspensions and 50 to 0 in expulsions from 2009 to 2013. Graduation rates from 2009 to 2014 (Figure 15.2) indicate great progress experienced at Lincoln High School when a trauma-informed model was implemented for our students, starting in the school year 2010–2011. It should be noted that our students averaged 3.5 ACEs in 2010–2011, 4.5 ACEs in 2011–2012, and 5.5 ACEs in 2012–2013, the year in which *Paper Tigers*, a documentary chronicling this work at Lincoln High, was filmed (Redford, 2013).

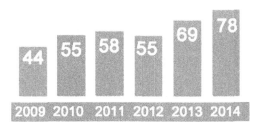

Figure 15.2 Lincoln High School graduation rates

Lincoln High research report

In 2013–2014, a study was conducted at Lincoln High to examine the impact of the trauma-sensitive practices we had introduced. The following is a summary of the Longhi *et al.* (2015) research report:

> On average, students at this school accumulated five out of ten Adverse Childhood Experiences (ACEs), about four times the average number of ACEs among students in Washington State (Longhi, 2010). Research has shown that these accumulated traumas result in students having not only a higher probability of behavioral and health disorders, but also tend to have greater difficulties in learning, all leading to a lower likelihood of academic success (Blodgett, 2012; Longhi, 2010; Shonkoff, 2012). Washington State reports and a recent national study have found that resilience can moderate some of ACEs' negative effects (Bethel *et al.*, 2014). This study tests the effects of specific practices and student experiences that lead to increased resilience, which then moderates ACE effects on school performance.
>
> In 2009–2013, a systematic attempt was made by teachers and staff at Lincoln High to transform the culture and interactions at the school in order to become sensitive and supportive of such heavily traumatized youth, and to increase their resilience and their capacity to learn. Four systemic "virtuous cycles" were identified as having been implemented at the school, each reinforcing different values and behaviors—among teachers and staff, between teachers/staff and students, and among students themselves—all supporting a safe, supportive learning environment. Since these changes were made, fewer discipline problems and suspensions have occurred, and the school has achieved a higher student retention rate. (p.1)

Students' voices at Lincoln High

> *"Yes, I struggled, with anger or depression, for weeks at a time. I felt there was no point in doing things I enjoyed because I was always alone. Now, not often; I have people to encourage me and share my experiences. I am determined to have something to be proud of. I am determined to go to [postsecondary] school…here I made friends quickly and I finally had people to rely on, support, and understand me. Or just be silly with."*
> *(Longhi et al., 2015, p.1)*

"The most significant change is that I finally figured out what I want to do with my life and that I have friends, students, staff, and my family (which may as well be the people of Lincoln as well as my parents) there to support me..." (Longhi et al. 2015, p.1)

Research conclusions

This study of Lincoln High quantitatively measured student resilience, both overall and in three underlying dimensions: supportive relationships, problem solving, and optimism. It assessed the increase in resilience for each student and its association with important student experiences, ones that were expected to occur due to changes in systemic, trauma-sensitive, school practices. Qualitative evidence on students' levels of resilience, based on student responses to open-ended questions, provided insights on student struggles with trauma and how resilience differed between students who remained trauma victims and those who were able to become survivors and thrivers.

The study then tested the relationship between resilience and school performance. Results confirmed that more resilient students had statistically significant better school outcomes on various measures of school performance: fewer absences, better reading and math scores on standardized tests, and, finally, higher grades.

Finally, the study found that, among the highly resilient students, about 70 percent of Lincoln High students with resilience-moderated ACEs were expected to have a negative impact on their school performance. Yet, these findings show that community-supported, systemic changes in school practices, ones developed to be sensitive to students' ACEs and involving interrelated "virtuous cycles," have beneficial effects by increasing student resilience for a majority of students and significantly improving school performance, even among students with disproportionately high ACEs.

Lincoln: A new school name and a new school culture

I had lived in the community long enough to know the negative labels that were used to describe Paine Alternative High School students (Lincoln's original name when I first became their principal). The last few weeks of school, I could feel that we had turned the corner and had momentum to start the new school year. I approached my staff with the idea of changing the school name and starting the new school year with the upward movement we began to see amongst our students. The staff presented the idea to the students and they bought into the idea of a new name and a new reputation. We lined a hallway with all the names that students had come up with, although there were a few names that we didn't include. It was our students that chose the name Lincoln Alternative High School, and they chose the Phoenix as the mascot.

Our teachers helped the students come up with a proposal to take to our school board requesting the change in name from Paine to Lincoln. The school board approved the change, and our journey started as Lincoln. The announcement was made in the local newspaper, and a few days later, a visitor came to see me. When I came out of my office to meet her, I was taken aback by a very kind, elderly woman who asked for a few minutes with me. As I welcomed her into my office, I noticed she had something in her hand that was wrapped. She shared that she wanted to give me a gift, and handed me a beautiful china plate with a hand painting of Lincoln High School in the middle of the plate.

This sweet lady explained that not many people in the community were aware that there was a Lincoln High School built on the same footprint as Paine in the latter part of the 1800s. The painting was an original, and over 100 years old. I shared with her that the kids had chosen the Phoenix as the mascot, and that it was a powerful story to know that Lincoln High School was reborn and its mascot symbolized coming out of the ashes. What a wonderful gift from one of our caring members of our community!

Recommendations for educators: A positive approach

- *Change of name:* As we started our new journey as Lincoln High School, we had meaningful conversations with students in regards to our new name, and what we needed to do as a school to begin a new culture that demonstrated to our community that we were a positive school doing positive things.

- *Outreach to community:* Students were placed into the community with our school colors, purple and silver. It's pretty hard not to notice kids in purple shirts. Students participated in community activities, allowing kids to be seen contributing in a positive manner, not as they had been previously labeled when we were Paine High School.

- *Creating a new culture*: Students were buying into our new culture, and we were adding programs and opportunities that made us look like a normal school with electives, sports activities, monthly assemblies, a school prom, and a yearbook class that designed the theme and format for our first hardcover student yearbook.

- *Media attention*: The community started to notice us as Lincoln High. We attracted the attention of our local newspaper, which started reporting the positive things we were doing as a school.

- *A classroom is for learning, not disrupting*: We were still dealing with behavior issues and we adopted the motto *Failure Isn't an Option* to address that the classroom was for learning, not disrupting. We developed the phrase: "When you come on Lincoln campus, you leave your gang colors on the curb, and when you are in school, it is for learning and supporting you to graduate from high school and beyond."

Conclusion

I refer to this time as a journey, because it took hard work and consistency to keep the momentum moving forward. Little did we know how Lincoln's transformation would come through learning about trauma-informed practices, and watching our students thrive. We were getting positive press, our community was standing behind us, but none of us could have predicted the outcomes when Lincoln High School became one of the first high schools in the country to become a trauma-informed school.

Once I became trauma-informed and grew a deeper understanding of what our kids were going through, I walked away from my strong traditional disciplinary practices. I learned quickly that the Zero Tolerance policies had no positive effect, and we were missing the root of the problem. Once I left my traditional past, what my students taught me about resilience transformed me. I learned the power of a caring adult relationship, and how we can influence a life path. When you look at Lincoln's statistical data and transformation, you will see the power of our paradigm shift and how it has impacted our students.

References

American Psychological Association Zero Tolerance Task Force (2008) 'Are zero tolerance policies effective in the schools? An evidentiary review and recommendations.' *American Psychologist 63*, 852–862.

Bethel, C.D., Newacheck, P., Hawes, E., and Halfon, N. (2014) 'Adverse Childhood Experiences: Assessing the impact on health and school engagement and the mitigating role of resilience.' *Health Affairs 33*, 12, 2106–2115.

Blodgett, C. (2012) *Adopting ACEs Screening and Assessment in Child-Serving Systems.* Available at http://ext100.wsu.edu/cafru/wp-content/uploads/sites/65/2015/03/Complex-Trauma-Research-ACE-Screening-and-Assessment-in-Child-Serving-Systems-7-12-final. pdf, accessed on 05/04/17.

Forbes, H.T. (2012) *Help for Billy: A Beyond Consequences Approach to Helping Challenging Children in the Classroom.* Boulder, CO: Beyond Consequences Institute.

Longhi, D. (2010) *The Relationship between Two Kinds of Adverse Experiences (AEs) and Academic, Behavorial, and Physical Health among Youth in Washington State.* Olympia, WA: Family Policy Council.

Longhi, D., Barila, T., Motulsky, W., and Friel, H. (2015) *Higher Resilience and School Performance among Students with Disproportionately High Childhood Adverse Experiences (ACE) in Lincoln High School, Walla Walla, Washington, 2009–2013: Research Report.* Walla Walla, Washington. Available at www.acesconnection.com/fileSendAction/ fcType/0/fcOid/419152459946645755/filePointer/419434030785671226/ fodoid/419434030785671222/LH%20report%20final.pdf, accessed on 05/04/17.

Losen, D. (2015) *The School to Prison Pipeline: What Research Says about Contributing Factors and Remedies.* Center for Civil Rights Remedies, at UCLA's Civil Rights Project. Available at http://cebcp.org/wp-content/CB2015/Losen.pdf, accessed on 09/13/16.

Maslow, A. (1966) *The Psychology of Science: A Reconnaissance.* New York: Harper and Row.

Maslow, A. (2013) *A Theory of Human Motivation.* Seaside, OR: Rough Draft Printing.

Medina, J. (2010) Keynote speech at Hope to Resilience Conference, Spokane, WN. Available at http://communityresiliencecookbook.org/tastes-of-success/the-walla-walla-washington-story, accessed on 07/18/17.

Medina, J. (2014) *Brain Rules: 12 Principles for Surviving and Thriving at Work, Home, and School, 2nd Updated and Expanded Edition.* Seattle, WA: Pear Press.

NoBullying.com (2015) *The Concept of Emotional Dysregulation in Children.* Available at https:// nobullying.com/emotional-dysregulation, accessed on 07/28/16.

Redford, J. (2013) *Paper Tigers.* KPJR Films.

Shonkoff, J.P. (2012) 'Leveraging the biology of adversity to address the roots of disparities in health and development.' *Proceedings of the National Academy of Sciences 109* (Supplement 2), 17302–17307.

Sporleder, J. and Forbes, H. (2016) *The Trauma Informed School: A Step-by-Step Implementation Guide for Administrators and School Personnel.* Boulder, CO: Beyond Consequences Institute.

Chapter 16

Love, Try, One

SUPPORTING RESILIENCE IN STUDENTS

Sara Truebridge

Looking out

As a professional in the field of resilience, I bring a strengths-based perspective to my work with students. This work focuses on the area of resilience in the context of education. In simple terms, resilience refers to the self-righting and transcending capacity to spring back, rebound, and successfully adapt in the face of loss, trauma, adversity, and/or everyday stress. Usually words flow, but not lately. I sit here in front of my computer today as I have days before and see a blank screen. Not because I have a blank brain, but rather because my brain is being overridden by a heavy heart.

This heavy heart is in response to the current news of the world—the news of the July 14, 2016 terrorist attack in Nice, France, that left 84 dead and 202 injured (Rubin *et al.*, 2016); the news of July 10, 2016 that elicited the *New York Times* headline to read "America Grieves, Tense and Wary" following three shootings: Alton Sterling in Baton Rouge, Louisiana; Philando Castile in Falcon Heights, Minnesota; and the attack by a lone shooter in Dallas, Texas, who gunned down police officers, leaving five dead (Achenbach *et al.*, 2016). These events come on the heels of another recent event recognized as the deadliest mass shooting in the United States and the nation's worst terror attack since 9/11. On June 12, 2016 a lone shooter entered a gay nightclub in Orlando, Florida, killing 49 people and wounding 53 (Ellis *et al.*, 2016).

Realizing the depth of impact of these events, I struggle to ground myself and my thoughts by using words that I embrace in my work with girls and boys—words like optimism, hope, reframing, resilience, and love. Children often express similar feelings of hopelessness, helplessness, and loss when exposed to personal challenging events and/or media input. These media events might not only create a challenging situation that requires children to access their resilience in the now, but may also re-trigger a past experience to deal with. Some get caught in a vortex of feelings resulting from the childhood losses Goldman presents in Chapter 1. These losses can include loss of lives, relationships, safety, privacy, and protection. Young people may ask themselves, as I do, the following questions: What do I do with all of this loss around me and within me? How do I tap into my resilience? How do I make sense of it all?

The biggest question I ask as an educator and researcher each and every day is: What about our students? What about their whirlwind of loss that can culminate with the loss of loved ones, control, trust, and innocence? How are they to tap into their resilience? How are they to make sense of it all?

Where to look for answers

As intellectual beings, we often look to research for answers. It is a continual goal to engage in research in order to apply findings into practice for the common good. Yet as I continue to read research in the areas of resilience and loss, I am reminded of a phrase that conveyed this meaningful message: *Some of the best and most popular research tells us what our grandmothers already did.* This specifically applies in the field of resilience and education. My own grandmother passed on to me some of the most prominent and powerful words and concepts I know: "love," "one," "believe," and "try." These simple concepts are an integral part of resilience work with children:

- *Love:* Love is everything.

- *One:* We are all one.

- *Believe:* Believe in the goodness of all.

- *Try:* Never be afraid to try.

These four words and concepts—*love, one, believe,* and *try*—keep reappearing in much of the "new and groundbreaking" research associated with resilience, loss, and education, albeit with different names and labels.

Resilience research

Research has an important role for individuals interested in increasing the positive outcomes and success of all students, especially those underserved in our school system. A deeper understanding of resilience research is especially beneficial for educators. As mentioned earlier, resilience refers to the self-righting and transcending capacity to spring back, rebound, and successfully adapt in the face of loss, trauma, adversity, and/or everyday stress.

In my book *Resilience Begins with Beliefs: Building on Student Strengths for Success in School* (Truebridge, 2014), I offer a more in-depth definition of resilience as

> the dynamic and negotiated process within individuals (internal) and between individuals and their environments (external) for the resources and supports to adapt and define themselves as healthy amid adversity, threat, trauma and/or everyday stress. (p. 12)

The internal process consists of tapping into one's personal strengths, attributes, past experiences, etc. The external process involves being surrounded by school, family, and community resources, supports, and services such as counselors and community-based organizations. The following illustration and explanation of resilience research findings provides the foundation for transferring resilience theory into practice.

Theory of resilience

Bonnie Benard, in her book *Resiliency: What We Have Learned* (2004), drew upon the work in resilience research and developed a theory of resilience, illustrated in Figure 16.1. It is followed by an explanation of Benard's theory of resilience as it situates itself in education.

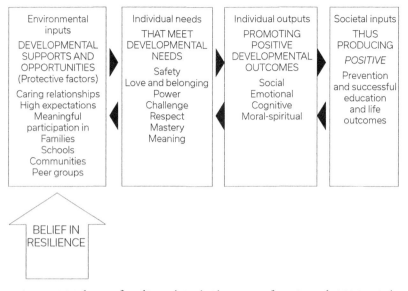

Figure 16.1 Theory of resilience (Truebridge, 2014, from Benard, 2004, p.31)

The theory of resilience recognizes that all individuals—children, youth, and adults—have basic human needs, which include, but are not limited to, the needs for safety, love, belonging, meaning, and accomplishment (Maslow, 1943).

The protective factors

Resilience research consistently finds that three inter-related protective factors (also known as developmental supports and opportunities) together in any single environment—home, school, community, or peer group—play a role in whether these needs are met. The following are the three protective factors:

- developing caring relationships

- maintaining high expectations

- providing meaningful opportunities for participation and contribution.

Once again, when these protective factors are present together in just any one environment—home, school, community, or peer group—the climate in that environment becomes one that is optimal for nurturing the resilience of a child, youth, or any individual. Having one protective factor in one environment and another protective factor in a different environment may be helpful, but Benard's theory of resilience stresses that all three protective factors need to be present in just one of the environments to be able to maximize the tapping and fostering of one's resilience.

Furthermore, having all three protective factors in one environment, such as in school, will compensate for the fact that some of the protective factors are not present in other environments such as the family, community, or peer group. This is exemplified by classroom teacher Kyle Schwartz in Chapter 3, and high school principal Jim Sporleder in Chapter 15, as they both share their use of these three protective factors in detail as a teacher and principal to meet the needs of many underserved students in their schools.

The protective factors are what provide the developmental supports and opportunities that mitigate and buffer the negative effect that any loss, trauma, adversity, and/or stress may have on an individual. As the illustration of the theory indicates, these protective factors contribute to the healthy and successful development and emergence of the individual's personal developmental competencies and strengths. They include strengths such as social competence (social skills involving relationships, responsiveness, flexibility, empathy, caring, communication, compassion, altruism, and forgiveness); the ability to problem solve (cognitive skills such as planning, flexibility, critical thinking, insight, and resourcefulness); autonomy (emotional skills fostering one's sense of self, including positive identity, internal locus of control, self-efficacy, initiative, self-awareness, and adaptive distancing); and sense of purpose and future (goal direction and moral and spiritual aspects, including sense of meaning, optimism, hope, imagination, creativity, motivation, educational aspirations, persistence, spiritual connectedness, and faith). It is then the student's strengths and outcomes that contribute to a reduction in his/her health risks and/or unhealthy behavior and a continued increase in that person's healthy development, positive well-being, educational success, and life success.

In addition to the positive outcomes that students experience, it is important to note that individual strengths and positive development outcomes also contribute collectively to an increase in successful community and societal outcomes. A good example of this would be that if students, teachers, staff, and parents in a school are supported in their own resilience, then the school itself, as a community, has the capacity to manifest its resilience in a time of difficulty or crisis. This has been evident in such trying times as the mass shootings in Newtown, Connecticut, and Littleton, Colorado, and with natural disasters as experienced by Hurricane Katrina in New Orleans and Hurricane Sandy in the Northeast. Jonathan Doll in Chapter 12 presents a strengths-based approach for schools, and underscores that the use of students' strengths in education is helpful "not just for students who are hurting, they are for everyone."

As mentioned earlier, the process of fostering resilience and being able to consistently provide the protective factors (caring relationships, high expectations, opportunities to participate and contribute) in any environment (home, school, community, or peer group), for ourselves or others, begins with beliefs.

Positive beliefs for educators

What are beliefs? Beliefs are thoughts and mindsets that affect our behaviors. They are socially constructed and often personal assumptions, judgments, generalizations, opinions, inferences, conceptions, conclusions, evaluations, and the like that we make about ourselves and the people, places, and things around us. Education research, as well as research in the medical field, law enforcement, and human services, continually informs us about how people's beliefs affect and influence their words, actions, thoughts, and behaviors. With specific reference to education, findings show that a teacher's beliefs can positively or negatively influence the academic and life outcomes of their students.

Three major environmental protective factors (developmental supports and opportunities) can be identified that mitigate adversities and nourish the personal strengths associated with resilience:

- *Caring relationships*—provide a sense of connectedness and belonging; demonstrate "being there"; exude compassion and trust.

- *High expectations*—convey a focus on strengths; stabilize routines; offer positive messaging in the belief of others as one is both challenged and supported at the same time.

- *Opportunities to participate and contribute*—contribute to personal power, inclusion, and self-efficacy; awaken the power and gifts of "service"; instill responsibility, voice, and choice.

The following are examples of positive beliefs for educators that can enable them to embrace, support, and nurture the resilience of students:

- Resilience is a process, not a trait. It is a dynamic process that involves how we interact and negotiate with ourselves, others, and our world, to find, engage, and navigate through the resources to help us thrive and move on a positive trajectory of success.

- All children and teens have the capacity for resilience. The question isn't whether or not one has resilience, but rather whether or not it has been tapped.

- Most young people *do* make it despite exposure to severe risk. Consistent with resilience research (Werner and Smith, 1992), at least 50 percent, and usually closer to 70 percent, of children and youth from high-risk environments overcome adversity and achieve good developmental outcomes.

- Coming from a risk environment does not determine individual outcomes. A child of color, born in poverty to a single mother who is abusing drugs, is not destined to become a gang member. Sporleder, in Chapter 15, underscores the transformation of young people who are in at-risk environments. They can achieve when concepts of love and caring are incorporated into a school environment. Students unfairly identified as "incorrigible" at his school rallied and overcame obstacles in a protected, caring educational climate.

- Bad behavior does not equate with being a bad person. Just because a student may display inappropriate behavior, such as hitting another student or cheating on an assignment, doesn't make that student a bad person. What he or she did was to display poor judgment and, as a result, he or she needs to be responsible for his or her actions. However, a person who displays bad judgment is not "forever" a bad person.

- One person can make a difference in the life of another person. One person—like a teacher, relative, or friend—can say something to us one day or believe in us in one way that can change our lives forever. Kyle Schwartz, in Chapter 3, exemplifies that one person as a classroom teacher made a huge difference for her students by loving them and acknowledging traumatic issues that impact learning.

- Challenging life experiences and events can be opportunities for growth, development, and change. Quite often our perseverance through tough times builds our confidence and makes us stronger.

- Many personal strengths (e.g., cognitive, social, emotional, moral/spiritual) are associated with resilience. These personal strengths not only foster resilience, but also manifest as outcomes of resilience.

- As an educator, it is *how* you do *what* you do that counts. For instance, as a teacher you can teach a difficult concept while being open to students' questions and supporting them for their persistence and determination in their attempt to understand a difficult concept, or you can inhibit, embarrass, or shame them for asking questions during a lesson.

- To help others you need to help yourself; resilience is a parallel process. It's the "oxygen mask on an airplane" analogy—in order for you to be able to help someone else, you first have to help yourself. Take care of the caretaker. You need to always find ways to support your own resilience while you are supporting the resilience of others.

- Resilience begins with beliefs. Our beliefs influence our actions. If you don't believe in the capacity of all students to have resilience, you run the risk of giving up on them.

    As Grandma and resilience research concur, we must continue to hold on to beliefs that recognize and affirm the core goodness and resilience that reside within all of us and in others.

Grandma's words with resilience: Research in action

It is fascinating how my grandma's words so beautifully align with the concepts brought forth in resilience research—the protective factors and beliefs. Yet as parents and educators, we know that words and phrases can only go so far. Most helpful are strategies and tools that can help show what words and phrases "look like" in action. Below I align my grandma's words with the three protective factors found in resilience research and offer concrete examples of what this looks like in the context of an educator's checklist (Truebridge, 2014).

Caring relationships

Love = Caring relationships: tapping into one's own heart and the heart of others. It's providing an authentic sense of connectedness and belonging and exuding sincere compassion, empathy, and trust.

An educator's checklist on caring relationships: What this may look like

- Creates and sustains a caring climate

- Models empathy and compassion

- Aims to meet developmental needs for belonging and respect

- Is available/responsive

- Offers extra individualized help

- Ensures a commitment to being culturally responsive

- Gets to know the life context of students

- Has long-term commitment

- Actively listens

- Shows common courtesy

- Respects others

- Uses appropriate self-disclosure

- Pays personal attention

- Shows interest

- Checks in

- Gets to know hopes and dreams

- Gets to know interests

- Shows respect for and acknowledges students' feelings

- Apologizes when mistakes are made

- Names and accepts students' feelings

- Is nonjudgmental

- Looks beneath "challenging" behavior

- Reaches beyond the resistance

- Uses humor/smiles/laughter

- Is flexible

- Shows patience

- Uses a community-building process

- Creates small, personalized groups

- Creates opportunities for peer-helping

- Uses cross-age mentors (older students, family/community members)

- Creates connections to resources:

  » Education

  » Cultural

  » Employment

  » Service

  » Recreation

  » Health, counseling, and social services

- Builds a sense of community in the classroom that is committed to all students being invited, valued, included, and having a voice

- Makes sure body gestures convey intentions (e.g., smiles, eye contact, nods)

- Keeps an open-door policy with students and family (if needed, select a specific time/day when you can be reached)

- Makes accommodations for interpreters if language is an issue during meetings

- Learns the names of all students and how to properly pronounce names

- Makes personal contact with students every day—something as simple as a hello or a smile

- Sets up peer support networks in the classroom to help new students and families acclimatize and be aware of all services/ programs available to them

- Talks with students to see how they access care/support (share what is being done in your grade, subject, or area with the rest of the school)

- Takes time to chat with students outside the classroom. (Adapted from Truebridge, 2014, pp.86–89)

High expectations

Try = High expectations: focusing on strengths while both challenging and supporting the effort to try new things in new areas. It's about reframing the word "FAIL" as "**F**irst **A**ttempt **I**n **L**earning."

An educator's checklist on high expectations: What this may look like

- Sustains a high-expectation climate honoring each student's unique strengths

- Conveys a "no excuses, never give up" philosophy (grit, persistence, determination)

- Models and teaches that mistakes and setbacks are opportunities for learning

- Provides descriptive and timely feedback to students about their work

- Recognizes progress as well as performance

- Aims to meet developmental needs for mastery, challenge, and meaning

- Believes in the innate capacity of all to learn

- Sees students as vital partners in school improvement

- Focuses on the whole child (social, emotional, cognitive, physical, spiritual)

- Understands the needs motivating student behavior and learning

- Sees culture as an asset

- Challenges and supports ("You can do it." "I'll be there to help.")

- Connects learning to students' interests, strengths, learning styles, experiences, dreams, and goals

- Provides appropriate wait time after questions for thinking and responding

- Encourages creativity and imagination

- Asks open-ended questions that encourage students to interpret, analyze, synthesize, and evaluate

- Uses a variety of assessments and evaluations including formative and summative ones

- Conveys hope and optimism

- Affirms/encourages the best in students

- Attributes the best possible motive to behavior

- Articulates clear expectations/boundaries/structure

- Provides clear explanations

- Holds students accountable

- Models boundary-setting
- Uses management and discipline that is consistent and fair
- Models and teaches adaptive distancing and conflict resolution
- Uses rituals and traditions
- Recognizes strengths and interests
- Mirrors strengths and interests
- Uses strengths and interests to address concerns/challenges
- Employs authentic assessment
- Groups students heterogeneously
- Continuously challenges "isms" (e.g., racism, sexism, ageism, classism, and homophobia)
- Helps to reframe self-image from "at-risk" to "at-promise"
- Helps to reframe problems and challenges into opportunities
- Conveys messages to students that they all have the capacity for resilience
- Sees students as constructors of their own knowledge and meaning
- Teaches critical analysis/consciousness
- Encourages mindfulness and self-awareness of moods, thinking, and actions
- Relates to family and community members with high expectations
- Calls home/communicates with home to report students' good behavior and achievements
- Helps family members see students' strengths, interests, and goals. (Adapted from Truebridge, 2014, pp.89–91)

Meaningful opportunities for participation and contribution

One = Opportunities to participate and contribute: understanding we are all one. It's acting upon the unity we have with each other as we awaken the power and gifts of participation and service by honoring and instilling responsibility, voice, and choice to create an environment of inclusion for all.

An educator's checklist on participation and contribution: What this may look like

- Builds a democratic, inclusive community

- Practices equity and inclusion

- Aims to meet developmental needs for power, autonomy, meaning, etc.

- Provides opportunities for voice

- Provides opportunities for decision-making

- Provides opportunities for problem solving

- Empowers students to create classroom norms/rules

- Is aware of being culturally responsive and creating a classroom that is culturally responsive

- Holds daily and as-needed class meetings

- Gives youth meaningful roles and responsibilities

- Infuses communication skills into all learning experiences

- Creates opportunities for creative expression:
  - » Art
  - » Music
  - » Writing/poetry
  - » Storytelling/drama
  - » Other

- Provides opportunities for students to use/contribute their:
  - » Strengths and interests
  - » Goals and dreams
- Includes and engages marginalized groups:
  - » Girls/women
  - » Students of color
  - » Students with special needs
  - » Other
- Infuses service learning into the program/curriculum
- Infuses active learning and project-based learning into the program/curriculum
- Uses cooperative learning
- Uses adventure/outdoor experience-based learning
- Offers peer helping
- Offers cross-age helping
- Provides ongoing opportunities for personal reflection
- Provides ongoing opportunities for dialogue/discussion
- Uses small, interest-based groups
- Uses restorative justice in place of punitive discipline
- Engages students—especially those on the margin—in a school climate improvement task force
- Invites the participation and contribution of family and community members in meaningful classroom activities (not just cooking/baking)
- Builds a sense of community in the classroom that is committed to all students and families being invited, valued, included, and having a voice:

> » Ensures *all* students are included in class activities and are aware of extra-curricular activities

> » Asks questions that encourage self-reflection, critical thinking, and dialogue

> » Asks students their opinions on issues and classroom challenges

> » Engages in technology support training

> » Engages students in setting their own goals

> » Gives students more opportunities and time to respond to questions

> » Makes learning more "hands-on"

> » Seeks training opportunities to work effectively with families and staff. (Adapted from Truebridge, 2014, pp.91–94)

These educational checklists can serve educators as a guide for school personnel to ensure a safe environment focused on love, caring, communication, and supporting resilience in our students. They provide a framework for creating and sustaining caring relationships, high expectations, and opportunities to contribute and participate.

Putting the resilience model into practice

It is incumbent on educators to support children by recognizing and naming their own personal strengths that support resilience, such as flexibility, humor, resourcefulness, optimism, and initiative. Goldman (2006) shares examples of students who manifest certain personal strengths that support resilience during challenging times, and are given opportunities to contribute and participate:

> Christina was a student in New York City during the 9/11 tragedies. Her school was a few blocks from the Twin Towers. She could hear the sounds, smell the smoke, and see the burning buildings from her classroom window. Christina wrote the following ideas about what was happening, and drew a picture about it [Figure 16.2] that exemplified her resilience. Her spiritual belief system was an important coping mechanism to help her through this difficult experience. (p.253)

once a real a pon a
time angels wr watching
god knew That
everuthina was fine.

Figure 16.2 Angels (Goldman, 2006, p.253)

Marie Moreno, school principal of Las Americas, explains in Chapter 6 her educational paradigm for underserved students, which seamlessly fits with the resilience model discussed: "Teachers must show *unconditional love while still holding high expectations.*" Marie warns that, despite testing and state accountability, educators should take into account the prior experiences of students when they enter school.

A majority of her school population did not speak English. Students were grouped by language proficiency rather than grade level, in order to create practical and high *expectations* for young people challenged by a new life, a new culture, and a new language. Accommodations were implemented so that all children learned the alphabet together, and could move through the levels of learning English at their own pace. Most of Marie's students were refugees, coming to America with trauma that led one boy to say, "I can't go on." This boy was *loved and cared for* enough to go on.

Las Americas provided social workers sensitive to students' past trauma, and funds for materials such as dictionaries and books that translate words from English into one of the 30 languages in this population. Student groups were created to help kids cope and provide the support needed for success. As Moreno states, "They have experienced grief and loss at many levels... They must feel that they are not alone."

Conclusion: Looking in

As mentioned earlier, some of the best and most popular research tells us what our grandmothers already did. I say this not to diminish or discredit anyone's research. Instead, I say this to support parents and educators who are searching for answers to questions about loss and resilience in an effort to untie some of the knots that are in all of our stomachs, heads, and hearts from current events and more. All too often we are compelled to look outward for answers. I contend that we need not be afraid to delve deep and look in. Like the Scarecrow, Lion, Tin Man, and Dorothy, in the very end, they actually possessed within themselves the knowledge and attributes they so fervently sought to acquire from the Wizard of Oz.

True wizards are not off in some far-away land. True wizards reside in our own backyards and very often are the ones who are on the front lines. In education, they are the parents raising our children and the educators who have the charge and privilege of spending sometimes over seven hours a day with our children, five days a week.

Research is important and has its place. Yet we must also believe in ourselves and tap into our own resilience, love, empathy, compassion, and intuition. As a community of caring wizards, parents and educators must not forget to look within and support each other as we dedicate ourselves to nurturing the head, heart, and spirit of children in an effort to unite and lift humanity—not only in times of loss but also each and every day. We need to give ourselves the permission to look deep in our own heads, hearts, and souls to find answers—or at least look to our grandmothers.

References

Achenbach, J., Wan, W., Berman, M., and Balingit, M. (2016) 'Five Dallas police officers were killed by a lone attacker, authorities say.' *Washington Post*, July 8. Available at www.washingtonpost.com/news/morning-mix/wp/2016/07/08/like-a-little-war-snipers-shoot-11-police-officers-during-dallas-protest-march-killing-five, accessed on 03/30/17.

Benard, B. (2004) *Resiliency: What We Have Learned.* San Francisco, CA: WestEd.

Ellis, R., Fanta, A., Karimi, F., and McLaughlin, E. (2016) 'Orlando shooting: 49 killed, shooter pledged ISIS allegiance.' *CNN*, June 13. Available at www.cnn.com/2016/06/12/us/orlando-nightclub-shooting, accessed on 03/30/17.

Goldman, L. (2006) *Raising Our Children to Be Resilient: A Guide to Help Children with Traumatic Grief.* New York: Taylor and Francis.

Maslow, A.H. (1943) 'A theory of human motivation.' *Psychological Review 50*, 4, 370–396.

Rubin, A., Blaise, L., Nossiter, A., and Breeden, A. (2016) 'France says truck attacker was Tunisia native with record of petty crime.' *The New York Times*, July 15. Available at www.nytimes.com/2016/07/16/world/europe/attack-nice-bastille-day.html?hp&action=click&pgtype=Homepage&clickSource=story-heading&module=a-lede-package-region&region=top-news&WT.nav=top-news&_r=0, accessed on 03/30/17.

Truebridge, S. (2014) *Resilience Begins with Beliefs: Building on Student Strengths for Success in School.* New York: Teachers College Press.

Werner, E.E. and Smith, R.S. (1992) *Overcoming the Odds: High Risk Children from Birth to Adulthood.* Ithaca, NY: Cornell University Press.

Chapter 17

Francis in the Schools

A NEW COMMUNITY PARADIGM FOR SERVING CHILDREN LIVING IN UNDERSERVED NEIGHBORHOODS

Linda Goldman and Terry Johnson

"We were treated royally the entire day… It was a magical day of beauty and learning and is a potential life-changing event in the lives of our children."

Ann Magovern, President, Saint Martin
de Porres School, Oakland

Introduction

Francis in the Schools is a free, fun-filled one-day educational outing offered to school children from inner-city neighborhoods. It provides opportunities for children to experience authentic caring relationships, be surrounded by sincere messages of high expectations, and engage in meaningful opportunities for participation and engagement. It is designed as a nonsectarian history lesson about: (1) the life and universal message of Francis of Assisi, the remarkable figure for whom the San Francisco Bay Area was named; (2) those who brought Francis's message to the Americas; and (3) those who deepen others' understanding of the universal principles lived by Francis.

Every Francis in the Schools event begins in the morning with a colorful musical play or concert, followed by a festive Faire with music, dancing, games, and treats. Since its founding in 2011 by Dr. Carol Weyland Conner, Francis in the Schools has hosted over 12,000 children at 22 events in San Francisco, Oakland, New York City, Baltimore, and Washington, DC (Johnson, 2016).

A program of joy that mitigates risk

Children in inner-city neighborhoods often grow up amid poverty, crime, and neglect. Yet growing up in a high-risk environment does not mean that a child is destined for less-than-successful education and life outcomes. Resilience, the ability to spring back from adversity, plays an important role in the development of all children. As Sara Truebridge discusses in Chapter 16, over 40 years of resilience research has identified specific environmental supports and opportunities— also known as protective factors—that mitigate and buffer risk, meet developmental needs, nourish personal strengths, and support a child's capacity to tap his or her resilience in the face of loss, trauma, adversity, and/or everyday stress.

The three most powerful protective factors often identified in resilience research are:

- developing caring relationships

- maintaining high expectations

- providing meaningful opportunities for participation and contribution. (Benard, 2004)

Resilience research consistently demonstrates that when these three interrelated protective factors are found together in any single environment—home, school, community, or peer group—a child's resilience—regardless of whether that child is from a high-risk environment or not—is supported, and positive and healthy education and life outcomes are promoted. Thus, it is incumbent upon all of us to be cognizant and intentional about providing these three protective factors in all environments, especially those identified as high-risk. Francis in the Schools is emblematic of a creative and meaningful program that does just that.

The protective factors at work at Francis events

It isn't too difficult to recognize the resilience protective factors at work in Francis in the Schools. An authentic caring relationship is fostered with every verbal and non-verbal interaction a child has with an adult. The volunteers are committed to demonstrating earnest respect for each child and, silently and unassumingly, wrapping each child in a safe and peaceful cocoon of love for the day. Following one

Faire, Frederica von Stade, international opera star and children's advocate, sent a note saying, "That was the most beautiful day ever, and I don't think the kids will ever forget it. The love and care and gentle generosity were like a gift from heaven, and to see so many beautiful faces and images! Thank you for giving everyone so much pure joy!"

Francis in the Schools welcomes kindergarteners through eighth graders. From the youngest to the oldest, the children can be seen behaving, cooperating, working with materials, and interacting with each other and with the volunteers in ways that are nothing less than stellar. After each Faire, volunteers can be heard commenting on how gracious and well behaved the children were. It is evident that their teachers, chaperones, and parents instilled in them high expectations of how they should handle themselves for the day. And their parent and teacher chaperones attribute the children's excellent behavior to the loving care and positive attention they receive from the volunteers and to the fact that the volunteers are asked to expect only the best from the children and not anticipate any behavior issues. The goal is to allow the children to feel completely welcome and at ease. After 22 events for more than 12,000 children, Francis in the Schools volunteers reflect on the students' exceptional manners toward each other and the volunteers. The children's thank-you notes often include a special and effusive note of thanks to their "Pied Piper," the costumed, flag-carrying Francis in the Schools escort who greets them in their classrooms in the morning and stays with them throughout the day.

When a child senses that someone truly cares and holds high expectations of him or her, that child will often rise to meet those expectations. In most cases, as these expectations are held, academically and socially, children not only rise to such expectations but also internalize them, thus holding those same expectations of themselves. Educator and author Nel Noddings states, "It is obvious that children will work harder and do things—even odd things like adding fractions—for people they love and trust" (1988, p.32).

One doesn't have to look far to see where the protective factor of providing opportunities to participate and contribute can be found in Francis in the Schools. The play is interactive. The actors, dancers, and singers invite audience participation. At a recent performance, the main character was feeling defeated and losing his confidence in his ability to do the right thing. He asked the audience what he should do.

Spontaneously children sweetly supported him by calling out a line from the beginning of the play. "Just do the best you can!" they said. Interacting, joining as one, being a unity are, in fact, what the program is all about—providing opportunities to experience joy, delight, and wonder. The children are the focus of an unforgettable day where they get to participate and contribute fully.

One day can change a life

Francis in the Schools founder Dr. Carol Weyland Conner has always had a special concern for the urban blight affecting many of our cities and visible nearly everywhere on their streets. She is especially mindful of the impact on children growing up in these areas. Francis in the Schools was created by Dr. Conner to bring to life the principles of the historical figure Francis of Assisi, who famously renounced material possession and comforts and found a life of "perfect joy" in serving others; the program is designed to strengthen within the children the timeless values lived and taught by Francis: kindness, brotherhood, service, and the essential unity of all life. Each Francis in the school event is made possible by the loving attention of hundreds of volunteers who work months to create one magical day for the girls and boys.

All students are provided free transportation to a beautiful setting where they are graciously welcomed by over 350 volunteers whose main objective as volunteers is to quietly exemplify the universal principles of kindness, compassion, selfless service, and respect and care for all. The children sense that the volunteers have organized the entire day with special regard for their happiness and safety. Upon their arrival, they are treated to a free, professional-quality performance, sometimes in the form of an original musical drama, sometimes in the form of a concert. The performance is historically accurate and beautifully staged. The actors, dancers, and singers are handsomely and colorfully costumed. The props and stage sets are artfully crafted to further enhance the production and inspire the children with the story and its message.

Following the performance, students are escorted by their Pied Pipers to a colorfully decorated Umbrian Renaissance-style Faire venue. Here they are served a tasty, nutritious lunch and spend the rest of the day enjoying a range of interactive games and festivities, including parachute and relay games, group dancing, face and hand painting, a delightful puppet show, flower arranging, creating wishes for the world at the Wishing Well, opportunities to meet and greet the characters from the performance, and more.

The Faire experience culminates with each child receiving a beautiful and delicious hand-made gift treat from Dr. Conner. She greets children by name, and personally thanks them for coming (Figure 17.1).

Figure 17.1 Greeting and thanking children

Francis in the Schools aspires to provide a vibrantly memorable day in which the children feel the love and respect they deserve. Above all, the day provides meaningful opportunities for children to participate and contribute in ways that nurture and support positive, internal change through their heart, rather than their intellect. It is exciting to consider the positive effect thousands of children whose hearts have been touched this way could have on the future of their cities, which need youth with strong, constructive, life-affirming self-identities. Children enjoy the experience (Figure 17.2); one child called it "the happiest day of my life," while another said, "I wish this day would never end."

Figure 17.2 Children enjoying their happy day

The power of volunteerism: Opportunities to participate and contribute—and more

The children are not the only beneficiaries of the Francis in the Schools program. There is a powerful parallel process happening at each event—the volunteers are also experiencing the effects of the three potent protective factors: caring relationships, high expectations, and opportunities to participate and contribute. Thus they are immersed in a day where, regardless of their background or living conditions, their resilience is nurtured alongside the children's.

Francis in the Schools is powered by hundreds of volunteers of all ages, faiths, and backgrounds. They include doctors, nurses, musicians, lawyers, artists, CEOs, bankers, computer technicians, engineers, writers, costume designers, and educators. They work for months and donate their time and own funds to make these events possible. They produce the dramas, prepare lunches for the children, arrange transportation, bake, decorate, and hand-wrap each gift treat, and plan and provide Faire activities.

Francis in the Schools events are striking examples of the power of volunteerism and what can be accomplished when we unite to serve others with love. The children come from public and private schools, neighborhood centers, YMCAs, Boys and Girls Clubs, and summer camps. The program has received support from San Francisco FAITHS Foundation, Bank of America, Whole Foods, Costco, the Cheesecake Factory, Catholic Charities CYO, Chevron, and KTGY Group, Inc.

Many of America's senior citizens are dedicating their later years to service. A large number of Faire volunteers are over 55, many are over 60, and some are over 70. The majority of these volunteers are retired and use retirement as an opportunity to serve their community. The founder, Dr. Conner, a retired psychologist, was in her late sixties when she conceived and launched the program in 2010.

Not just fun; it's educational too!

The most obvious educational component of the Francis in the Schools program is the nonsectarian history lesson about Francis of Assisi, San Francisco Bay Area's namesake. The program is designed to complement and supplement the elementary school history and social science curriculum framework outlined by the California Department of Education (2004). In this framework, children in the earlier grades (2–5) are encouraged to study biographies that bring to life the stories of "people who make a difference." Francis in the Schools provides an innovative approach to history education using the arts and theater so that children may learn through experience and feeling. Interactive approaches include girls and boys meeting and talking to the "characters" from the play, visiting all day with their Pied Pipers, creating wishes for the world, and interviewing characters from Faire vignettes that expand on parts of the morning play.

Most schools barely have time or adequate funding to cover basic curriculum instruction. As a result, important enrichment programs— including theater arts, music, and dance—are challenging to afford and integrate into the learning experience. Francis in the Schools plays always include beautifully choreographed dances, fine-quality acting and singing, breathtaking costumes, and ten-foot puppets to play "imposing" characters (Figure 17.3).

Figure 17.3 Puppet

Beyond history: Embracing social/emotional learning

There is a growing recognition that students with strong, clear values and social-emotional skills become resilient, dedicated, life-long learners. In a national teacher survey (CASEL, 2013) conducted by Hart Research, over 600 teachers were polled, and 75 percent believed that a greater focus on social and emotional learning would greatly benefit students to be successful in the world. These teachers defined the concept of social and emotional learning as "the ability to interact or get along with others"; "teamwork or cooperative learning"; "life skills or preparing for the real world"; and "self-control or managing one's behaviors."

Research has also found that school-based social and emotional learning programs improve students' classroom behavior, reduce bullying and other conduct problems, and deepen connections between students and teachers, according to analysis of 213 programs published in the journal *Child Development* (Durlak *et al.*, 2011). Schools that incorporated social and emotional learning also showed gains in student academic achievement—on average, a gain of 11 percentile points. Equally important, children are more likely to express their creativity, curiosity, and empathy in environments where they feel included and safe (Adams, 2013).

Beyond the four walls of the classroom

Increasingly educators across the nation have sought ways to nurture and support social and emotional skills, not merely by teaching them, but by modeling them. Francis in the Schools brings to life and models many of these crucially important skills. It is a real-life example of providing social and emotional learning outside the confines of a classroom and still within the context of a learning environment.

The theatrical productions provide rich opportunities for children to take the perspective of another person, witness deeply felt empathy, appreciate diversity, and recognize and understand social and ethical norms. Many scenes reinforce these principles in songs. The Faire includes creative activities and non-competitive group games, where all participants cooperate and there are no "winners" or "losers." The joy is in collaborating. Relay races and giant-ball tosses with a colorful parachute are favorite Faire activities. A San Francisco middle school teacher, Dorothy Vigna, sent a thank-you note saying, "A simple 'thank you' is really not enough for all you provided for our children. They had a spectacular time. You helped our students feel the spirit of Francis. The love of Francis was modeled for us. As a teacher, I can talk about who Francis was and what he was about, but you exhibited it for us. Thanks to you, Francis has become more than a historical figure. He has become a person of the present moment, a great man of our time."

The children say thank you

The Francis in the Schools program has been a "day of perfect joy" for thousands of children who have experienced the program. It has been a day of transforming love that many of them had never experienced before. They've sent hundreds of handmade thank-you cards. What follows is a sampling of what they have to say:

> "The trip was great because the people treated me like family."

> "Thank you for a wonderful and caring field trip, I can't stop thanking you."

> "I loved the wonderful activities you prepared for us, and the funny dance you taught us. Thank you for the fun-filled day!"

> "…an entertaining, inspiring, and very fun experience."

"At first I thought that we would be doing something boring at the beginning of the day, but I was completely wrong. Thank you. This day is what I'll never forget in my life."

Leaving the final Faire activity and walking toward her bus, a fifth grade girl gazed into the distance and said, more to herself than to anyone around her, "This was the best day of my life. It sounds silly, but I feel like a real princess here. I really do. But it's over now, and we have to go back. But we will *always* have today."

Conclusion

Francis in the Schools shares the story of Francis of Assisi, a great historical figure whose life and universal message have inspired Martin Luther King, Jr., Mother Teresa of Calcutta, Mahatma Gandhi, and countless others. In a world plagued by religious and secular conflict, poverty and violence, and abuse and neglect, the nonsectarian Francis in the Schools transcends differences and life circumstances to bring children, volunteers, and donors of all faiths, races, and backgrounds together in harmony to work toward a united goal—to serve, honor, inspire, and encourage the sense of self-worth of children whose life situations don't always provide such opportunities for growth.

Program founder Dr. Carol Weyland Conner shared the following meaningful perspective from a correspondence to the author:

All children are members of the one human family. It behooves us, then, to offer to each child, to all children, the very best we have. That "best" may be translated as the most nourishing and delicious lunches or games and activities well thought through and calculated to capture the children's spontaneous interest, drawing upon their developing intellect and moral values. It may also include a personal greeting for each child, paired with each child's name, that I, as the hostess, offer before the children get on the buses at the end of the day. Of course, along with that comes a carefully prepared gift to take home, an outstanding gift treat especially beautifully prepared. Most important, among the "best" that we have to offer, is the broad universal love that extends to each child, without exception, throughout the day.

In this atmosphere, we find that these children from backgrounds of privation, neglect, and even violence don't quarrel nor do they exhibit emotional turmoil. All of this defies prevailing psychological theory that nearly all educators and health workers are trained in. When children are embraced in a net of universal love, which extends humor, delight, stimulation, and respect to each child, every child is perfect.

It is the hope of Francis in the Schools that this unique and loving experience will inspire the children to internalize Francis's timeless principles of compassion and selfless giving. If so, they may help birth and nurture a kinder, more compassionate, and more understanding world culture. The event is designed to deliver a powerful message to the children: *If such a day as this is possible, then anything is possible.*

References

Adams, J.M. (2013) 'Social and emotional learning gaining new focus under Common Core.' *EdSource*, May 15. Available at http://edsource.org/2013/social-and-emotional-learning-gaining-new-traction-under-common-core/32161, accessed on 03/30/17.

Benard, B. (2004) *Resiliency: What We Have Learned.* San Francisco, CA: WestEd.

California Department of Education (2004) *Science Framework for California Public Schools: Kindergarten through Grade Twelve.* Available at www.cde.ca.gov/ci/cr/cf/documents/scienceframework.pdf, accessed on 03/30/17.

CASEL (Collaborative for Academic, Social, and Emotional Learning) (2013) Available at www.casel.org/library/2013-casel-guide, accessed on 03/13/17.

Durlak, J., Dymnicki, A., Taylor, R., Weissberg, R., and Schellinger, K. (2011) 'The impact of enhancing students' social and emotional learning: A meta-analysis of school-based universal interventions.' *Child Development 82*, 1, 405–432.

Johnson, T. (2016) *Francis in the Schools.* Available at www.francisintheschools.org, accessed on 03/30/17.

Noddings, N. (1988) 'Schools face crisis in caring.' *Education Week 8*, 14, 32.

Conclusion:
And a New Beginning

"People will forget what you said, people will forget what you did, but people will never forget how you made them feel."

Maya Angelou[1]

Our underserved youth often live a life of marginalization in a pervasive culture of exclusion and accountability denial. It is required of educators, parents, clinicians, and all caring adults to become the voice of respect and adaptation for those young people unable to advocate for themselves and their life circumstances. Numerous girls and boys carry an enormous burden, many times disenfranchised from a system that too often neglects the needs of innocent children.

The magnitude of challenges they face is enormous, and the task before us can be overwhelming. Yet how can we *not* serve all children, real children, facing struggle and pain as students in our educational system? How can we *not* provide, ensure, and demonstrate effective interventions to relieve the struggles associated with the array of complex difficulties highlighted in each chapter? How can we *not* seek to provide for the concerns of *all* children with courage, caring, and advocacy?

Each and every child is an integral part of our global human family with intrinsic rights to dignity and justice. Pope Francis, in his speech to the U.S. Congress (2015)[2], called attention to "the most vulnerable,

---

1   Maya Angelou (n.d.) Quote retrieved February 13, 2017 from BrainyQuote.com website: https://www.brainyquote.com/quotes/quotes/m/mayaangelo392897.html

2   Transcript: Pope Francis's speech to Congress. September 24, 2015. Washington Post. Available at https://www.washingtonpost.com/local/social-issues/transcript-pope-franciss-speech-to-congress/2015/09/24/6d7d7ac8-62bf-11e5-8e9e-dce8a2a2a679_story.html?utm_term=.8c0f504a0e97, accessed on 07/18/17.

the young…trapped in a hopeless maze of violence, abuse and despair. Their problems are our problems." Together we can seek solutions that make the impossible possible…the dream that every child feels loved, comforted, understood, and respected in their classrooms, homes, community, and world.

> *"We are powerless to control the losses and catastrophic events our children may need to face. But by honoring their inner wisdom, providing mentorship, and creating safe havens for expression, we can empower them to become more capable and more caring human beings."*

Linda Goldman (2006)[3]

---

3   Linda Goldman (2006) *Raising Our Children to be Resilient.* New York: Routledge.

Contributor Biographies

These authors have contributed a body of knowledge through their experience, expertise, and passion to help all children become the best they can be.

Jennifer Baggerly is a professor in the Counseling program at the University of North Texas at Dallas, a Licensed Professional Counselor Supervisor, and a Registered Play Therapist Supervisor. She is a former Chair of the Board of Directors for the Association for Play Therapy. Dr. Baggerly has taught and provided counseling for children for 18 years.

Eve Birge serves as the human trafficking liaison in the Office of Safe and Healthy Students at the U.S. Department of Education. She also works with schools nationwide to develop systems that improve behavioral outcomes and learning conditions. Before coming to the Department, Eve was the director of membership and programs at the Coalition for Juvenile Justice.

Eliza Byard, Ph.D., the Executive Director of GLSEN (the Gay, Lesbian & Straight Education Network), holds a B.A. from Yale University and a Ph.D. from Columbia University. As GLSEN's primary spokesperson, she has has appeared on shows such as ABC 20/20 and National Public Radio's Talk of the Nation. Dr. Byard currently serves on the Board of Trustees of the America's Promise Alliance, and has served on Mayor Bloomberg's Commission on Runaway and Homeless LGBT Youth. www.glsen.org

David Cohen is Director for Strategy and Research at Sesame Workshop, where he coordinates formative and summative research for domestic television series and outreach projects, including *Sesame Street*, as well as multiple Sesame Workshop outreach initiatives. Prior to Sesame Workshop, David studied anthropology at the University of Chicago and graduate studies in anthropology at New York University with a focus on cross-cultural child development. David taught at the Bank Street College of Education's Family Center, and served as Assistant Producer on Classroom Prodigy. www.sesame.org

Amalia Cortina is the Executive Director of Get on the Bus. She has worked in restorative justice, prison ministry, and with families and children of the incarcerated for many years. Amalia received the Voices of Courage Award from the Women's Refugee Commission for her work with the immigrant community. Her experience has led her to be invited to give presentations in different states of the country, including Georgetown University and Loyola University in Chicago. www.getonthebus.us

Susan E. Craig, Ph.D., is a lifelong student of trauma and its effects on learning. Her texts *Reaching and Teaching Children Who Hurt: Strategies for Your Classroom* (2008) and *Trauma-Sensitive Schools: Learning Communities Transforming Children's Lives* (2015) are best sellers among educators. She provides training in schools throughout the country.

Lynda Davis, Ph.D., is presently the Chief Veterans Experience Officer for Veterans Affairs. Lynda previously served as Executive Vice President at the Tragedy Assistance Program for Survivors (TAPS), the Deputy Undersecretary of Defense for Military Community and Family Policy (Department of Defense), the Deputy Assistant Secretary for Military Personnel Policy (Department of the Navy), and faculty of the Department of Psychiatry (USC).

Jonathan J. Doll, Ph.D., is a passionate school violence prevention advocate. He extensively researched and authored the book *Ending School Shootings—School and District Tools for Prevention and Action* (2015). He has also written a bullying prevention bill in Massachusetts, and articles for the *Huffington Post*. Dr. Doll is a Harvard University Strategic Data Project alumnus.

Rocio Galarza serves as Assistant Vice President of the Sesame Workshop. Rocio manages the development of educational content for a wide range of multimedia projects. As an expert in early childhood educational development, Rocio works with advisors to ensure that the content of Sesame Street's initiatives is age-appropriate, engaging, and effective. www.sesamestreet.org

Linda Goldman, MS, FT in Thanatology, has been adjunct faculty at Johns Hopkins Graduate School and King's University College at Western University, as well as grief therapist for children and adults, for 30 years. Linda has authored many books, including *Children Also Grieve* (2005), *Great Answers to Difficult Questions About Death* (2009), and *Life and Loss, 3rd Edition* (2014). www.grievingchildren.net

Eric Green, Ph.D., is a faculty associate in the School of Education at the Johns Hopkins University in Baltimore, MD. Dr. Green is the author and co-editor of *The Handbook of Jungian Play Therapy* (2014) and *Counseling Families* (2015). www.drericgreen.com

Terry Hogan Johnson has served as the Director of Francis in the Schools since its inception. She received her graduate degree in educational psychology at the University of California at Berkeley and has taught fifth grade for 35 years. Since 1994, Ms. Johnson has been the music director of several performing choruses. She has been active in community service since her youth. www.francisintheschools.org

Kari Hudnell is an award-winning public relations professional with more than a decade of experience in education, public health, and civil rights. She helps people and organizations that are improving the world around them amplify their work through communications. Previously, Kari oversaw all messaging and media for GLSEN, including developing the organization's student leaders, volunteers, and staff into sought-after experts and storytellers. www.karihudnell.com

Kathy Kater is an internationally respected psychotherapist, author, and consultant who has specialized in the treatment and prevention of body image, eating, fitness, and weight-related concerns for over 30 years. She is the author of the *Healthy Bodies: Teaching Kids What They Need to Know* (2012) curriculum. www.bodyimagehealth.org

Michael Lotz, MSEd, is a doctoral student in Counseling Psychology at Purdue University in West Lafayette, IN. Michael has worked with youth in primary schools, as well as with adolescents at the high-school level, through his school counseling efforts. Previously at Purdue, Michael served as Dr. Eric Green's research assistant and co-presented on play therapy.

Juan Martinez is an entrepreneurial, practical, and committed executive with 25 years of experience. He has spent a large portion of his career working in K-12 and postsecondary education, including as Chief Communications & Advocacy Officer for GLSEN. Juan was a journalist and editor for over a decade and now leads JMart Strategies, a management consulting firm helping organizations improve brand, culture, and outcomes.

Marie Moreno has been the school principal at Las Americas Newcomer School for the past 12 years and an educator for the Houston Independent School District for the past 22 years. Marie has traveled to other countries to learn and advocate for English Language Learners. www.houstonisd.org/lasamericas

Ronnie Nowicki is a school counseling graduate student at Purdue University's College of Education in West Lafayette, IN.

Ruby K. Payne, Ph.D., is an educator, consultant, author, and speaker. She is an expert on the mindsets of economic class. Her book *A Framework for Understanding Poverty, 5th Edition* (2013) has sold over 1.8 million copies. She holds a Ph.D. from Loyola University, Chicago. She speaks nationally and internationally (India, China, Australia, Slovakia, etc.). www.ahaprocess.com

Kyle Schwartz is a public school teacher in Denver, CO. In addition to teaching, Kyle is a dedicated advocate for students. She has spoken internationally about supporting students and building strong communities in classrooms. Kyle authored *I Wish My Teacher Knew: How One Question Can Change Everything for Our Kids* (2016). www.iwishmyteacherknewbook.com

Jim Sporleder is the retired principal of Lincoln High School, nationally recognized as a "Trauma Informed" school. In the first year of implementation of trauma-informed strategies, Lincoln experienced an 85 percent reduction in out-of-school suspension days. Director Jamie Redford filmed a documentary on Lincoln High School, *Paper Tigers*, during the school year 2012–2013. Jim has authored (with Heather Forbes) *The Trauma Informed School* (2016).

Sara Truebridge, Ed.D., is an education consultant specializing in the area of resilience. She is the author of *Resilience Begins with Beliefs: Building on Student Strengths for Success in School* (2013) and was the education consultant for the documentary films *Race to Nowhere, Beyond Measure,* and *Love, Hate Love.*

Sandra Trutt has a Bachelor of Science degree from the University of Southern California and a Master of Arts degree from Azusa Pacific College, in Azusa, CA. She taught elementary school with Los Angeles Unified School District for 12 years. Sandra was an Elementary School Librarian with Tucson School District in Arizona, and presently serves as an active volunteer with the League of Women Voters of Los Angeles and Get on the Bus.

Subject Index

Page numbers in *italics* refer to figures and tables.

Author Index